# CONSTRUCTING CHRISTOPHER MARLOWE

From Greene's 'mad and scoffing poet' to Greenblatt's flaunter of his 'society's cherished orthodoxies', Marlowe's putative personality has licensed and informed disparate and often conflicting readings of his writings. This book illustrates and challenges the ways in which the writer has been constructed by the prejudices of readers, critics and directors.

Taking nothing on trust, the authors review what is known about Marlowe's life, the publication of his plays, conditions in Elizabethan theatre, and his reputation among his contemporaries and late-twentieth-century critics. Their essays will disturb some cosy preconceptions by tackling major aspects of Marlowe's dramaturgy, his use of magic, the homoeroticism of the plays, his female characters, twentieth-century performances of his plays, and the radical nature of his narrative poem *Hero and Leander*. Together they contribute to the critical effort to construct a fuller understanding of the poet and playwright.

PROFESSOR J. A. DOWNIE is Pro-Warden (Academic) and Professor of English at Goldsmiths College, University of London. His major publications include: *Robert Harley and the Press: Propaganda and Public Opinion in the Age of Swift and Defoe* (1979), *Jonathan Swift, Political Writer* (1984), *Shakespeare. Amleto* (1991), *Telling People What to Think: Early Eighteenth Century Periodicals from 'The Review' to 'The Rambler'* (1993), and *To Settle the Succession of the State: Literature and Politics 1678–1750* (1994).

DR J. T. PARNELL is lecturer in English at Goldsmiths College, University of London. He has edited a critical edition of *Tristam Shandy*, he is editor of *Defoe and the Novelists* for the *Scriblerian* and he is currently writing a literary biography of Sterne.

# CONSTRUCTING
# CHRISTOPHER MARLOWE

EDITED BY

J. A. DOWNIE and J. T. PARNELL

CAMBRIDGE
UNIVERSITY PRESS

PUBLISHED BY THE PRESS SYNDICATE OF THE UNIVERSITY OF CAMBRIDGE
The Pitt Building, Trumpington Street, Cambridge, United Kingdom

CAMBRIDGE UNIVERSITY PRESS
The Edinburgh Building, Cambridge CB2 2RU, UK
40 West 20th Street, New York, NY 10011–4211, USA
10 Stamford Road, Oakleigh, VIC 3166, Australia
Ruiz de Alarcón 13, 28014 Madrid, Spain
Dock House, The Waterfront, Cape Town 8001, South Africa

http://www.cambridge.org

First published 2000

Typeset in Baskerville 11/12.5pt   [CE]

*A catalogue record for this book is available from the British Library*

*Library of Congress Cataloguing in Publication data*
Constructing Christopher Marlowe / edited by J. A. Downie and
J. T. Parnell.
p.   cm.
Includes bibliographical references and index.
ISBN 0 521 57255 X (hardback)
1. Marlowe, Christopher, 1564–1593 – Criticism and interpretation.
I. Downie, J. A. (James Alan), 1951– .   II. Parnell, J. T.
PR2674.C65   2000
822'.3–dc21   99–16604   CIP

ISBN 0 521 57255 X hardback

Transferred to digital printing 2004

To the Memory of Gareth Roberts

# Contents

# Illustrations

# Contributors

JULIAN M. C. BOWSHER, Museum of London

GEORGIA E. BROWN, Queens' College, Cambridge

JANET CLARE, University College, Dublin

J. A. DOWNIE, Goldsmiths College, University of London

JOANNA GIBBS, Goldsmiths College, University of London

LAWRENCE NORMAND, Middlesex University

J. T. PARNELL, Goldsmiths College, University of London

LOIS POTTER, University of Delaware

RICHARD PROUDFOOT, King's College, University of London

GARETH ROBERTS, formerly University of Exeter

SIMON SHEPHERD, Goldsmiths College, University of London

CLAUDE J. SUMMERS, University of Michigan-Dearborn

RICHARD WILSON, University of Lancaster

# Editors' note

Although there are many editions of Marlowe's plays, there is no standard edition. Unless indicated otherwise, quotations are from Christopher Marlowe, *The Complete Plays*, J. B. Steane (ed.) (Harmondsworth: Penguin Books, 1969), and references to act, scene, and line are given in the body of the essay within parentheses (e.g. *Tamburlaine Part II*: 1.6.80–4).

# Abbreviations

Bartels      Emily Bartels, *Spectacles of Strangeness, Imperialism, Alienation and Marlowe* (Philadelphia: University of Pennsylvania Press, 1993)

Bredbeck      Gregory W. Bredbeck, *Sodomy and Interpretation: Marlowe to Milton* (Ithaca, NY: Cornell University Press, 1991)

Cartelli      Thomas Cartelli, *Marlowe, Shakespeare, and the Economy of Theatrical Experience* (Philadelphia: University of Pennsylvania Press, 1991)

Dabbs      Thomas Dabbs, *Reforming Marlowe: The Nineteenth-Century Canonization of a Renaissance Dramatist* (Lewisburg, London and Toronto: Bucknell University Press and Associated University Presses, 1991)

Dollimore      Jonathan Dollimore, *Radical Tragedy: Religion, Ideology and Power in the Drama of Shakespeare and his Contemporaries* (Brighton: Harvester, 1984)

Greenblatt      Stephen Greenblatt, *Renaissance Self-Fashioning From More to Shakespeare* (Chicago: Chicago University Press, 1980)

Kastan and Stallybrass      David Scott Kastan and Peter Stallybrass (eds.), *Staging the Renaissance: Reinterpretations of Elizabethan and Jacobean Drama* (New York and London: Routledge, 1991)

Keach      William Keach, *Elizabethan Erotic Narratives: Irony and Pathos in the Ovidian Poetry of Shakespeare, Marlowe, and Their Contemporaries* (New Brunswick, NJ: Rutgers University Press, 1977)

Shepherd      Simon Shepherd, *Marlowe and the Politics of Elizabethan Theatre* (Brighton: Harvester, 1986)

Smith             Bruce R. Smith, *Homosexual Desire in Shakespeare's England: A Cultural Poetics* (Chicago: University of Chicago Press, 1991)

Steane           J. B. Steane, *Marlowe: A Critical Study* (Cambridge: Cambridge University Press, 1965)

# Introduction

*J. T. Parnell*

The title of this book can be understood in at least a double sense. To a greater or lesser extent, all the contributors engage with the ways in which Marlowe has been constructed by the critical discourse that has developed around his works. At one extreme, this process of construction has given us a 'Marlowe' who sometimes appears to be little more than the product or projection of the preconceptions and preoccupations of his commentators. Yet it would be a bold or foolish critic who claimed objective access to the 'real' Marlowe and the definitive meanings of his plays and poems. The essays gathered here aim, therefore, to contribute in a positive sense to the critical effort to construct a fuller understanding of the poet and playwright, but with a keen awareness that such a project is necessarily ongoing and incomplete.

While the modern formal academic essay bears little resemblance to Montaigne's sceptical and digressive discourses, his conception of the form as a provisional means of 'trying out' ideas and arguments nevertheless sheds light on the aims of the essays in this volume. By their very nature, single-authored monographs tend to be driven by one informing thesis. A collection of essays, on the other hand, not only eschews final and potentially reductive closure, but is able to offer a productive dialogue between positions. Accordingly, while the contributors to *Constructing Christopher Marlowe* are united in their rejection of biographical approaches and their attention to more nuanced and flexible readings of the complexities of Marlowe's texts and culture, one of the strengths of the book is that it does not impose methodological or interpretative homogeneity across the essays. As well as presenting the reader with essays on key areas of contemporary debate in Marlowe studies, the collection highlights both the range of Marlowe's concerns and the variety of perspectives from which they can be illuminated.

Superficially, at least, Marlowe seems to invert Michel Foucault's dictum that 'the author is the principle of thrift in the proliferation of meaning'.[1] From Robert Greene's 'mad and scoffing poet'[2] to Stephen Greenblatt's flaunter of his 'society's cherished orthodoxies' (Greenblatt, p. 220), Marlowe's putative personality has licensed and informed disparate and often conflicting readings of his writings. And yet, of course, the return to 'Marlowe' betrays the desire for a centre around which the ambiguities and complexities of his plays and poems can be resolved. If such an interpretative strategy is now less likely to be damned, in Roland Barthes' terms, as the dogmatist's search for 'a final signified',[3] it remains peculiarly suspect in Marlowe's case. As J. A. Downie reminds us in the first chapter in this collection: 'We know next to nothing about Christopher Marlowe. When we speak or write about him, we are really referring to a construct called "Marlowe".'

To be sure, as Downie acknowledges, all authors are inevitably partially constructed by their commentators, but myths of Marlowe the man, regardless of their provenance, have had a special force in Marlowe studies from their beginnings in the nineteenth century to the present day. The continuing potency of the biographical approach can be gauged from the opening paragraph of David Bevington's and Eric Rasmussen's World's Classics edition of *Doctor Faustus and Other Plays* (1995):[4]

From first to last in his brief and meteoric career, Marlowe appears to have been fascinated by challenge of the established order in its cosmic and human dimensions. We sense in this, as we read or experience his plays in the theatre, the projection of a self that was no less daring, yet at the same time caught up in guilt and remorse. Even though we cannot interpret the plays as straightforward autobiography, no body of dramatic literature in the Renaissance makes us more curious to know the dramatist himself, for the plays seem to us intensely personal.

While it is difficult to gainsay this reading on the level of reader or audience response, it is just as difficult to believe that such conclusions could be derived from the plays alone. Behind the 'meteoric career' lingers the myth of Marlowe the Romantic artist, who lived as he wrote in one gloriously short and inspired burst. So the biographical 'facts' of rumoured transgressions neatly fall into place in the image of Marlowe as a guilt-ridden aesthete for whom it is entirely appropriate to elide life and works. Circular reasoning thus reduces textual complexities and questionings to the personality traits of a hypothetical 'Marlowe'.

Given the traditional nature of such reasoning in Marlowe criticism, and the undiminished appetite for biographical conjecture evident in the recent work of Charles Nicholl and others, Downie's account of the few verifiable biographical facts is salutary. Teasingly elliptical and suggestive as it may be, the documentary evidence neither supports the commonplaces about Marlowe's involvement in espionage, his alleged atheism and homosexuality, nor adds up to anything like a meaningful biography. If free-wheeling critical speculation is required to flesh out a 'life' that will make sense of the plays, Downie's scepticism takes us in a different direction by reminding us of the disturbing fact that not even the plays were 'unambiguously attributed to [Marlowe] prior to his death'.

Turning to a similarly shadowy area of our knowledge of the historical Marlowe, Julian M. C. Bowsher offers an archaeologist's perspective on the playhouse most clearly associated with early performances of the two parts of *Tamburlaine, Doctor Faustus, The Jew of Malta* and *The Massacre at Paris*. Although, significantly, 'there remains no documentary evidence' of Marlowe's personal association 'with the London playhouses', the regular performances of the plays at the Rose attest to their popularity, if not to the playwright's fame. Indeed, that the papers of the Rose's owner and manager, Philip Henslowe, name the plays but make no mention of Marlowe himself alerts us to important differences between our own assumptions about authorship and the priorities of Elizabethan acting companies and audiences.

The survival of Henslowe's papers has, as Bowsher notes, long given the Rose 'a unique documentary status amongst its contemporaries', but the Museum of London's excavation of the playhouse in 1989 adds a new dimension to the picture by revealing 'for the first time the physical context in which the plays of Marlowe, and his contemporaries, were performed'. Two distinct stages of the theatre's physical development were uncovered by the excavations. The redevelopment of the Rose (probably in 1592) to improve staging conditions and increase audience capacity parallels similar developments at the Theater, and suggests, according to Bowsher, keen competition among the London playhouses, 'all of which were striving to attract audiences, acting companies, and playwrights'. Interestingly, the second phase of development did little to enlarge a stage space that was 'small even by contemporary standards'. The extension of the yard, however, 'produced a greater "thrust" and thus greater contact with the groundlings'. It is in this intimate arena that Edward Alleyn famously 'stalked and roared' as Tamburlaine and made the roles of Barabas and Faustus his own.

Having begun by establishing both certainties and uncertainties in our efforts to reconstruct a historical Marlowe, the collection moves on, with the chapters of Richard Proudfoot and Gareth Roberts, to consider some of the interpretative ramifications of the no less vexed area of Marlovian bibliography. In a chapter which offers an overview of the fortunes of the plays in the hands of editors and publishers, Proudfoot begins with a consideration of William Mountfort's rendering of *Doctor Faustus* as farce. A high point in what Robert D. Hume calls the 'farce boom' of the Restoration, Marlowe scholars, nevertheless, have often viewed Mountfort's *Faustus* as 'a dreadful object lesson in textual instability and the corrosive effect of the players on the play'. Yet, Proudfoot argues, the late and posthumous *publication* of *Doctor Faustus* 'and the clear indications that neither A- nor B-text is unadulterated "Marlowe" should allow theatrical history a greater importance than is usually accorded to it in editions of the play'. Although it is not a matter of a simple choice between the comic emphasis of seventeenth-century traditions and a twentieth-century tendency to downplay or simply drop the scenes of 'low' comedy, the tonal alternations on which the play depends were better understood, suggests Proudfoot, when *Faustus* 'remained . . . a play for acting, not a text for academic study'.

Accepting the unresolvable nature of certain textual questions, our ignorance about the dating of Marlowe's plays, and the sequence in which they were written, Proudfoot draws attention to the comparable cases of contemporary playwrights such as Robert Greene and George Peele. Necessarily fragmentary though it is, the 'theatrical history of [Marlowe's] time' offers as 'rich a context' as any for the plays. Thus the essay concludes with a call for a more daring approach to the editing and performance of plays, for 'anthologies that juxtapose Marlowe with other plays from the repertoires of the Admiral's and Pembroke's Men . . . and a Marlowe theatre festival at which his repertoire might be extended to take in *Dido* and *The Massacre*, and even . . . to juxtapose . . . seventeenth-century versions of *Doctor Faustus*'.

Focusing too on *Doctor Faustus*, Roberts finds significant parallels between critical attempts to comprehend the meaning of 'magic' in the play and those of editors to reconstruct Marlowe's 'original' text: 'The hope of recovering an "authentic" text might be as fallacious as recovering "magic" in the play . . . As there are variant readings in scenes of magic in *Doctor Faustus* and . . . two distinct plays, so it might turn out that we have to acknowledge different discourses of magic in the Renaissance.' Beyond these crucial editorial problems, Roberts' discussion of how, for example, we might best read Faustus' claim that 'These metaphysics of magicians/ And necromantic books are heavenly' opens up broader questions about the play's much debated orthodoxy or subversiveness. While it is possible to discover authorial irony behind the epithet 'heavenly', which might then guide a reading of the play's essential orthodoxy, Roberts points out that 'juxtapositions of magic and religious thought' are not necessarily 'uneasy and ironic' in the early modern period.

Indeed, Roberts argues, the issue is made problematic by the typical discursive entanglements of religion and magic in the Renaissance, and further complicated by the differing inflections of three distinct discourses about magic: 'orthodox demonology, high magic, and popular belief'. We might look to demonologies to bolster an orthodox reading of *Doctor Faustus*, but while the conservative position is evident in, for example, 'the voices of the Prologue and the Good Angel', it is 'not the only or dominant viewpoint in the play'. What the play does, according to Roberts, is to mobilise 'different discourses about magic and [set] them at odds'. This characteristic Marlovian strategy denies the reader or viewer the security of either a straightforwardly orthodox or a straightforwardly subversive interpretation of the play.

While a number of important studies of Marlowe from David Bevington's *From Mankind to Marlowe* (1962) to Clifford Leech's *Christopher Marlowe, Poet for the Stage* (1986) have argued that the plays are best understood as theatre, there are also strong traditions in Marlowe scholarship in which primarily textual analysis implies the secondary and almost incidental nature of performance. Moreover, for all the popularity of the plays in performance in the late sixteenth and seventeenth centuries, Marlowe's plays have only been selectively and occasionally revived in the twentieth century. There are a number of possible reasons for this relative neglect, but among them the perceived unfamiliarity of the plays' dramatic idioms and Marlowe's continuing ability to disturb rank high. The chapters of

Janet Clare and Lois Potter thus join important debates about Marlowe as dramatist. Like several of the other contributors to this volume, Clare points to the value of attending to Marlowe's dramaturgy on its own terms, while Potter demonstrates the relationship between stage history and broader issues of interpretation.

For Clare, the 'combination of Renaissance eloquence and extreme acts of aggression' found in the plays makes it both necessary and difficult to 'find an appropriate vocabulary for Marlowe's dramaturgy'. Since 'character' in the plays seems to have little to do with 'either humanist or determinist notions of psychology and agency', Clare suggests that biographical readings of the plays are necessarily 'unreliably premised'. In addition, Clare argues, attempts to understand the violence of the plays in terms of its ideological and social implications ignore the 'limitations in Marlowe's representations of power, shorn in its reduction to violence of its other attributes'. Writing within the relatively new context of purpose-built theatres, which made increasing 'claims to be recognised as [places] of dangerous effects and emotions,' Marlowe extended traditional stage violence to a level of 'on-stage, amoral intensity'.

Because the aesthetics of Elizabethan critics like Sidney, Puttenham, and Lodge are 'grounded in didacticism', they have 'little to say about the effects and implications' of the plays' 'violent enactments'. Sensitive to the historical milieu of Marlowe's plays, Clare, nevertheless, finds a more appropriate model for his dramaturgy in Antonin Artaud's conception of the theatre of cruelty. In particular, Artaud's call for a theatre built on 'extreme action pushed beyond all limits', which might serve 'as a liberating vent to extreme passions and cultural nightmares' finds an analogue in Marlowe's 'excesses of . . . spectacle', his 'sensory assault on the spectator and the violation of any predictable moral or emotional responses'. In his sensual use of word and image and his eschewal of psychologically complex character construction, Marlowe solicits a 'radical audience response'. Such a response has little to do with moral exempla or empathy with his protagonists. By 'surrendering the ethical to the aesthetic', Marlowe, Clare argues, invites his audience to complete his texts, 'to formulate their own responses'.

Potter's account of key moments in the history of the revival of Marlowe's plays reveals a number of trends that often parallel the preoccupations of academic commentary. The tendency, before the opening of the Swan Theatre in Stratford-upon-Avon in 1986, to justify 'many Marlowe revivals' on the grounds of 'comparison with Shakespeare' has its counterpart in literary criticism and suggests, perhaps, the limitations of selective literary history as much as the cultural value of the bard. The critical fascination with Marlowe's brief life and especially his violent death is echoed in the theatre in such plays as R. H. Horne's *The Death of Marlowe* (1837) and Peter Whelan's *The School of Night*, which opened in Stratford in 1993. A more welcome, but, perhaps, no less double-edged, manifestation of the relationship between professional criticism and performance is the fact 'that most Marlowe revivals (those of *Tamburlaine* and *Dido* in particular) have happened in academic or experimental contexts'.

Of Marlowe's 'four major plays', *Faustus* has been the most frequently produced, perhaps because of a perception of the 'time-less' nature of the Faust myth. The other plays have been more obviously interpreted in the light of urgent contemporary concerns. Thus, for example, post World War II productions of *Tamburlaine* have sometimes identified the hero 'with the military leaders whose ambition kills civilians and soldiers alike'. Similarly, Barry Kyle's 1988 *Jew of Malta* alluded to the Holocaust, and by suggesting parallels with 'religious conflict, in Ireland [and] the Middle East, gave Marlowe's fantastic plot a new relation to real life'. Of all the plays, *Edward II* has been the most 'affected by outside events, particularly the disappearance of pre-performance censorship in 1968'. Since the late 1960s, Potter notes, 'productions have become so explicit about both the hero's homosexuality and the nature of his death that it is hard to believe that the play was once able to make its effect in any other way'.

Clearly, productions of the plays on the twentieth-century stage raise inevitable questions about the relationship between contemporary appropriation and the historical integrity of Marlowe's texts. Yet, as much as it might like to rise above such questions, the critical discourse of twentieth-century Marlowe scholarship is fully implicated in them. The critical revolution which followed from the importation of the *nouvelle critique* in the late 1970s and 1980s brought about a much-needed re-thinking of traditional assumptions about English literature in general. Because the study of the Renaissance was seen to be especially burdened with ideological baggage, its literature became and remains a subject of lively contestation. The sense that all critical positions are interested ones and that the

'norms' and 'universals' of traditional criticism resulted in monolithic and yet partial constructions of the 'Renaissance' legitimated
re-readings of canonical texts by critics who wore their political
agenda on their sleeves. Yet for all the excitement of new and
productive insights, there is some danger that we have merely
swapped one interested orthodoxy for another. The truism that each
generation necessarily re-reads the literature of the past in the light
of its own concerns is borne out by the reception of Marlowe as
much as Shakespeare. Seductive as it might be, however, the logic of
total relativism is worth resisting, not least to prevent another fall
into the kind of critical narcissism in which Renaissance texts merely
reflect back to us what we already know. Partly in response to such a
threat, the chapters of Simon Shepherd and Richard Wilson attend
to Marlowe's critical fortunes in the wake of the theoretical reassess-
ments of the last two decades.

The felt need to counter liberal-humanist interpretations of
Renaissance drama led in the 1980s to a new critical emphasis on
the period's 'other' sides, especially those transgressive and marginal
discourses which were perceived to challenge the dominance of
oppressive orthodoxy. For Shepherd, however, the 'search for transgression in Renaissance drama' is coloured both by 'a rage against
literary fuddy-duddies and English nationalism', and the fantasies of
critics themselves. The focus on transgression not only provides
vicarious pleasures for study-bound academics, but also adds a
spurious sense of engagement with earthy 'reality'. More troubling
still, Shepherd argues, are the unrigorous elisions which allow critics
to make marginal cultural practices stand for the whole culture and
to conflate representation and reality. At the same time, the newly
theorised 'Marlowe' suspiciously resembles the old sublime trans-
gressor whose presence is everywhere felt in the plays.

Apparently sensitive to questions of performance and audience
response, critics such as Greenblatt, James Shapiro, Thomas Cartelli, and Emily Bartels paradoxically move, in their zeal to access
Renaissance 'realities', further and further away from the particularities of Marlowe's texts and 'the praxis of theatre'. Thus when
Greenblatt alludes to the RSC's 1964 production of *The Jew of Malta*
to demonstrate the audience's complicity in Marlowe's dismantling
of moral values, he tellingly ignores the fact 'that Marlowe never
wrote a scene showing the nuns dying'. By concentrating on the
scene of Abigail's confession, which is framed by the briefest of

references to the dying nuns, Shepherd shows how Marlowe's 'dialectical dramaturgy' is considerably more complex in its effects than the readings of Greenblatt and Bartels allow. Turning to the fifth scene of the final act of *Edward II*, Shepherd similarly sets the particular nuances of Marlowe's dramaturgy against the efforts of a number of critics to historicise the conception of homosexual identity that emerges from the play. In Shepherd's reading, the 'specifically sensual complexity of the stage' belies critical efforts to confine the scene 'to being a gesture of homosexual inscription'.

Wilson, like Shepherd, argues that the Marlowe of the 1990s is to some extent a projection of the ' "mercenary drudge" on campus', but his major concern is the playwright's role in the development of the critical discourse of New Historicism. Where 'Shakespeare came to be the template on which New Historicism played out its game of subversion and containment', Wilson suggests, 'it was Marlowe who prompted its Foucauldian lament that "limit and transgression depend upon each other", and that if power is inscribed in signs, there can be no escape from the prison-house of words'. Concentrating primarily on Margery Garber's and Greenblatt's seminal treatments of Marlowe, Wilson argues that these critics 'effectively laid down the parameters within which Marlowe criticism . . . would develop in the last quarter of the century'. Thus was born the postmodern Marlowe, a 'Marlowe' who uncannily anticipates post-structuralism's anxieties about both language and sexual identity.

In spite of the popularity and influence of *Hero and Leander* in the late sixteenth and early seventeenth centuries, and its high reputation in the nineteenth century, twentieth-century critical interest has focused largely on the plays. Apart from the poem's own considerable merits, however, *Hero and Leander* is valuable for the fuller picture it affords of Marlowe's broader skills and concerns as a writer. As Claude J. Summers argues, the poem 'is a remarkable achievement, principally because of its curious tone, an unusual blend of apparently affectionate but actually scathingly unsentimental comedy and iconoclastic realism in its depiction of love'. By revealing the 'utter arbitrariness of desire', Summers suggests, Marlowe 'destabilises his society's ideas about sexuality'. Against the Christian orthodoxy that condemns homosexuality as sodomitical, Marlowe sets 'classical culture's acceptance of homoerotics'. In the blazon devoted to Leander and the handling of Neptune's desire for the young man, the 'power to shock and titillate' thus derives 'from the satiric view of homosexuality' that Marlowe's Ovidian stance 'delightfully' mocks.

Marlowe's attack on the 'sexual conventions of his day' is as much in evidence in the poem's sympathy for Hero as it is in his handling of same-sex desire. While the poem's plot is finally about Hero's humiliation, Summers argues that 'the process of humiliation is less revealing of any personal failure on her part than of the deficiencies of an erotic economy that valorises women as trophies of male virility but devalues and even despises expressions of their own desire'. A 'pivotal work in the literary representation of sex' and profoundly influential on the love poetry of the late Renaissance, *Hero and Leander*, Summers concludes, initiated 'the transition from Petrarchan to Ovidian attitudes toward love'.

Sharing with Summers the sense of Marlowe's radical treatment of gender issues, Georgia E. Brown reads *Hero and Leander* in the context of some of the literary debates of the 1590s. Contrary to New Historicist assumptions about the equivalence between literary and non-literary discourses, Brown argues that while the poem 'does do political work' Marlowe was 'also in the process of discovering and elaborating purely aesthetic institutions and traditions'. Where the humanist critics of the 1590s would have literature fulfil a didactic role, *Hero and Leander* 'develops a new kind of defence of literature, one which does not deny the traditional association of literature with the trivial and peripheral, but capitalises upon it, and uncovers the paradoxical value of marginality, error, and game'. In a way which resonates with Clare's intuition that Marlowe's theatre stands in an antagonistic relation to the critical discourses of the anti-theatrical-ists, Brown places Marlowe's poem in a developing anti-didactic and avant-garde literary tradition. Adapting Ovid for his own ends, Marlowe's poem, Brown argues, connects 'sexual explicitness, mod-ernity, and literariness' and in doing so challenges both contempo-rary poetics and traditional assumptions about the relationships between genre and gender.

While questions of sexual identity and issues of sexual politics have become increasingly prominent in Marlowe scholarship in the last ten years, critics have had surprisingly little to say about the representation of women in the plays. Joanna Gibbs suggests that such neglect derives from implicit presuppositions about Marlowe's apparent misogyny, and from anachronistic conceptions of gender relations in the playworlds. Thus, Gibbs argues, it is not Marlowe but his commentators who assume a straightforward dichotomy between the public world of male politics and the private, emotional sphere allotted to women. Rather than assuming this simple binary division, Marlowe reveals the interconnections between the ostensibly emotional actions of such women as Isabella, Dido, and Olympia and the broader social and political structures which disempower them. Tempting as it has been for critics to subsume all of Marlowe's women within the same stereotypical patterns, Marlowe, Gibbs suggests, makes a distinction between uncomprehending victims of male power like Zenocrate, Edward's niece and Abigail and those like Isabella who have the 'ability to comprehend the operations of power and to intervene accordingly'. Focusing on key moments in *Edward II*, *Dido* and *Tamburlaine* that might be read as endorsements of Marlowe's own unquestioning acceptance of women's marginality, Gibbs demonstrates how the plays themselves complicate this reading.

In the final chapter in this collection, Lawrence Normand, too, is concerned with Marlowe's handling of the nexus between sexual and state politics. Reading Marlowe's *Edward II* in the light of Derek Jarman's film version and vice versa, Normand explores the relationship between early modern and postmodern conceptions of homoeroticism. Whereas Jarman's handling of the Gaveston–Edward relationship is fully sexualised and informed by a modern conception of homosexual identity, Marlowe's play has 'no one dominant discourse' that explains the relationship in unequivocal terms. Instead, Normand argues, homoerotic 'desire appears in the play as one strand in discourses that are not simply sexual: namely, sodomy, friendship, and patronage'. Importantly distinct in these and other respects, Marlowe and Jarman similarly engage in the social and political concerns of their respective historical moments. Where Jarman responds to the homophobia of Thatcher's government in his film's political thesis that 'English state power had depended since at least the time of Edward II on the repression of homosexuality', Marlowe 'repeatedly dramatises the instability and violability of the social order to demonstrate that social and political values are expedient'.

Comparing Edward's death in the film and the play, Normand argues that both Jarman and Marlowe depart from their sources 'to diminish homophobia'. The 'staged death with a spit' becomes in Jarman's film the stuff of a nightmare from which Edward awakes to

'find Lightborn transformed from murderer to lover'. Suggesting
that Marlowe is more concerned with power than sex in his
treatment of Edward's death, Normand, like Shepherd, questions
the critical assumption that the king dies by means of the red-hot
poker. Developing Stephen Orgel's reading of the death, Normand
concludes that Marlowe's primary concern is to dramatise 'Edward's
responses as king in the face of a designedly low and treacherous
death'.

If the directions in which Marlowe studies will move in the next
century are necessarily impossible to predict, then Normand's
chapter at least suggests a way out of some of the confusions between
present concerns and Marlowe's historical moment which Shepherd
and Wilson identify in broadly New Historicist readings of the plays
and poems. Respecting the historical integrity of both Jarman's self-
conscious appropriation of *Edward II* and Marlowe's play, Normand
opens up a mutually illuminating dialogue between the 1590s and
the 1990s.

# CHAPTER I

# Marlowe: facts and fictions

## J. A. Downie

> You must and will suppose (fair or foul reader, but where's the difference) that I suppose a heap of happenings that I had no eye to eye knowledge of or concerning.
>
> Anthony Burgess, *A Dead Man in Deptford* (1993), p. 3

> Is this a true story?
>
> Yes, in the sense that it is fact rather than fiction. The people in it are real people, the events I describe really happened, the quotations are taken verbatim from documents or books of the period. Where there is a dialogue I have reconstructed it from reported speech. I have not invented anything.
>
> Charles Nicholl, *The Reckoning* (1992), p. 3

We know next to nothing about Christopher Marlowe. When we speak or write about him, we are really referring to a construct called 'Marlowe'. The same might of course be said about all writers. Truly 'modern' critics are only too well aware of 'the historicity of texts and the textuality of history'. But Marlowe/ 'Marlowe' poses the problem in a peculiarly acute form. The recent spate of fictions published about Marlowe, in which category one is forced to include Charles Nicholl's book about Marlowe's murder, are merely the latest manifestation of a (dis)honourable tradition.[1] For whatever reason, writers and critics seem particularly predisposed to pontificate about Marlowe's life, his character, and his artistic intentions, regardless of the exiguity of the documentary evidence on which they base their accounts. Given these circumstances, it is scarcely surprising that researchers' hunches quickly become transmogrified, as a consequence, into hard 'facts'.[2]

Nicholl, for instance, claims at the outset of his narrative that his is 'a true story . . . in the sense that it is fact rather than fiction' (Nicholl, *The Reckoning*, p. 3). It is nothing of the kind. For all his digging in the official records of Elizabethan England, what we are offered by Nicholl is an account of *what might have been* the 'facts' of Marlowe's life – but what, equally clearly, might be nothing more than a fiction of his own constructing. Nicholl writes a lot about the importance of 'evidence', but he doesn't actually provide any for his tendentious suggestion that Marlowe was murdered on the orders of the Earl of Essex as part of the wider power struggle in which Essex was engaged with Sir Walter Ralegh, and the increasing resort to *credo* is a giveaway. So many sentences and phrases begin with the words, 'I believe', particularly towards the end of Nicholl's book, that it assumes the character of a nervous tic.

Given this tendency to embellish the 'facts' of Marlowe's life, it might be salutary to remind ourselves just how little we know for certain. Born in Canterbury, 'Christofer the sonne of John Marlow' was christened on 26 February 1564.[3] Subsequently, on 14 January 1579, 'Chr[ist]ofer Marley' was admitted to one of the scholarships provided for 'poor boys, both destitute of the help of friends, and endowed with minds apt for learning'[4] at the King's School, Canterbury. Then, on 17 March 1581, 'Chrof. Marlen' matriculated at Corpus Christi College, Cambridge.[5] As Frederick S. Boas remarks: 'of Christopher's home life not the faintest echo remains either in tradition or in his writings'.[6]

Already, however, we have several of the variants on Marlowe's surname in the scanty documentary evidence which have caused problems for biographers. There were soon to be others. The name of 'Christof. Marlyn' appears in a list of Corpus Christi undergraduates admitted to the degree of BA in 1584, while 'Marley' is listed 199th out of 231 graduates on the 'Ordo Senioritatis' in the Grace Book of the University of Cambridge for 1583–4.[7] That was not the end of Marlowe's university career, however. His Parker scholarship, restricted to a native of Canterbury who had attended the school there, was for a period of six years, and Marlowe carried on studying for his MA. By 1587 he had held it for virtually the maximum permitted duration, which implies, as Boas points out, 'that he intended to take holy orders' (Boas, *Christopher Marlowe*, p. 15).

But Marlowe was not in attendance at Corpus Christi for the whole of this time. His scholarship carried with it an allowance of twelve pence a week, and there are numerous entries in the buttery books and college accounts relating to his expenditure. These suggest that he was absent for several weeks during the academic years 1581–2 and 1582–3, and again in 1584–5 and 1585–6.[8] Marlowe's absences assume significance in the light of the famous entry in the Privy Council Register dated 29 June 1587:[9]

Whereas it was reported that Christopher Morley was determined to haue gone beyond the seas to Reames and there to remaine, Their Lordships thought good to certefie that he had no such intent, but that in all his accions he had behaued him selfe orderlie and discreetlie wherebie he had done her Majestie good service, & deserued to be rewarded for his faithfull dealinge: Their Lordships request was that the rumor thereof should be allaied by all possible meanes, and that he should be furthered in the degree he was to take this next Commencement: Because it was not her Majesties pleasure that anie one emploied as he had been in matters touching the benefitt of his Countrie should be defamed by those that are ignorant in th' affaires he went about.

Does this refer to the Christopher Marlowe known to posterity? After all, a Christopher Morley of Trinity was a contemporary of Marlowe's at Cambridge, although he took his MA in 1586. While some scholars have been cautious about the identification of Marlowe as 'Morley', others have been less circumspect. 'This is definitely Marlowe', insists Nicholl, 'and this certificate of good behaviour drawn up on a summer morning in 1587 is the earliest record of his involvement in confidential government work' (Nicholl, *The Reckoning*, p. 92). What sort of work? Here Nicholl is equally confident. At Rheims was the English College, a Catholic seminary at which young Catholics were trained in order that they might return to England and work for the restoration of Catholicism as the national faith. 'On the surface Marlowe appears to be a Catholic sympathiser, but this is only a pose', Nicholl explains. 'In reality he is the government's man, working in some way against the Catholics. This is the only possible interpretation of the Council's wording' (Nicholl, *The Reckoning*, p. 93).

The *only* possible interpretation? Scarcely. However, assuming that the Privy Council's letter does refer to Marlowe, who took his MA degree in July 1587, it seems that rumours had evidently been circulating that he had converted to Catholicism, and had 'gone . . . to Reames . . . there to remaine'. New light on the significance of these rumours has recently been supplied by Peter Roberts, who draws attention to 'the residential requirements for students and fellows' at Cambridge in the 1580s, which allowed for 'discontinuance' between the BA and the MA provided that the Vice-

Chancellor received confirmation that they had 'lived soberly and studiously the course of a scholar's life' during their absence from College. 'The Privy Council testimonial', Roberts concludes, 'was presumably a substitute for the landlord/parson certificate'.[10] Apparently Marlowe had been absent from Cambridge for some weeks early in 1587, as only 5s 6d was paid from his Parker scholarship during the Lent term. Perhaps this was the source of College gossip. To set the record straight, the Privy Council insisted this was not the case. Marlowe had been employed in unspecified 'matters touching the benefitt of his Countrie'.

And that is all we *know* about Marlowe's activities prior to the middle of 1587, although it has not prevented speculation about what he *might* have been doing. Attention has been drawn to the sharp increase in the scale of his spending in 1585, as recorded in the buttery books. Where did he get the money, not only to spend eighteen or twenty-one pence a week in the college buttery, but to kit himself out in such lavish style for his celebrated portrait? I do not pretend to know the answer to the first question, although it should be pointed out that there are clear discrepancies in both the college accounts and the buttery books.[11] As for the second, it must be stated, quite categorically, that there is *not one iota of evidence* that Marlowe is the subject of the portrait found in builders' rubble at Corpus Christi in 1953. Similarly, it is simply not safe to assume that Marlowe was a twenty- or twenty-one-year-old spy in the middle of the 1580s, and that that is the burden of the entry in the Privy Council Register.

Circular arguments of considerable ingenuity have been constructed not merely to 'prove' that the portrait is of Marlowe, but that it offers evidence to indicate that, by 1585, he was already a 'spy'. How else is one to account for the sitter's costly apparel? Rash reasoning of this sort is rife in Elizabethan scholarship in general, and Marlovian scholarship in particular. As the lavishness of the costume attests, the portrait is evidently of a wealthy young man. Marlowe was a cobbler's son, at Corpus Christi as a Parker scholar: he is therefore highly unlikely to be the subject of the controversial portrait, which must fairly be described as a portrait of an unknown young man.

During the late 1580s Marlowe is also confidently believed to have had another occupation ostensibly remote from the world of espionage. 'By the summer [of 1587] *Tamburlaine* was on-stage in

1 Christopher Marlowe: a putative portrait, from Corpus Christi College, Cambridge. The College cannot vouch for the identity of this portrait and 'it must be stated, quite categorically, that there is *not one iota of evidence* that Marlowe is the subject'.

2  Christopher Marlowe: the 'Grafton' portrait, from the John Rylands University
Library of Manchester

London', writes Nicholl with his customary lack of scholarly
caution, 'and Marlowe was launched on his career as a "play-
maker"' (Nicholl, *The Reckoning*, p. 100). On the basis of the
evidence of Greene's *Perimedes The Blacke-Smith*, published in 1588,
scholars assume that *Tamburlaine* was staged in 1587, although the
extant printed text, which states that the two parts of the play '*were*

*sundrie times most* stately shewed upon Stages in the Citie of London. *By the right honorable the Lord Admirall his seruantes*' was 'newly published' in 1590.

*Tamburlaine* is the only play now attributed to Marlowe that was published during his lifetime. Unfortunately, it is also the only play now attributed to Marlowe that is not attributed to him on the title-page, either by his full name, or by the abbreviation '*Ch. Mar.*'. But Greene, alluding to 'two Gentlemen Poets' whose verses have 'latelye' appeared 'vpon the stage in tragicall buskins', not only refers to them as 'daring God out of heauen with that Atheist *Tamburlan*', but as 'such mad and scoffing poets, that haue propheti-call spirits as bred of *Merlins* race'.[12] Critics assume that this refers to Marlowe, the man with many names. 'Merlin' would have been pronounced 'Marlin' in Elizabethan England and, after 'Morley', 'Marlin' was perhaps the commonest corruption of Marlowe's surname. Thus the fact that 'the dramatist's name was often known as Marlin' is sufficient for Boas to insist that it 'can leave no reasonable doubt that Marlowe is here attacked as the writer of *Tamburlaine*'. Well, it's possible. And, with Boas,[13] we can always choose to ignore the fact that, apart from the passage I have just quoted, there is no external evidence that Christopher Marlowe wrote *Tamburlaine* dating from before his death.

The way in which *Tamburlaine* was first attributed to Marlowe by literary scholars is illuminating. It was neither the result of the references in *Perimedes The Blacke-Smith* nor Gabriel Harvey's similarly ambiguous allusion to '*Tamberlaine*' in 'Gorgon, Or the Wonderfull Yeare' (1593).[14] As Thomas Dabbs notes, '[i]n the eighteenth century, Malone had assigned the authorship of *Tamburlaine* to Nashe' (Dabbs, p. 61). It was John Payne Collier who first insisted not only that Marlowe was its author, but that he was an actor, too – just like his famous contemporary, Shakespeare. And Collier went to extraordinary lengths to 'prove' that Marlowe wrote the play, down to forging an entry in Philip Henslowe's diary that had 'escaped the eye of Malone'.[15]

Collier was reacting to the comments of the editor of the 1826 Pickering edition of Marlowe's works, who 'concluded that *Tambur-laine* "cannot be laid to Marlowe's charge"' on the basis of Thomas Heywood's prologue to *The Jew of Malta* (1633) (quoted in Dabbs, pp. 61–2):

> We know not how our play may pass this stage,
> But by the best of poets in that age,
> The Malta Jew had being and was made;
> And he then by the best of actors play'd:
> In Hero and Leander, one did gain
> A lasting memory: in Tamburlaine,
> This Jew, with others: th' other wan
> The attribute of peerless, being a man
> Whom we may rank with (doing no one wrong)
> Proteus for shapes and Roscius for a tongue.

Heywood's verses are every bit as obscure as Greene's and Harvey's references to '*Tamburlaine*', and therefore no more conclusive on the question of authorship. Clearly it is Marlowe who has gained a 'lasting memory' on account of *Hero and Leander*. But it is far from clear whether the allusion to Tamburlaine refers to the play or to the character, to the playwright or to the actor – whether, in short, it refers to Marlowe or to Edward Alleyn.

However, although we have no information whatsoever on his actual movements between leaving Cambridge[16] and the fracas in which he was involved in the autumn of 1589, we know for certain from a very different kind of source that Marlowe *was* moving in theatrical circles in London in the late 1580s. By this time, Marlowe was evidently a neighbour of the poet and playwright Thomas Watson, in the district of Norton Folgate, near Shoreditch, close to the Theater and the Curtain. We know this because Watson and 'Christoferus Marlowe nuper de [Norton Fowlgate] yoman' were arrested and committed to Newgate prison on 18 September 1589[17] on suspicion of the murder of William Bradley in Hog Lane in the parish of St Giles without Cripplegate. The inquest on Bradley's death was held the following day, but it was only on 1 October that 'Christopher Marley of London, gentleman' was bailed. His sureties for the sum of £40 were 'Richard Kytchine of Clifford's Inne, gentleman, & Humfrey Rowland of East Smithfeilde in the county aforesaid, horner'. Watson was subsequently found to have killed Bradley in self-defence, and Marlowe was duly discharged on 3 December 1589 at the Old Bailey where, presumably, he appeared in person to save his bond.

Like all other documentary references to Marlowe, the Hog Lane incident prompts a number of questions, but offers few answers.

How did the fight between Marlowe and William Bradley begin? Why did Marlowe take no further part in it once Watson intervened? Why was Marlowe, a graduate of Cambridge, described as 'yoman' in the Middlesex Sessions Roll, but as 'generosus' when admitted to bail? Why was bail set at such a high sum? What was the nature of the relationship between Marlowe and Watson? After all, the dedication to the Countess of Pembroke of the posthumous edition of Thomas Watson's *Amintæ Gaudia*, entered in the Stationers' Register on 10 November 1592, is signed 'C. M.', and *Edward II* was acted by the Earl of Pembroke's servants.

If the connection between Marlowe and the Pembroke circle is worth pursuing, so are Watson's connections with others who have their place in Marlowe's story. Watson was, for instance, a friend of Thomas Walsingham, dedicating *Meliboeus* to him in 1590. *Meliboeus* was an elegy on Walsingham's cousin, Sir Francis Walsingham, who, until his death in that year, had been Elizabeth I's Secretary of State and spymaster-in-chief. Sir Francis would therefore have been in a position to know the circumstances behind the famous entry in the Privy Council Register concerning Christopher Morley, although he was not present at the meeting held on 29 June 1587. And when 'E. B.' – presumably Edward Blount – dedicated *Hero and Leander* to Sir Thomas Walsingham in 1598, he reminded him of his interest in the poet:

I suppose my selfe executor to the unhappily deceased author of this Poem, upon whom knowing that in his life time you bestowd many kinde favours entertaining the parts of reckoning[18] and worth which you found in him, with good countenance and liberall affection.

It was from Thomas Walsingham's house at Scadbury in Kent that Marlowe would ride to Deptford on 30 May 1593 to a meeting with Ingram Frizer, Robert Poley, and Nicholas Skeres.

After 3 December 1589, however, Marlowe's name once again disappears from view in the official records until Sir Robert Sidney, Sir Philip Sidney's younger brother, writes to Lord Burghley, the Lord Treasurer, on 26 January 1592 from Flushing, about a 'scholer' called 'Christofer Marly' who had been taken up for coining in Flushing along with one Gifford Gilbert.[19] They had been shopped by their 'chamber fellow' Richard Baines – a name otherwise familiar to Marlowe scholars on account of his 'note Containing the opinion of on[e] Christopher Marly Concerning his Damnable

Judgment of Religion, and scorn of Gods word'. In this document, Baines also alleged that Marlowe had affirmed that 'he had as good Right to Coine as the Queene of England, and that he was acquainted w[th] one poole a prisoner in newgate who hath greate Skill in mixture of mettals'.[20] 'The men being examined apart never denied anything', Sidney assured Burghley, 'onely protesting that what was done was onely to see the Goldsmiths conning.'

This sounds like our man. The most interesting piece of information to arise from Sidney's letter, however, concerns Marlowe's alleged connections with much bigger fish than Richard Baines and John Poole. According to Sidney:

> The scholer sais himself to be very wel known both to the Earle of Northumberland and my Lord Strang. Baines and he do also accuse one another of intent to goe to the Ennemy or to Rome, both as they say of malice one to another. Hereof I thowght fitt to advertis yowr Lo: leaving the rest to their own confession and my Anciants report.

For the second time, then, documentary evidence exists of Marlowe's intention either to defect to the enemies of Elizabeth I's England or to convert to Roman Catholicism or both. In order to get out of trouble this time, however, Marlowe insinuated that he was connected in high places. For Nicholl, this scrap of second-hand evidence becomes the clinching argument for Marlowe's membership of Ralegh's 'School of Night', to whom, according to Richard Cholmeley, he read his 'atheist lecture'. Nicholl puts it thus: 'Marlowe himself said, in early 1592, that he was "very well known" to Northumberland' (Nicholl, *The Reckoning*, p. 52). Once again, then, circular reasoning allows us to postulate hard 'facts' about Marlowe. Cholmeley claims that Marlowe was an atheist associated with the so-called 'School of Night'. 'Fortunately', writes Nicholl, 'we do not have to rely on Cholmeley's word alone' (Nicholl, *The Reckoning*, p. 52). Marlowe evidently told Sidney that he was 'very wel known both to the Earle of Northumberland and my Lord Strang'. Northumberland, in turn, 'was a close associate of Sir Walter Ralegh' (Nicholl, *The Reckoning*, p. 52). *Ipso facto*, Marlowe was part of the 'School of Night'.

Alas, it is not that simple. Arrested for coining – a crime which carried the death penalty – 'Christofer Marly' told his interrogator that he knew powerful men like Northumberland and Strange. Why should he do this if, as Nicholl and others contend, he was a government agent? What are we to conclude from Sidney's letter to

Burghley? That Marlowe was well in with Northumberland and Strange, and 'part of that free-thinking, philosophical clique, centred on Ralegh, called the "School of Night" ' (Nicholl, *The Reckoning*, p. 52)? Or that 'Christofer Marly' was trying to impress Sidney with his connections and escape the consequences of being caught in the act of 'uttering' a counterfeit Dutch shilling?

What, then, is the evidence for Marlowe's association with Northumberland and Strange?

Anxious to establish an 'early connection between Marlowe and Northumberland' which would reveal the former at work as a 'poet-spy' in the latter's household (Nicholl, *The Reckoning*, p. 201), Nicholl makes much of the fact that Thomas Watson dedicated two pieces of work (one unpublished) to Northumberland. And of course Marlowe knew Watson. Further, there was an eighteenth-century tradition known to Thomas Warton and Edmond Malone that Marlowe translated one of these, *Helenae Raptae*, 'into English rhyme' in 1587 (Nicholl, *The Reckoning*, pp. 192–3). (What this proves I am not quite sure, and of course Malone thought *Tamburlaine* was the work of Thomas Nashe.) Thwarted but apparently undismayed by the lack of evidence, Nicholl then simply assumes that Marlowe 'had perhaps served as a government listener in the Northumberland circle' (Nicholl, *The Reckoning*, p. 232). Why? Because he believes Marlowe's murder was a political job, engineered by the Earl of Essex.

While other evidence of Marlowe's association with Northumberland is simply lacking, Henslowe's diary, as Julian Bowsher notes, records performances of both *The Jew of Malta* and *The Massacre at Paris* by Lord Strange's Men at the Rose theatre in 1592 and 1593. 'In May 1593, Kyd recorded that he and Marlowe had been "wrytinge in one chamber twoe years synce" ', Bowsher continues. 'Marlowe was working (or rather, writing) for the "plaiers" of a certain Lord, unidentified, but thought to be Lord Strange' (see below, p. 33). If the Lord to whom Kyd refers is indeed Strange, then once again we encounter evidence which is difficult to interpret. Kyd's description of Marlowe's relationship with 'his Lordship' is hardly that of a favourite, much less a friend:[21]

My first acquaintance w^th this Marlowe, rose vpon his bearing name to serve my Lo: [Lord] although his Lp never knew his service but in writing for his plaiers, ffor never cold my L. endure his name, or sight, when he had heard of his conditions, nor wold in deed the forme of devyne praiers used duelie in his Lp' house haue quadred w^th such reprobates.

In what sense, then, was Marlowe claiming to be 'very wel known' to Strange?

In either case, Marlowe's claim to be connected with North-umberland and Strange apparently cut no ice with Sidney, who sent Marlowe and Gilbert (but *not* Baines) 'over unto [Burghley], to take their trial as you shall think best'. What Burghley thought best we do not know, although Sidney's letter was endorsed: 'S*ir* Robert Sidney to my L. He sendes over by this bearer his Auntient one Evan Lloyd, and 2 others Christopher Marley and Gifford Gilbert a goldsmithe taken for coynage, to be tryed here for th*at* fact. There hath bene only one dutch shilling uttered, the metall playne peuter.'[22]

Whether Marlowe was tried, whether he was punished, or whether he was shielded by Burghley because he was a government agent,[23] he was at liberty in May 1592 when he was arrested for making threats against the constables of Holywell Street in Shore-ditch. According to the record, Christopher Marlowe of London, gentleman, was put upon his recognisance on 9 May 1592 to appear at the Michaelmas Middlesex Quarter Sessions of October 1592.

Revealingly, Mark Eccles called this 'the second definite record of Marlowe's life as a playwright in London' (Eccles, *Christopher Marlowe in London*, p. 114), with the affray in Hog Lane the first. It is an interesting point. Marlowe may well have been the author of *Tamburlaine* and other plays, but there are no documentary records of his authorship dating from his lifetime. In addition, Thomas Kyd, under interrogation in May 1593, referred to the time when he and Marlowe were 'wrytinge in one chamber twoe yeares synce', but Kyd was in fear of his life, and trying to explain how certain 'waste and idle papers . . . fragmentes of a disputation tochinge that opinion affirmed by Marlowe to be his' were found in his, Kyd's, possession. These dangerous papers, which we now know not to have been written by Marlowe at all, but to have been part of a treatise by John Proctor published in 1549 called *The Fal of the Late Arrian*, supposedly got 'shufled w^th some of [Kyd's]', without Kyd's knowledge.[24]

'When we next hear of Marlowe after the seizure of Kyd's papers in May a year later', Eccles pointed out, 'the Council is ordering him arrested at the house of Mr Thomas Walsingham in Kent' (Eccles, *Christopher Marlowe in London*, p. 106). However, one of the very few new pieces of information about Marlowe to have come to light since the publication of *Christopher Marlowe in London* in 1934 reveals that he was involved in a third violent *contretemps* prior to his encounter with Ingram Frizer, Robert Poley, and Nicholas Skeres on 30 May 1593 in Deptford. According to the Plea Roll of Canterbury Civil Court, on 15 September 1592 Marlowe 'did by force of arms [*vi et armis*], viz., with staff and dagger, make an assault upon the aforesaid plaintiff [William Corkyn], and against the Peace of the said Lady the Queen' near the 'central crossroads of Canterbury' (Urry, *Christopher Marlowe*, pp. 65, 66).

Marlowe's father stood bail for his son for the princely sum of 12*d*. (Why did Marlowe, the successful playwright, government agent, and friend of Northumberland and Strange, not have such a sum at his disposal?) In the meantime, his attorney, John Smith, prepared an indictment against William Corkyn for the quarter sessions which began at Canterbury on 26 September, in which Marlowe, in turn, unsuccessfully accused Corkyn of an assault on his person. Marlowe's civil case duly came up on 2 October, was first adjourned, and then dismissed a week later on the 9th. As William Urry notes: 'Christopher Marlowe's dismissal from court on 9 October 1592 marks his last recorded appearance at Canterbury and indeed is the last precisely dated evidence for his whereabouts until his arrest and death the following May' (Urry, *Christopher Marlowe*, p. 67).[25]

Marlowe was arrested in May 1593 as a direct result, it appears, of the apprehension (on or before the 12th) and subsequent interrogation of Thomas Kyd. We do not know what Kyd was taken up for, although papers found in his chamber led to the suspicion that he was an atheist. Kyd fingered Marlowe. On 18 May 1593 the Privy Council issued a warrant to a messenger 'to repair to the house of Mr. T. Walsingham in Kent, or to anie other place where he shall vnderstand Christopher Marlowe to be remayning, and by virtue hereof to bring him to Court in his companie, and in case of need to require ayd'.[26] The Privy Council, then, knew that Marlowe was likely to be staying at Thomas Walsingham's house at Scadbury. But Marlowe was not arrested and kept in confinement. Instead, after appearing before the Council on 20 May, he was released on bail, and ordered to report daily.

Ten days later, as everybody knows, Christopher Marlowe was 'in the house of a certain Eleanor Bull, widow', in Deptford Strand, from 'about the tenth hour before noon . . . until the sixth hour after noon' on 30 May 1593, in the company of Ingram Frizer, Robert Poley, and Nicholas Skeres. In the early evening they came in from the garden and had supper. Then they argued over '*le recknynge*'.

According to the affidavits, Marlowe attacked Frizer with his own dagger. Frizer fought back, 'and so it befell in that affray that the said Ingram, in defence of his life, with the dagger aforesaid to the value of 12*d*. gave the said Christopher then & there a mortal wound over his right eye of the depth of two inches & of the width of one inch'.[27] Marlowe's death was evidently instantaneous.

The inquest on Marlowe's death opened on 1 June, with William Danby, Coroner to the Royal Household, presiding. (Marlowe had been killed 'within the verge', in close proximity to Greenwich Palace and the body of the Queen.) Sixteen jurors found that Frizer had killed Marlowe in self-defence. Marlowe was buried in an unmarked grave in St Nicholas' churchyard the same day. For some reason, as if determined that the ambiguity over documentary evidence relating to Marlowe should dog him to his death and beyond, the parish register reads: 'Christopher Marlow slaine by Francis Frezer.'[28] A writ of *certiorari* was issued on 15 June to summon the case into Chancery, and on 28 June a pardon was issued to Frizer as he had acted 'in defensione ac saluacione vite sue'.

And so the 'historical' Marlowe disappears from view, unless one is prepared to entertain the preposterous theory that he was not killed at all, that the 'recknynge' was a clever way of 'disappearing' Marlowe for some reason that is not immediately apparent, but that was not unconnected with espionage. That the unusual circumstances of Marlowe's death should tease the scholar into thought is understandable. As soon as the affidavits were discovered in the 1920s, speculation began as to whether the 'affray' could have happened as alleged, and whether Marlowe's wounds were consistent with the events described by Frizer, Poley, and Skeres. Conspiracy theories have been woven around the connections of Marlowe's companions, and the suspicious ease with which Frizer was pardoned. Is this not indicative that he had friends in high places? But so far all that these theories amount to is mere speculation. Announcing the discovery that Frizer had indeed 'one more [friend] than has been suspected', not Walsingham or Burghley or Essex, but Paul Banning, sometime elected Sheriff of London, Arthur Freeman puts it thus: 'the "conspiracy theory" . . . seem[s] less necessary than before. Marlowe may even have been murdered, as his earliest biographers believed, in a brawl' over the reckoning.[29]

After duly weighing all the documentary evidence for the historical Marlowe which has been presented over the years, I see no

reason to contradict Frederick S. Boas's admirably balanced judgement on the death of Marlowe: 'Is it legitimate, from the natural
desire to shield the name of a great poetic playwright, and to redress
the balance of contemporary prejudice against a revolutionary
thinker, on account of some difficulties in the case, to reverse the
verdict in posterity's court of appeal?'[30] I think not.

What, then, are we left with? Marlowe was born in Canterbury,
educated at the King's School, Canterbury, and Corpus Christi,
Cambridge, where he took BA and MA degrees. He was absent from
his college from time to time prior to 29 June 1587, when he took his
MA, apparently on account of nameless 'matters touching the
benefitt of his Countrie'. He was arrested and imprisoned on
suspicion of murder in September 1589, but subsequently released.
He was arrested on a charge of coining in the Low Countries in
January 1592, and deported to England. He was arrested in May
1592 for threatening behaviour in Shoreditch. He was arrested once
more in Canterbury on 15 September 1592 for an assault on William
Corkyn. Such conduct, taken in conjunction with the account of his
alleged attack on Ingram Frizer on 30 May 1593, might be taken to
corroborate Kyd's account of Marlowe's 'other rashnes in attempting soden pryvie iniuries to men'.

In the intervals between his court appearances, Marlowe apparently wrote some plays, although none of them was unambiguously
attributed to him prior to his death. He also wrote some poems.
'Marlowe's poems and translations are traditionally assigned to his
Cambridge years', writes Stephen Orgel, 'though there is in fact no
evidence to support this view'.[31] Once again, none of the poems
appears to have been published prior to his death. Greene's
*Menaphon* (1589) paraphrases *The Passionate Shepherd*, although the
earliest extant printed version is from 1599 when it appeared in *The
Passionate Pilgrim. Hero and Leander: Begun by Christopher Marloe; and
finished by George Chapman*, with a dedication to Sir Thomas Walsingham signed 'E. B.', was published in 1598. None of the surviving
clandestine editions of Marlowe's translations of Ovid's *Amores* is
dated, although the book was banned by Archbishop Whitgift and
burned in the yard of the Stationers' Hall on 4 June 1599. The
Huntington Library copy is entitled *All Ovids Elegies: 3. Bookes*, by
'C. M.', and was supposedly published 'At Middlebourgh'.[32] Finally,
*Lucans First Booke Translated Line for Line, by Chr. Marlovu,* appeared in

1600, with a dedication by Thom. Thorpe to Edward Blount, 'his kind, and true friend', '*in the memory of that pure Elementall wit* Chr. Marlow; *whose ghoast or* Genius *is to be seen to walke the* Churchyard *in (at the least) three or foure sheets'*.

It is difficult to judge how seriously to take Thorpe's pun. Clearly it is suggesting that Marlowe was a published author '*whose ghoast or* Genius' could still be found if one were to take the trouble of visiting the booksellers at St Paul's Churchyard. Assuming that Thorpe's purpose was not to insinuate that he knew or suspected that some of the works attributed to Marlowe between 1593 and 1600 by his initials or by the abbreviation '*Ch. Mar.*' were not actually written by Marlowe at all, but were 'ghosts' – booksellers' ploys to cash in on the sensational manner of his death, Thorpe nevertheless implies that Marlowe was known as the author not of a large body of plays, but of '*(at the least) three or foure sheets'*. This might mean as little as three or four broadsheets or at least 96 pages, assuming the format was duodecimo – about the length of *Hero and Leander*, for instance.

We can name certain of Marlowe's associates, some with more confidence than others. Clearly, in addition to Walsingham and Blount, he knew the poets and playwrights Thomas Watson and Thomas Kyd, as well as Thomas Nashe and Robert Greene. He may also have been connected with the Earl of Pembroke. Although both Kyd and Richard Baines associate Marlowe's name with that of Thomas Harriot, 'S$^r$ W[alter] Raleighs man', Kyd's apparently second-hand account is the only source for Marlowe's conversations 'w$^{th}$ . . . Warner, Royden, and some stationers in Paules churchyard'. Similarly, although it seems to be the basis of Nicholl's conspiracy thesis, Sir Robert Sidney's letter to Burghley is the only source connecting Marlowe with the Earl of Northumberland and Lord Strange, as well as being the only suggestion that Marlowe was personally known to Burghley. (True, *The Jew of Malta* and *The Massacre at Paris* were acted by Lord Strange's men, but that is no proof that Marlowe and Strange were personally acquainted – indeed Kyd's testimony would rather suggest the reverse.)

Finally, there are of course the strong traditions concerning Marlowe's atheism. Kyd's references to 'marlowes monstruous opinions' – 'to iest at the devine scriptures[,] gybe at praiers, & stryve in argum$^t$ to frustrate & confute what hath byn spoke or wrytt by prophets & such holie men' – correspond closely to those of Richard Baines, Marlowe's 'chamber-fellow' in Flushing when he was arrested for coining. Baines claimed that Richard Cholmeley 'Confessed that he was perswaded by Marloe's Reasons to become an Atheist'. Cholmeley was alleged to have said 'that one Marlowe is able to show more sound reasons for atheism than any divine in England is able to give to prove divinity, & that Marlowe told him he hath read the atheist lecture to Sr Walter Ralegh & others'. Several other traditions deriving from a single source suggest that Cholmeley was not the only one to be persuaded to atheism by Marlowe. According to Eccles, they 'go back to Simon Aldrich, whose home was in Canterbury and who was for many years a scholar and fellow at Cambridge, so that he heard what was said about Marlowe both by his fellow-townsmen and by the gownsmen of the university' (Eccles, *Christopher Marlowe in London*, p. 61). But, on their own, do these accounts – second-hand at best – make Marlowe an 'atheist'? On the contrary, accusations of atheism and sodomy were common contemporary methods of blackening a man's character – as they were until at least the later twentieth century.[33]

Of more significance, does any of this help us to interpret Marlowe's plays? They, too, are massively ambiguous documents. Although it is highly unfashionable to write of an author's intentions, I suspect that they were *intended* to be ambiguous:

> View but his picture in this tragic glass,
> And then applaud his fortunes as you please.

In this context, the words of the Prologue to *Tamburlaine* seem to have been chosen with particular care.

# CHAPTER 2

# Marlowe and the Rose

### Julian M. C. Bowsher

Much about Christopher Marlowe is enigmatic. Very few facts are known about his life, and even the events surrounding his death are occasionally disputed. However, Marlowe's dramatic legacy has remained a cornerstone of Elizabethan theatrical history. His association with the Rose theatre consists in the fact that most of his plays were performed there to great acclaim over a number of years. Philip Henslowe, the owner of the Rose, which was situated on the Bankside in Southwark, left diaries which provided details of performances, accounts, and the relationship with acting companies. Henslowe's papers, the only such surviving accounts of theatrical life from this period, have given the Rose a unique documentary status amongst its contemporaries.[1] The archaeological excavation of this playhouse in 1989 by the Museum of London (Figure 3) has doubled the importance of the Rose by revealing for the first time the physical context in which the plays of Marlowe, and his contemporaries, were performed. Although only the foundations remained, the excavations were able to determine the layout of the building in different phases. Most important, the stage area was clearly defined and the results of the excavations now allow us a clearer insight into where these performances took place.[2] This chapter examines the relationship of Marlowe and his plays both with the Rose, and with other Elizabethan playhouses.

Marlowe (and Shakespeare for that matter) apparently came to live in London in 1587, the same year that the Rose playhouse was built. However, it is assumed that he went to live in Shoreditch where the two most successful and earliest of the playhouses were situated – the Theater and the Curtain built ten years earlier. A number of other actors and playwrights are known to have settled in the area,[3] and Marlowe is recorded as living in Norton Folgate in 1589. He was

3 Overhead photograph of the Rose theatre excavations in May 1989.
The eastern edge remains unexcavated and clusters of concrete piles from the 1950s
still disfigure the site. The stage area can be seen at the northern end, with the
building alterations of Phase Two.

sharing lodgings with Thomas Kyd, perhaps in the same area, in the summer of 1591, and was certainly in this vicinity (Holywell Street) in May 1592 when he was arrested after an affray (see above, p. 24). It is important to realise that the distance between Shoreditch and the Bankside was (and is) less than an hour's walk across London Bridge – the only bridge across the Thames in London at the time. In sixteenth-century terms London was very small, and such distances would have been considered almost negligible. Furthermore, London Bridge was the gateway to the south and the road to Marlowe's home town of Canterbury.

In Elizabethan England, plays were usually written for specific companies rather than for specific venues, as the former moved about so much at this time, and their composition was constantly changing. Elizabethan actors achieved great fame, perhaps greater than the playwrights. It has even been questioned whether the bulk of the audiences knew who had written the plays they flocked to see. Henslowe's diary records the names of plays rather than their authors. Other than the performance of his plays, therefore, there remains no documentary evidence of Marlowe's association with the London playhouses.[4]

The chronology of Marlowe's plays is still uncertain, but it is probable that his earliest works of the late 1580s were performed by the Admiral's Company, almost certainly at the Theater. In November 1587 a member of the audience was accidentally shot and killed during the performance of a play by the company. This has been associated with *Tamburlaine*, performed by the Admiral's Men at the Theater.[5] The company was named as the players of *Tamburlaine* when the play was entered in the Stationers' Register in 1590, and it is thought that they were also performing it at the Theater in the same year.

The Admiral's Men might also have performed *Doctor Faustus* at the Theater during this period. Thomas Middleton recorded an undated episode when 'the old Theater crackt and frighted the audience' watching *Faustus*.[6] Another late source records *Faustus* being performed at the Bel Savage theatre in Newgate Hill 'in Queen Elizabeth's dayes', although the company concerned remains uncertain.[7] However, there is no definitive record of the play being performed elsewhere until put on at the Rose by the Admiral's Men in October 1594.

Not all of Marlowe's later plays were linked to the Rose. *Edward II* was entered in the Stationers' Register in July 1592, where it was associated with Lord Pembroke's Company which might have been playing at the Theater. It is completely absent from the repertoire of plays performed at the Rose. Perhaps this was because, as Tucker Brooke has noted,[8] Edward II was not the sort of role usually played by Edward Alleyn, who took the lead in most of Marlowe's other dramas performed by the company at the Rose. *Dido, Queen of Carthage* is another play which cannot be connected with the Rose. It seems to have been finished off or edited by Thomas Nashe and was first published in 1594. The title page claims that it was 'Played by the Children of her Majesties Chappell', but it remains uncertain where, or when, the play was performed.[9]

In November 1590 the Admiral's Men amalgamated with Lord Strange's company, before quarrelling in May 1591 with James Burbage, the owner of the Theater, over receipts. On leaving the Theater they moved, almost certainly, straight to the Rose, probably taking many of their plays with them. In January 1589 Edward Alleyn, their chief player, had bought certain playbooks from a fellow player, Richard Jones.[10] The identity of these plays remains uncertain, but Alleyn was to accumulate a number of texts throughout his varied life and, as *Tamburlaine, Doctor Faustus*, and *The Jew of Malta* were regarded as old plays when they were performed at the Rose by the Admiral's Men a few years later, the company's repertoire may well have included some of Marlowe's works.

Edward Alleyn played some of the greatest roles that Marlowe created and, as he owned copies of some of them, it has been suggested that they were written specifically for him. However, there is no documentary proof of Marlowe's relationship with Alleyn, nor indeed of his relationship with Philip Henslowe, whose stepdaughter Alleyn married in late 1592. Rutter notes that Henslowe did not even mention Marlowe's death in a letter written to Alleyn dated 1 August 1593, only two months after the tragedy in Deptford.[11] (Alleyn was on tour in the provinces at this time.) Nevertheless, Marlowe's death was probably as much of a social as a professional loss to Alleyn.

In May 1593 Thomas Kyd recorded that he and Marlowe had been 'wrytinge in one chamber twoe years synce'. Marlowe was working (or rather, writing) for the 'plaiers' of a certain Lord, unidentified, but thought to be Lord Strange. In January 1592 Marlowe himself was reported to have claimed 'to be very wel known' to Strange (see above, pp. 21–4). All of this occurred around the very time when Strange's company was about to start playing at the Rose. The principal evidence for Marlowe's association with the Rose derives from Philip Henslowe's diary which begins in February 1592, five years after the Rose was built. It is uncertain which playwrights or acting companies were associated with the playhouse before this time. However, the first recorded performances in the diary at the newly refurbished building (see below, p. 36) were by Lord Strange's company.

The Jew of Malta is one of many plays known to have been privately owned by Alleyn since he sold it to Henslowe in January 1602. It had hitherto been played by a number of companies all associated with him, although it is uncertain when he first acquired it.[12] The first (known) performance of the Jew by the company at the Rose was on 26 February 1592. Marlowe was certainly not present for on that very day he was arrested and deported from Flushing (see above, pp. 21–23). If he spent time in prison, he would have missed the performances of the Jew on 10 and 18 March, and 4 and 18 April. Four days after the performance held on 5 May, however, he was involved in the well-known affray in Holywell Street. After this he was again bound over so probably missed the Rose performances of 11, 20 and 30 May and that of 14 June. Nevertheless, Marlowe may have taken some comfort in the fact that the performances of The Jew of Malta clearly attest to the play's popularity.

From June until the end of December 1592, the Rose was closed, and the Jew was not performed there again until 1 February 1593. Marlowe is known to have been in Canterbury in September 1592 (see above, p. 25), but his movements for the rest of that period are unknown. On the re-opening of the theatres, however, The Massacre at Paris, played by the Admiral's Company, was performed at the Rose on 26 January 1593. Henslowe marked the play as 'ne'. This notation is usually regarded as indicating a new play and it would seem that this was its first performance. Unfortunately, the playhouse closed once again a few days later. It was not to re-open until 27 December of that fateful year, by which time of course Marlowe was dead. His movements in the early part of 1593 are unknown, although it would have been entirely reasonable that he would have wanted to see the first performance of his latest work.

During the closure of the Rose, it is probable that Marlowe spent much time at Scadbury, the Kent seat of his patron, Thomas Walsingham. In his recent play, The School of Night, Peter Whelan imagines a meeting between Marlowe and other conspirators at the empty playhouse towards the end of this period.[13] The Rose re-opened at the end of December 1593 and, despite various further closures, survived until early 1606. Throughout this period Marlowe's plays were still being performed alongside a profusion of new works. Excavation of the building shows that it wore its popularity well.

Henslowe's partnership agreement with one John Cholmley dated 10 January 1587 mentions that the playhouse was 'now in framing', which would suggest that the superstructure was already being constructed.[14] Although it was described as 'ye new plaie house' in April 1588, the Rose was certainly hosting performances by October 1587 when complaints were made about playing on the Sabbath on Bankside, as it was the only playhouse there at the time.[15]

The archaeological excavations undertaken in 1989 uncovered two distinct phases of building. The first, which we presume is the original construction of the playhouse in 1587, is a simple affair. The building was a slightly irregular polygon whose frame comprised two parallel rings of walls that formed the galleries, surrounding an open yard. There was an entrance at the southern end and a stage projecting into the yard at the northern end. The surviving remains of this first stage (Figure 4) reveal an irregular shape tacked on to the inner wall of the frame. Its rear therefore was clearly the same inner wall whose angles mirrored the external wall of the frame, thus providing, it seems, five planes. It had a broad but tapered frontage and covered an area of about 490 square feet. There were perma-nent footings at the front of the stage, although it is possible that these supported trusses which, in turn, supported the actual boards. The actual height of the stage – perhaps five feet like the stage of the Red Lion[16] – is, of course, unknown. No evidence was found to suggest the greater supports which would have been needed for a roof or 'cover' over this stage, and it seems to have been open to the elements. As noted above, the stage back or *scenae frons* appears to have had five planes and there would have been at least two doors here, perhaps a larger third one in the centre. The 'tiring house', where the actors would get 'attired', was clearly that area of the frame of the building behind the stage, which would have been useless for an audience.

The second phase of construction involved the remodelling of the playhouse's northern half, its stage end, which gave it a much more

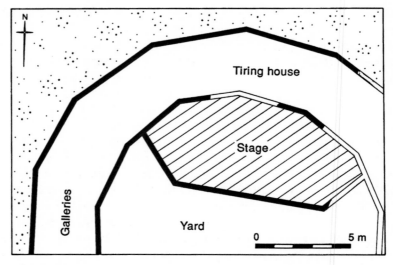

4  The northern part of the theatre in Phase One showing the stage. Black lines
are those walls found, white ones are restored.

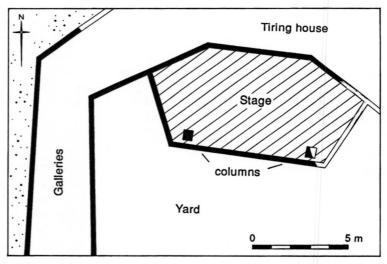

5  The same northern part of the theatre showing the stage and gallery alterations
of Phase Two moved a little to the north. Black lines are those walls found, white
ones are restored.

irregular shape. This phase has been associated with the £105 that Henslowe spent on 'suche carges as I haue layd owt a bowte my playe howsse' in February 1592.[17] This large entry in Henslowe's diary had previously been thought by some scholars simply to relate to repairs, but a sum of £105 seems excessive for such work, and the archaeological excavations reveal substantial structural changes. It is interesting to note that, at the same time, the Theater in Shoreditch was also undergoing (equally unspecified) alterations recorded as 'further building & reparacions'.[18] It would seem that this period was one of competition between the London playhouses, all of which were striving to attract audiences, acting companies, and playwrights through new building designs.

The excavations reveal that this phase of building at the Rose involved the inner and outer walls of the frame moving outwards from either side of the stage, which was itself moved back. The reason for this new layout is explained by the discovery of the bases of two columns that would have supported a 'cover' over the new stage, so that the galleries either side had to be moved outwards in order to allow unimpeded sight of the stage itself from the upper galleries. Such a view would have been impossible in the first phase of construction had there been a roof or 'cover' over the original stage.

The new stage (Figure 5) was not much larger in area than the original but, with the extension of the yard on either side, it produced a greater 'thrust' and thus greater contact with the groundlings in the yard. This second stage certainly had three planes to its stage back or *scenae frons* and it is hard to deny the implication that here there were three corresponding openings on to the stage. Amongst the expenditure that Henslowe recorded at the time was also payment for 'payntinge my stage'. No trace has been found of the back, northern, wall of the building in this phase, almost certainly because of disturbance in this area caused by later-seventeenth-century industrial installations. However, the tiring house must have been located in the same area as it was in the first phase of building, as no evidence has been found to indicate that it was ever a separate structure like that seen on a 1596 drawing of the nearby Swan playhouse.[19]

Two months after this rebuilding, Henslowe recorded payment for the construction of a 'penthowsse shed at the tyeringe howsse doore' and to 'sellynge the Rome ouer the tyerhowsse'.[20] These entries imply that the 'tiring house' was limited to the ground floor. Such an area would have been a little cramped and the new shed (of which no identifiable trace was revealed in the excavations) may have been designed to provide more working space. The 'sellynge' or sealing/plastering of the room over the tiring house may have related to a balconied area such as seen at the Swan, used either for musicians, richer patrons or even as a playing area for the 'above' scenes within certain plays. However, as an entry in Henslowe's diary dating from March 1598 refers to costumes being 'Leaft above in the tier-house in the cheast', some ambiguity remains as far as the area actually defined as the tiring house is concerned.[21]

Surviving documentary evidence from other playhouses reveals that the Rose stages were small even by contemporary standards,[22] although actually bigger than the 'downstage centre' area (i.e., that seen by the whole auditorium) of a proscenium stage. It is probable that the Rose stage is represented – as a single line – in the famous drawing of a performance of *Titus Andronicus*, which was first performed at the Rose on 23 January 1593.[23] Henslowe's diary provides details of a repertoire known to have been performed at the Rose, and there have been a number of modern studies dealing with the stage and the staging of these plays.[24] Now that the dimensions of the actual stages have been revealed, these studies can be enhanced. However, as it is generally recognised that the eventual publication of play scripts usually took place some time after their original performances, any printed 'staging directions' which are included may not actually have related to a play's first performance.

The size of the stage at the Rose would seem to preclude large scene properties and it must have remained a simple affair. Henslowe's well-known list of properties (with costumes and accoutrements) belonging to the Admiral's Men in 1598 may well have covered only small, easily removable items.[25] Whether there was a trap door in the boards of the stage could not, of course, be determined by the excavations, but any space below it would have been a little cramped. In fact, an analysis of the list of plays performed at the Rose has led to the suggestion that there was no need for a trap door at the theatre.[26]

Even before the actual size of the stage at the Rose was known, scholars had suggested that the yard could have been used for dramatic play. Simmons, for example, thought that, in performances of *The Jew of Malta*, Barabas was thrown over the front of the stage into the yard, and that the Turks entered into the yard via an *ingressus*. For these to have taken place, part of the yard would have had to have been roped off.[27] There was certainly no indication on the surface of the yard (during either building phase) of any structural elements suggestive of partitioning. There could, as noted above, have been access through the front of the stage through trusses above the footings. An *ingressus* into the galleries from the yard was, however, found in a similar position to that depicted at the Swan. The mortar surface of the original yard was rather eroded near the stage front. In the absence of any other information, this is thought to have been caused by the crush of groundlings towards the stage. The surface of the yard remaining from the second phase of construction appears to have been rather better laid as no such erosion was detected.

It should be noted that nothing was found amongst the artefacts recovered during the excavation that would have been unduly out of place in the archaeological assemblage of any other sixteenth-century urban building, such as coins, pottery, and other domestic debris. However, fragments of two swords – the hilt of one and a scabbard belonging to another – were found in the debris overlying the original stage, under that built during the second phase of construction at the Rose. They could have been stage props. Swords were needed for a number of plays, including *Doctor Faustus*, that predate 1592. What was possibly a replacement for one or other of these items, a 'long sworde', is recorded amongst the properties belonging to the Admiral's Company in 1598.[28]

Despite the absence of documentary information Marlowe obviously knew Alleyn and Henslowe. He certainly knew other contemporary playwrights, and together they must have been acquainted with the London, and possibly the provincial, playhouses. Nevertheless, the little that is known of Marlowe suggests a thoroughly metropolitan figure who enjoyed the company and delights that the capital had to offer. The Rose was the leading playhouse in London in the 1590s, its popularity clearly demonstrated not only by its wide-ranging repertoire but the income recorded by Henslowe in his diary.

Marlowe would have known the Rose in both of the building phases uncovered by the excavations, which have been associated with the playhouse's original construction in 1587, and the alterations recorded in Henslowe's diary in 1592. The overwhelming impression provided by the layout of Phase Two is that it was dictated by a perceived need for a studied improvement in staging conditions. A welcome consequence of the new stage arrangements was an increase in audience capacity. The drive for improvement may have been as much one initiated by the dramatic community as one pursued by Henslowe in order to maintain the pre-eminence that the Rose had acquired by this time.

Although the London playhouses themselves were probably of a roughly similar size, the dimensions of the Rose stage, smaller than its contemporaries, does not seem to have hindered its repertoire or diminished its popularity, and it is probable that the well-known stentorian delivery of Alleyn, especially when performing Marlowe's greatest roles, would have had a great impact in 'this small circum-ference'.[29] This setting, therefore, was clearly one known and appreciated by Marlowe, especially after Alleyn and his company were permanently established at the Rose.

The popularity and prestige of the Rose, attested by Henslowe's papers, was to continue for many years after Marlowe's death. Indeed his plays continued to be performed there to great acclaim throughout the Elizabethan period. Nevertheless, the lack of new works by Marlowe slowly resulted in a change of repertoire and Alleyn himself (temporarily) retired in 1597. Although we know much more about the Rose than any other London playhouse of the time, the death of Marlowe – and the survival of Shakespeare – has meant that it has been accorded a subordinate position to that of the Globe in theatrical history. In the light of the new information resulting from the excavations of the remains of the playhouse, the association of Christopher Marlowe with the Rose must now be seen as at least as great as that of Shakespeare with the Globe.

# CHAPTER 3

# Marlowe and the editors

### Richard Proudfoot

In 1964, Marlowe's 400th birthday was heralded by academic conferences, special publications, and theatrical revivals, especially of his (then) less performed plays. In 1993, his fourth lifetime ran out to the knell of academic conferences and special publications, a production of *Dido, Queen of Carthage* at his old school and a spate of imaginative recreations – theatrical, novelistic, and documentary – of the man, his life, and his death.

Marlowe is being used in old ways, though sometimes under novel disguises. His name would seem to have gained in commercial value to publishers. His plays have been commandeered for a variety of theoretical purposes, while theatrical companies are still as likely as ever to rely on star casting of leading roles or on bending the texts in the direction of real or factitious topicality to draw audiences, and they still assume an *oeuvre* of only four plays (although productions of those plays have been unprecedentedly frequent).

For his fourth lifetime the hitherto faceless Marlowe acquired a likeness. A portrait of a young gentleman, dated so as to indicate that the sitter was the coeval of Marlowe, Shakespeare and the rest of their year-group, was astutely identified by the then Master of Corpus Christi College, Cambridge (where it was discovered in the 1950s on a heap of builder's rubble) as representing the face that launched the Marlowe industry. To this day the College's imaginable motives for having acquired, commissioned or even accepted the gift of a portrait of one of its less than satisfactory graduate students remain obscure. The 'portrait', however, supplied a felt need, not least by reinforcing the anti-Stratfordian (and more recently the anti-Shakespearean) camp with an icon of the anti-Bard more humanly prepossessing than the man with two right shoulders of the 1623 Folio frontispiece or the prosperous butcher of the Stratford memorial.

Can't we keep Shakespeare out of it? Much as we might wish to, it is hard to see how. Robert Greene started it, after all, though his passionate warning to his fellow poet-graduates of the dangerous rival who was emerging from the ranks of their collaborative commercial antagonists, the players, has long yielded to different kinds of definition of the relation, human (if any), theatrical, and poetic between the man who died in May 1593 and the man who survived him by just under twenty-three years. I shall refer to Shakespeare again, but my initial occasion for mentioning him is my title, 'Marlowe and the editors'. The works of Marlowe are being edited into ever-increasing conformity with those of Shakespeare. We have a Cambridge Marlowe and a New Cambridge Shakespeare; an Oxford Marlowe and three Oxford Shakespeares; a Revels Marlowe, in a series modelled by its founding general editor, Clifford Leech, on the Arden Shakespeare (and initially published by the same firm, Methuen); and we have New Mermaid and other occasional Marlowes, including, of course, a one-volume Everyman Marlowe and a two-volume Penguin Marlowe as against the New Penguin Shakespeare's one text per volume policy.

There are naturally significant differences. The university presses offer a scholarly Marlowe. Cambridge does so in Bowers' austere two-volume set (Cambridge, 1973; 2nd edn. 1981), textual in emphasis, definitive in appearance, and based on the principles devised for Bowers' other Cambridge editions, of Dekker and of the plays in the Beaumont and Fletcher canon. Roma Gill's recent Oxford Marlowe is more innovative and more approachable. The first two volumes usefully challenge any monolithic vision of Marlowe. Volume 1, entitled 'Translations' (Oxford, 1987), certainly raises questions about two of its contents, *Hero and Leander* and *Dido, Queen of Carthage*, neither easily definable as merely a translation, but it also achieves a welcome realignment of those texts with the humanist face of Marlowe familiar in most critical accounts and separates *Dido* from the miseries of enforced marriage with *The Guise* – as in the Revels volume (ed. H. J. Oliver [1968]), which lumps them together as short, and by implication minor, Marlowe. The devotion of Volume 2 (Oxford, 1990) exclusively to *Doctor Faustus* has also a clear appropriateness; the play remains Marlowe's most popular work, requires editorial attentions of a different kind from the rest, and has had a theatrical and publishing history very unlike theirs.

Readers and students of Marlowe are unquestionably much better off today than they were in 1964 (though C. F. Tucker Brooke's single-volume *Works of Christopher Marlowe* [Oxford, 1920] continues to offer a practical old-spelling edition which has as yet no obvious replacement). What is more disturbing for students of Elizabethan drama is that the rise of Marlowe studies may be seen as among the contributory causes of a sharp decline in availability of cheap editions or anthologies of the works of his contemporaries and immediate predecessors. The name of Marlowe retains its drawing power, even in the popular imagination, while a discredited mythology which cast him as John the Baptist to Shakespeare's 'something else thereby' has yielded to an apter but still over-defining antagonistic relationship based on anxiety of influence and the political need for an opponent to a politicised Shakespeare. 'Let Marlowe be Shakespeare!' is not, perhaps, a very new cry, and Calvin Hoffmann has by now few disciples, but the desire to crown the better parts of Shakespeare in Marlowe all too readily recalls the ironies of Shakespeare's *Julius Caesar.*

In 1993 we commemorated the 400th anniversary of the death of Christopher Marlowe. Who, I wonder, on 9 December 1992, commemorated the death, 300 years before, of the 28-year-old actor-dramatist William Mountfort? Mountfort's death was more openly and more circumstantially reported than Marlowe's:[1]

Last night lord Mohun, captain Hill of collonel Earles regiment, and others, pursued Mountfort the actor from the playhouse to his lodgings in Norfolk Street, where one kist him while Hill run him thro' the belly: they ran away, but his lordship was this morning seized and committed to prison. Mountfort died of his wounds this afternoon. The quarrell was about Bracegirdle the actresse, whom they would have trepan'd away, but Mountfort prevented it, wherefore they murthered him thus.

I mention the chivalrous death of Mountfort because, of course, he has been cast in an altogether less attractive role in the textual and theatrical history of Marlowe's plays. In 1697, five years after he was murdered, there was published:

The LI[F]E and DEATH of *Doctor Faustus*, Made into a FARCE. By Mr. MOUNTFORD. WITH THE Humours of *Harlequin* and *Scaramouche*: As they were several times Acted By Mr. *LEE* and Mr. *JEVON*, AT THE Queens Theatre in *Dorset* Garden. Newly Revived, At the Theatre in *Lincolns Inn Fields*, With *Songs* and *Dances* between the ACTS.

This was the last 'edition' of *Doctor Faustus* before revived literary and antiquarian interest collected it for what, in the nineteenth century, began to grow into a 'Marlowe canon'. Doubt exists whether Mountfort's role was fully authorial or whether he was mainly associated with the play as a principal actor in it. Certainly MS notes beside the list of 'ACTORS Names' in the British Library's copy of the previous edition of *Doctor Faustus*, that of 1663 (shelfmark: 644. b. 69), cast 'Mr Baterton' as Faustus and 'Mr Munfert' as Mephostophilis. Mountfort's farce probably dates from about 1688 (when he was 24) and it seems as likely that these casting notes refer to it as to an earlier revival of the B-text in the somewhat altered form represented by the 1663 edition (which presumably reflects stage practice in the immediate aftermath of the Restoration of Charles II). In the 1663 version, the Pope and Rome were replaced by the Sultan and Babylon in a sequence of scenes whose action draws also on the final scenes of *The Jew of Malta*. The Empress of Babylon affords female attractions for Faustus. Elsewhere in the 1663 text extra lines are added to the scene between the Hostess and the Clown.[2]

Mountfort's farce of *Faustus* is an easy target for satirical or dismissive comment. In its opening scene Faustus moves nimbly from conjuring to repentance, by way of the expected signing of the bond and two appearances by the Good and Bad Angels. The scene also incorporates Helen – a first prize on the now feminised stage rather than a final consolation. There are no books in this play and if the scope for actresses remains small (they gain Pride but lose Lechery) there is compensation for the audience in the form of the Scaramouche/Harlequin extension of the servant scenes of *Doctor Faustus*. These scenes draw on some familiar routines: for instance, the first encounter of Scaramouche with Harlequin stands midway between those of Trinculo and Caliban in *The Tempest* and Papageno and Monostatos in *The Magic Flute*.

For Marlowe scholarship, Mountfort's text, when it is mentioned at all, represents the end of a catastrophic story of decline, a dreadful object lesson in textual instability and the corrosive effect of the players on the play. Looked at from the point of view of a different scholarship, that of Restoration theatre, *The Life and Death of Doctor Faustus, Made into a Farce* comes up shining. Robert D. Hume refers to it at some length:[3]

The final document in this progress of farce is Mountfort's adaptation, *The Life and Death of Doctor Faustus, Made into a Farce* (c. March 1688) . . . In his hands, the work becomes a catalogue of foolery. We are offered thunder and lightning (2); a giant who flies into pieces (13–14); a flying table (14); Harlequin using 'a Chamber-pot of Piss, and a Lamp of Oyl' to make a salad dressing (15); the pantomimers caught in trick chairs and squirted with milk by devils (16; cf. *The Citizen Turn'd Gentleman*); the horse-courser pulling Faustus's leg off (17); a magic wand; horns grown on Benvolio's head (20) – and so forth. At the end, Faustus's limbs are torn asunder, but in Hell they rejoin, and Mountfort concludes with 'A Dance, and Song' (26). The staging tricks put even *The Lancashire Witches* to shame. Mountfort's *Faustus* is the grand culmination of the farce boom, neatly combining magic, machinery, pantomime, and horseplay: what it aims to do, it does well.

The ending merits fuller quotation:[4]

*Enter old Man and Scholar.*

OLD M.　　Come, Friend, let's visit *Faustus*: For such a dreadful Night
was never seen.

*Scene discovers* Faustus*'s Limbs.*

SCHOL.　　O help us, Heav'n; see here are *Faustus*'s Limbs,
All torn asunder by the Hand of Hell.

OLD M.　　May this a fair Example be to all,
To avoid such Ways which brought poor *Faustus*'s Fall.
And whatsoever Pleasure does invite,
Sell not your Souls to purchase vain Delight.

[*Exeunt.*

*Scene changes to Hell.*
Faustus *Limbs come together. A Dance, and Song.*

The final stage direction is either the last infirmity of ignoble theatre or a caution to us about habitual ways of thinking and writing about *Doctor Faustus*. I think it might even be pressed into service for my present purposes as an emblem of Marlowe scholarship – and in particular of the editing of Marlowe. Of course, as a disciple of the New Bibliography, I would have to rewrite the stage direction: '*Scene changes to Heaven*. Marlowe's *Texts come together. A Dance, and Song*'. The pavan of Dr Greg and Mr Bowers would indeed be a stately and celestial affair, a celebration of the accomplishment of truly heroic tasks on whose basis we, coming after them, still repose while we repine. Less frivolously, the incorporation and canonisation of the *disjecta membra* of the literary and theatrical remains of Christopher Marlowe is a curious phenomenon, even more so than with other major English playwrights of the period we loosely call Elizabethan.

Before leaving poor Mountfort and the end of the play, I should like briefly to reminisce about my experience of *Doctor Faustus* in the theatre. I first met Marlowe in the form of anthologised excerpts in a book of English verse. Among them was the final speech of Faustus. Its impact was immediate, even if its verses didn't seem to scan (among the hazards of a classical education is the development of a metronomic ear for regularity in verse). I longed (for many years) to see the play, imagining the power that speech must have in context. Some seven theatrical experiences later I am still longing, still imagining. At least three of the productions I have seen were very good, with actors who gave life to Faustus in radically different but equally compelling and persuasive ways. But, for me at least, the 'big speech' did not work. Disbelief lost its suspension and power was regenerated only by visual means after the speech. I may just have been unlucky (and I'll go on trying and hoping), or I may have been looking for the wrong thing, but what lingers in my memory of each production is not the effect of the speech but a visual image.

Two such memories are particularly strong.

At Stratford-upon-Avon in 1968 Eric Porter, as Faustus, fell flat on his face after 'I'll burn my books'. Such was the violence of his fall and so long the pause after it that there was time for the thought that terror had indeed induced a massive heart attack. But no – slowly, fearfully, Faustus raised his head, and as he looked around at the still empty stage fear yielded to incredulous joy. It was at this moment that the back wall of the set crumbled inward onto the stage, revealing the teeth of a stylised Hell-mouth over which the grotesque, medievally-costumed devils swarmed towards their prey. I have to rely on another witness for what followed: 'Mephostophilis, now viciously demonic, yet laid a hand on Faustus' head in an almost tender farewell, while the latter uttered his final "ah *Mephastophilis*" as an agonized cry for help'.[5] A quite different effect was achieved at the end of a more recent production by the Medieval Players. After the speech Faustus, broken and beaten, was conducted back into his curtained 'study'. On the night I saw it, the curtain was finally re-opened, after the epilogue, to reveal, not scattered limbs, but Faustus hanged (I am told that this explicitly suicidal ending was not invariably used).

The simple proposition behind the anecdotage is of course that, in the case of *Doctor Faustus*, the inevitable gap between text and performance yawns into a gulf. Mountfort's Faustus shows an extremity of adaptation in one available direction, presumably designed to keep the old play on the boards. John Barton in his 1974 production for the RSC, which removed many of the comic scenes but supplied their absence with 'extracts from P. F.'s *Damnable Life*', was hardly less extreme, though his aim was the opposite of Mountfort's: 'though in theory the sub-plots provide a complementary comment on the main action by showing the abuse of necromantic powers in trivial pranks, in practice they tend to trivialize the tone of the play itself'.[6]

Will the *real* Doctor Faustus please stand up? Do we have to choose between the 'trivialisation' of a seventeenth-century tradition for which the comic scenes in *Doctor Faustus* clearly constituted a principal source of its theatrical appeal, and a late twentieth-century solemnity which is so afraid of the play's fragility that its high seriousness has to be shored up and sandbagged against comic scepticism? My question is rhetorical and its simple binary formulation false. The play, as is by now fairly generally accepted, depends on the alternation of tones and moods. For my money, though, the seventeenth-century tradition had a firmer grasp on this awareness than our own century has always shown – but that is presumably because *Doctor Faustus* remained then a play for acting, not a text for academic study. At least we may suspect that the late publication of *Doctor Faustus* and the clear indications that neither A- nor B-text is unadulterated 'Marlowe' should allow theatrical history a greater importance than is usually accorded to it in editions of the play – and textual analysis, perhaps, correspondingly less.

Turning to some of the broader issues implicit in my catch-all title, my image for the editing of Marlowe, 'Faustus' Limbs come together', recommends itself, I trust, beyond comic aptness because it enables a comparison with the strikingly different case of his deplorably successful coeval. We all recall the words of John Heminges and Henry Condell in the First Folio of 1623 deprecating certain earlier publications of the plays of their dead fellow William Shakespeare and recommending their own wares to the great variety of readers with the claim[7]

so to have publish'd them, as where (before) you were abus'd with diverse stolne and surreptitious copies, maimed, and deformed by the frauds and stealthes of injurious impostors, that expos'd them: even those, are now offer'd to your view cur'd, and perfect of their limbes.

The image of cure is simple enough (and it is used with some justice of the contents of the 1623 Shakespeare Folio): that of exposure

seems more confused. I have always taken it to allude to the ancient
Greek practice of exposing (and thus killing off) babies unlikely to be
viable. To maim first and then expose is an act of peculiarly wanton
savagery (except, I suppose, in the celebrated case of swell-foot
Oedipus. At least, like Oedipus, the Shakespearean 'bad quartos',
uncertain of their paternity, have recently returned to plague the
inventor). Less often quoted is the earlier comment in their dedica-
tory epistle that Heminges and Condell have acted as literary
executors of 'so worthy a Friend, & Fellow . . . as was our SHAKE-
SPEARE' in procuring 'his Orphans, Guardians' (sig.A2ᵛ).

The rhetoric in each instance is designed to ease the metamorphosis of play into text. The tact of Heminges and Condell in
seeking noble guardians for Shakespeare's orphaned 'Comedies,
Histories & Tragedies' doubtless owed something to the ridicule
attracted by Ben Jonson's self-presentation in the 1616 folio of his
*Works*. By the time Humphrey Moseley heralded his 1647 folio
collection of the unpublished plays of 'Beaumont and Fletcher' into
the world the ice had been broken and no apology was needed for
salvaging the textual flotsam of the grounded playhouses. The
smaller collections of Lyly and Marston published in the 1630s
reprinted plays by private theatre authors who, like Jonson, had
shown some care for the preservation of their own dramatic texts.

The case of Marlowe was, of course, radically different. Before
1593 plays accounted for a minuscule proportion of the output of the
London printing-houses. The conditions of commercial playwriting,
which entailed the author's loss of control of his copy, reinforced a
climate in which publication must more often have been seen as a
hazard than a hope. The publishing history of Marlowe's plays is not
wholly untypical and certainly resists any easy attempt at general-
isation (even on the assumption, open to obvious challenge, that we
have enough of the evidence to serve as a basis for any hypothetical
structure).

The story starts with the publication of *Tamburlaine* in 1590,
doubtless a reflection of the play's impact on audiences and dramatists alike in the late 1580s. R. Jones, the publisher, made the curious
claim to have[8]

(purposely) omitted and left out some fond & frivolous Jestures, digressing
(and in my poore opinion) farre unmeet for the matter, which I thought,
might seeme more tedious unto the wise, than any way els to be regarded,
though (happly) they have bene of some vaine conceited fondlings greatly

gaped at, what times they were shewed upon the stage in their graced deformities.

Depending on our estimate of his veracity, this either means what it says, affirming the learned appeal of at least parts of a popular play, or it is Jones's excuse for not printing what he had no copy for. (I note in passing that the identification of the lost manuscripts behind surviving printed editions of Marlowe seems not to have been the most fruitful area of study of his texts.) The reprint of 1593, depending when exactly it appeared, may or may not have been occasioned by Marlowe's sensational exit from world and stage. This would seem to offer a more secure explanation for the hum of activity in 1594, when *Dido*, *Edward II*, and probably *The Massacre at Paris* were all published and *The Jew of Malta* was entered on the Stationers' Register (though no edition for Nicholas Ling and Thomas Millington, who entered it on 17 May, has yet surfaced). *Tamburlaine* went through further reprints in 1597 and 1605–6; *Edward II* in 1598, 1612, and 1622: *Dido* and *The Massacre* did not.

These facts hardly suggest that Marlowe's plays were best-sellers, though the Jacobean revival of interest in *Tamburlaine* and *Edward II* is noteworthy. Certainly none of his plays began to equal the popularity of *Hero and Leander*, which went through nine editions between 1598 and 1637. *Doctor Faustus* followed in 1604 (unless an earlier lost edition followed the Stationers' Register entry to T. Bushell on 7 January 1601), and was twice reprinted in the 'A-text' before it was superseded in 1616 by the 'B-text', itself reprinted five times by 1631. The earliest – and only surviving – seventeenth-century edition of *The Jew of Malta* in 1633 is confidently described in the *STC* 2 as 'not the first'.

The theatrical success of *The Jew*, *The Massacre*, *Doctor Faustus*, and *Tamburlaine* is attested by Henslowe's diary: again interest would seem to have run high after Marlowe's death. Though there is little reason to believe that authors' names meant much to audiences (if indeed they even knew them), it still seems possible that the tendency to read Marlowe's alleged personality into his plays may have originated early and may thus have lent some factitious significance to the authorship of *The Jew*, *Faustus*, and *The Massacre* (and, I suppose, *Tamburlaine*, if the universal assumption that he wrote it was likewise of early origin). Thomas Nashe, activated, as Roma Gill supposes, by '[a] proper sense of the duty owed to a recently deceased friend',[9] may have elected himself literary executor and got

*Dido* into print – but only if he possessed a copy of it (which he may well have done if there is any substance to the title-page's claim for his co-authorship). It is perhaps as likely that the early printing of *Dido* and of *Edward II* was facilitated by the disgrace or dispersion of the companies that had acted them, 'the Children of her Majesties Chappell' and the Earl of Pembroke's Men. The printed editions of *Tamburlaine, The Massacre,* and *Faustus* all mention performance by the Admiral's Men – and *The Massacre* and *Faustus* have been the texts most regularly stigmatised with allegations of inauthenticity or corruption. The revival of *The Jew* at the Drury Lane Cockpit and at court that occasioned its publication must have taken place in the late 1620s or early 1630s and was given by Queen Henrietta's Men.

What we do not know is as significant as what we do. We do not know when the plays were written, though 1584–93 seems a likely estimate of the outer limits and *Tamburlaine* can be no later than 1587–8. We do not know what precisely were Marlowe's relations with the playing companies, although some continuity of dealings with Philip Henslowe and Edward Alleyn is strongly implied. We are unsure of the sequence in which the plays were written, although critical readings regularly assume a greater degree of confidence in this matter than is attainable on present evidence.

This kind of ignorance need not surprise us. The plays of George Peele and Robert Greene raise similar unanswered – perhaps unanswerable – questions. Of his immediate contemporaries it is perhaps Peele whose activities as a dramatist most resemble Marlowe's: a classical play for a boys' company, a two-part tragedy of high seriousness (Marlowe's historical, Peele's biblical), an English history, a modern European tragedy. Peele may have written more for the court and for the boys (assuming on the basis of its *dramatis personae* that *The Old Wife's Tale* must have originated with a boys' company despite its explicit association with the Queen's Men) and Marlowe may have achieved a greater and more lasting popular success, but both represent the application of university education to the most lucrative trade available to the unemployed graduate of literary bent.

Like Marlowe, Peele was mythologised in the decade after his death, in his case as a jest-book hero and, by derivation, as the foiled trickster George Pieboard in Middleton's early comedy *The Puritan* (which, to bring the wheel full circle, contains a hilarious parody [in Act 4, Scene 2] of the conjuring in *Doctor Faustus*).

Marlowe's plays find at least as rich a context in the fragmentary theatrical history of his time as in the critical readings which variously build them into relation with that short life about which we have so much, and in many ways such unhelpful, information. A secure conclusion to be drawn from the past three decades of experience of Marlowe is that he was as much professional play-wright as inspired poet. This conclusion has not, however, been of very great service to editors. Marlowe's plays do not add up to a volume of dramatic works: they are six very different kinds of play, having in common their excitingly innovative subject-matter, their sceptical engagement with orthodoxies, and their capacity to keep audiences guessing. Just how striking those qualities are can best be appreciated by reading (or performing) Marlowe in the context of the other surviving plays from his lifetime.

When Fredson Bowers edited Marlowe's works in the early 1970s he wrote:[10]

It would be pretentious to claim that the present edition has done very much more than, by a fresh survey, to offer fuller records of the textual transmission and the edited tradition, and in some respects, perhaps, to refine the wording. When a dramatist and poet like Marlowe has been edited so many times by scholars, startling upsets and illuminations are likely to be rare indeed. As with Shakespeare, an editor can but re-order a few details in the presentation of the text and occasionally glean a new reading after the gathering of the sheaves or, as in *Hero and Leander*, remove a persistent corruption or two in the several texts.

The answer to any reader irreverent enough to reply 'Why bother, then?' came on the next page: 'Critical views of the play [*Doctor Faustus*] may be clarified, perhaps, by the new account of the contents of the original play and of its revised 1602 version, which has some bearing also on the authorship of previously debated parts of the comic and farcical sections and also of the concluding scene.'[11]

Bowers stood at the end of a tradition of editing Marlowe which, to caricature it only mildly, took on the rest as an excuse for making a push at *Doctor Faustus*. That tradition is epitomised by the epigraph Greg used for the 'Conjectural Reconstruction' of *Doctor Faustus* which he published as a parergon of his parallel-text edition: 'Where there is great or complicated divergence between the editions, as in the case of Marlowe's *Faustus*, the production of a resultant text which may be relied upon to represent the ultimate intention of the author is well-nigh impossible'.[12] We all know what has happened since the publication of Bowers' edition in 1973: standing or falling by its treatment of *Doctor Faustus*, Bowers' edition fell. Having argued forcefully that, contrary to the conclusions of Greg, the B-text *does* incorporate the late additions for which Henslowe paid Samuel Rowley and William Bird, Bowers still chose to *print* the B-text, on the traditional grounds that the A-text was memorially contaminated.

The demolition of Greg's solution of the problem of the texts of *Faustus* has run parallel with the erosion of the received eclectic texts of some major Shakespearean plays, primarily *King Lear*. Many reasons have been found, or revived, for calling in question any notion of an 'ultimate intention of the author' in so volatile a medium as the Elizabethan theatre. So A is A, and B is B again, and never the twain shall meet (except in so far as the 1611 reprint of A contributed to the printer's copy for B, 1616). If *Faustus* was the Everest of Elizabethan dramatic editing (and this was clearly Greg's view) it was so *only* if you assumed that reconstruction of a single text was both theoretically desirable and practically attainable. With something of a sigh of relief we are now back where we started: as Gareth Roberts' chapter graphically illustrates (see below, pp. 55–59), Everest is besieged by queues of editors – now mostly choosing the shorter ascent afforded by the A-text – and John Jump's 1962 Revels edition of the B-text (immortalised by Simon Shepherd as 'an edition that claims to be as authoritative as others' [Shepherd, p. 92]) has just been ousted by the two-man team of David Bevington and Eric Rasmussen, securely roped, who present both A- and B-texts, though in tandem rather than in parallel.[13]

Editing Marlowe isn't, I take it, quite as humdrum an activity as Bowers made it sound. True, for the most part it does consist (as does very much other editing) of making the best of a single witness and trying hard to discern what your predecessors may have missed. But there are still unanswered questions which, though they won't re-write the plays, may promote fresh thought, especially about the nature of Marlowe's activity as playwright and about the character and status of the manuscripts of his plays from which the surviving early editions were printed.

I offer a sample of such questions. Who printed *Tamburlaine* in 1590? Is the current readiness to deny Nashe a share in *Dido* based on evidence, rather than convenience? Did Marlowe collaborate elsewhere? (Bevington and Rasmussen are not the first to assign him an anonymous collaborator for the A-text of *Faustus*, while Roma Gill[14] thinks it was completed by A. N. Other *after* 30 May 1593.) Was *The Massacre* certainly printed as early as 1593, or might the traditional date of *c.*1603 for its undated first edition still be plausible, and still bolster the theory of memorial reconstruction by allowing that the Guise's dying speech may evoke not only the historical Julius Caesar but Shakespeare's representation of him: 'Thus Caesar did go foorth, and thus he dyed' (xxi. 87)? If the manuscript leaf of variant text of *The Massacre* is neither in Marlowe's hand (which, *pace* Bowers, the arguments of R. E. Alton render tolerably certain), nor – despite some continuing claims such as that of Thomas Dabbs (Dabbs, pp. 69–70; 151, *nn.* 41–3) – a forgery by J. P. Collier (on the satisfying grounds that at the date of its discovery Collier's skills as a forger were still seriously inadequate to the task of producing it), then *what* is it? And what implications has it for our understanding of the text of that play? What if one stylometrist's subdued murmur that *The Jew of Malta* comes up much more like Kyd than Marlowe were to become a shout? When we see him, *do* we know Samuel Rowley? Who *did* write *Tamburlaine*?

Marlowe scholars, perforce, live dangerously. The edifice of assumption and conjecture on which, for instance, the chronology of composition of his works is based might easily be shaken. My hope would be that they might live even *more* dangerously, that they might look for more ways of opening up what sometimes threatens to become a dizzyingly centripetal operation. I am most grateful for what has been achieved in the past thirty years. Among my miscellaneous and random hopes for the next thirty would be: anthologies that juxtapose Marlowe with other plays from the repertoires of the Admiral's and Pembroke's Men; a set of facsimiles of the earliest editions of Marlowe's works; and a Marlowe theatre festival at which his repertoire might be extended to take in *Dido* and *The Massacre*, and even, perhaps, to juxtapose the two, or three, or four, seventeenth-century versions of *Doctor Faustus*. Editing can be humdrum, but the challenge of presenting Marlowe's plays as plays is still a fresh one – and Tucker Brooke's 1910 edition is still the only one since 1663 where you will find the speech from *Faustus* with the memorable first line 'Welcome *Mephostophilis* from the siege of *Malta*' – though Tucker Brooke's editorial care did not extend to pointing out that '*Mephostophilis*' must be a compositor's misreading of

'*Mustapha*' in his copy, induced by the sudden introduction of a leaf or two of manuscript in the midst of printed copy and by the failure of the preceding stage direction to give names to two entirely new characters, the two bashaws who attend the Sultan on his first entry, one of whom is called Mustapha (as the said compositor was soon to notice).

# CHAPTER 4

# Marlowe and the metaphysics of magicians

## Gareth Roberts

I

My point of departure is located fifty lines into *Doctor Faustus*. The context is a scholar in his study turning from dissatisfaction with orthodox knowledge and divinity to a fall – or an ascent? – to magic:[1]

> Divinity, adieu!
> [*He picks up a book of magic.*]
> These metaphysics of magicians
> And necromantic books are heavenly,
> Lines, circles, signs, letters, and characters –
> Ay, these are those that Faustus most desires.

This is the first time, apart from the Chorus' condemnation, that magic appears in the play, and it does so verbally and visually: Bevington and Rasmussen were surely right to make explicit the stage-direction. Faustus' words adumbrate what makes magic desirable to him: philosophical investigation not only of physical but also non-material entities, and a series of inscriptions in a book. Faustus and audience speculate on what magic might be, before Faustus enthusiastically imagines what magic might do.

These lines immediately involve us in the play's problems and contested issues: editorial, critical, and epistemological. First, what editorial decisions should we take, say, about the catalogue of magical inscriptions in 1.1.53: the A-text or the B-text, or a modern edition which may follow neither? Here are some of the choices:[2]

(1)  Lines, circles, sceanes, letters and characters:
(2)  Lines, Circles, Letters, Characters:
(3)  Lines, circles, letters, and characters:
(4)  Lines, Circles, Signes, Letters and Characters
(5)  Lines, circles, schemes, letters and characters

(6)  Lines, circles, scenes, letters, and characters
(7)  Lines, circles, seals, letters and characters

Second, Faustus' lines evoke in particular cases large critical issues about the play: is there irony in the juxtaposition of 'metaphysics' and 'magicians', and how can we be sure? Irony, which 'requires a sense opposite to that which is spoken',[3] must rely on our secure sense of a system against which that irony plays. The application of the epithet 'heavenly' to books of magic is ironic only if we all agree that such books are the very opposite of heavenly and the adjective is ironically misapplied to something orthodoxly understood to be hellish.

The question of irony in this passage has its place in sets of questions about the persistent use of religious language in *Faustus*, the relation of magic and religion in the play, and those in turn within the debate, which has a long history, about whether the play as a whole is orthodox or subversive.[4] What we make of magic is important in all these questions, just as it is in making individual editorial decisions. Leo Kirschbaum saw the play, at least in the B-text, as contained within an orthodox frame, and thought that 'there is no more obvious Christian document in all Elizabethan drama'.[5] There might be in the play an analogous frame of orthodox ideas about magic, perhaps consonant with and contributing to the enclosing moral frame sensed by Kirschbaum.

Third, epistemological questions about 'the metaphysics of magicians' provide a field within which to consider the issues already rehearsed. Are there metaphysics of magicians in the play, that is, some coherent and identifiable system and understanding of magic in the Renaissance and represented in the play, in which we could situate *Doctor Faustus*, to which we could appeal to settle critical issues and even help with editorial decisions? Wilbur Sanders thought not and was taken to task for this by West.[6] The problems are like those involved in talking about the 'atheism' of Faustus, or for that matter Marlowe. Is Renaissance atheism identifiable and coherent or is it 'a much broader range of phenomena'; or was 'atheist' just a general smear more or less synonymous with godless, evil-living, irreligious or sensual?[7]

II

I want to work up from the local problems in 1.1.50–4 to the larger issues, although the former are always implicated in the latter.

Scholars necessarily appeal to a knowledge and understanding of magical theories and practices in the early modern period to help make editorial decisions in *Doctor Faustus*. One may take three examples of editorial choices in 1.1.53, their associated annotations, and the magical authorities invoked: other examples will occur incidentally in the course of this essay. For 1.1.53 Roma Gill offered 'Lines, circles, schemes, letters and characters!' glossing 'schemes' as 'diagrams' in her 1989 New Mermaids edition and in her Oxford edition (p. 57), and citing as her authority Helen Gardner's note on some lines in Donne's elegy, 'The Bracelet', which describes the practices of a conjurer. Keefer in his 1991 edition gives us 'Lines, circles, seals, letters and characters', glossing 'seals' as 'talismanic symbols of the planets and of the angels' (pp. lxx–lxxi, 8). And although the first word, 'Lines', is not a problem, as it is the reading of both A- and B-texts, the Ormerod-Wortham edition explains 'lines' as those used in geomancy (p. 6). Gill's reading leads us into a small editorial maze. The lines from Donne she cites are:

> Or let me creepe to some dread Conjurer,
> Which with fantastique schemes fulfills much paper
> Which hath divided Heaven in tenements.

In a rather dizzying circular argument, in which editorial decision and a sense of early modern magical practice are interrelated, Gardner preferred the reading 'schemes' in the 1633 edition of Donne's poems to 'scenes' in the 1635 edition and two manuscripts, appealing partly to 'the misreading "scenes" for "schemes" . . . in *Dr. Faustus* (A text, 1.81)'.[8] It seems to me that Gardner was actually right in reading 'schemes' in 'The Bracelet', as the poet imagines consulting a conjuror who will cast the lost bracelet's horoscope ('scheme') in a diagrammatical representation of the heavens and their houses extant in numerous manuscripts. If so, then the rightness of the reading 'schemes' in 'The Bracelet' makes 'schemes' the wrong reading in *Doctor Faustus*. Keefer's 'seals', his only major departure from the A-text, seems an instance where knowledge of magic has actually got in the way of a more likely reading, and the appeal of the Ormerod-Wortham's edition to geomancy to gloss 'lines' seems perverse: Faustus is fascinated with conjuration, not divination, here. It seems sensible to follow Greg's judicious emendation, 'signs', so that the line reads 'Lines, circles, signs, letters and characters'. As evidence of magical practice one could cite internally from the play, as Bevington-Rasmussen do, 'Characters and signs of erring stars' in the conjuration (1.3.11), and externally the depiction of the magical 'signs' (*signa* and *signacula*) in a book on magic such as Agrippa's *De Occulta Philosophia* where, especially in the 1567 edition, one may find illustrated in some profusion lines, circles, signs, letters, and characters.

Magic is involved in debates about large editorial decisions, too. Perhaps one ought not to be surprised at the recent interesting alliance between bibliography and magic. Editing and 'high' magic, certainly cabalistic magic, are both intensely textual practices and have long sought for the virtue of the 'authentic' or 'original' text. It may be no accident that some Renaissance humanists (such as Ficino, Pico della Mirandola, Reuchlin, and Agrippa) were intensely interested in the power of words, editing, the restoration of authentic texts, and magic. The definition of some cabalistic practices, especially temurah ('systematic replacement of letters in a word with other letters'), could serve almost equally well as a description of editing. The desire to reconstruct an original text promising access to its author[9] might be analogous to cabalistic attempts to rediscover the secret name of God by which he authored (or author-functioned) creation.

The editions by Ormerod and Wortham, Keefer, and Bevington and Rasmussen not only pay attention to magic in their introductions and annotations, but implicate considerations about magic in decisions about texts. A number of articles which are primarily bibliographical adduce considerations about magic in arguments about the virtues of the A- and B-texts.[10] Michael Keefer argued for the superiority of the A-text on the basis of a critical preference partly grounded on an appeal to ideas about magic, for 'in one important respect – the handling of verbal magic – the B version is fundamentally incoherent'. His argument is partly based on what he sees as the inconsistency and incoherence of the treatment of the power of words in B. On the other hand, A presents the play 'as a whole in a form which is both more authentic . . . and aesthetically superior' and (and because) it ironically shows Faustus' early aspirations about the transitive efficacy of words proved increasingly empty by the play (Keefer, pp. 324–6).

Clearly, what we understand about the play's magic is important to its editing. But *are* there 'metaphysics of magicians' in the play: that is, is there a coherent theory of magic in the Renaissance and univocally represented in A or B or both? What would this be? Attempts to establish a text or texts of *Doctor Faustus* would become even more problematic if they were based on an assumption that the play presented consistent magical theory, when in fact the play's representations of magic were plural or incoherent. The hope of recovering an 'authentic' text might be as fallacious as recovering 'magic' in the play: both projects might be flawed in their assumption that there is one to be found, or rather *one* to be found. One might not be able to appeal to the monolith, 'Renaissance magic', to adjudicate the critical disputes. As there are variant readings in scenes of magic in *Doctor Faustus* and, so editors and critics increasingly argue, two distinct plays, so it might turn out that we have to acknowledge different discourses of magic in the Renaissance. *Doctor Faustus* may rather be seen as the site of the interplay of different and sometimes competing, contestatory and contradictory perceptions of magic, which may also be perceived in the early modern world outside the play.

### III

Irony too involves contradictory perceptions and a contest over the meaning of words. Irony can be one of the ways in which orthodoxy deploys its power in an implicit assumption of values that contain and so license Puttenham's 'trespasses in speach'. Puttenham included irony among figures that draw the ear and mind 'to a certaine doublenesse', and Peacham expressed irony's Janus-faced reversibility: 'by this fygure we . . . commend that that is worthy of disprayse, and disprayse that, that is worthy of high commendation'.[11] Analogous contests over words were taking place in the Renaissance over religion and magic, such as the efficacy of the words of consecration in the Mass and of Roman Catholic sacramentalia; whether the words of charms had an innate power or derived it through the devil's co-operation. The slippages possible are indicated by some meanings of 'conjuration' and 'conjure' in the sixteenth century. The noun can mean a solemn adjuration by something sacred; the verb, to call a spirit to appear by the invocation of a sacred name, or for Protestant Reformers to consecrate in the Roman Mass (*OED*: 'conjuration', *sb.* 2; 'conjure', *v.* 5a and 7).

The critical question about irony in the play, especially in the

play's use of religious language, is often about a struggle over words
between religion and magic. Differences of opinion over the possibility of licit magic and its relation to religion offer a perspective on
the play's use of religious language. Although critics may understandably discern irony in juxtapositions of magic and metaphysics,
and heavenly necromantic books in 1.1.50–4, it is important to
remember that juxtapositions of magic and religious thought and
language are not *necessarily* always uneasy and ironic ones in some
Renaissance thought. Voices may be heard claiming that it was
possible to be profound in the magic art and yet not damnable.
Although he may have been rhetorically provocative, Pico was not
being ironic when he proclaimed: 'There is no branch of knowledge
that assures us more of Christ's divinity than magic and cabala.'[12]
Agrippa was equally sincere when he said that 'the name of magic
was received by philosophers, praised by theologians and even not
unpleasing to the Gospel itself' (*De Occulta*, sig. α2). King James knew
and disapproved of claims, such as those of the conjuring-book the
*Liber Juratus*, that magic was somehow heavenly, 'for this same name
magyan dothe signefy in the grike twonge a philosopher, and in the
hebru twunge a scrybe, and in the latten twunge it signefyeth
wyse'.[13] James's orthodox spokesman, Epistemon, tells Philo-
mathes:[14]

This worde *Magie* in the *Persian* toung, importes as muche as to be ane
contemplator or Interpretour of *Divine and heavenlie sciences* [my italics]:
which being first vsed amongst the Chaldees, through their ignorance of the
true divinitie, was esteemed and reputed amongst them, as a principall
vertue: And therefore, was named vnjustlie with an honorable stile.

When Faustus peruses his book of magic and enthusiastically looks
forward to the Sidneian 'profit and delight' it promises to the
studious artisan (1.1.55–7), this is not *necessarily* an ironised view of
magic as *utile* and *dulce*, any more than the same humanistic promise
to the reader in the preface to Agrippa's *De Occulta*: 'you shall receive
much profit and pleasure from this book' (sig. α2ᵛ).

   In magical praxis, the appeal to the sacred is not simply a means
of claiming that the magician's art is licit. Success – and safety – in
high magical operations depends on a reverent mobilisation,
through rehearsal and reminiscence in the words of the conjuration,
of the power contained in divine names, epithets, and events.[15] A
modern reader may find them indecorous, but adjurations of spirits
are in earnest when they use the names of God, recall events in the

life of Christ, invoke his mother's virginity, and echo the liturgy. The language of conjuring books often has a pious, even devotional tone especially when it recalls the most sacred moments of Christian history. An English magical treatise, the *Ars Memorativa*, enjoins spiritual and corporal purity, fasting, prayer, hearing divine service and the saying parts of the ordinary of the Mass and the *Ave Maria* (BL Harley MS 181, fols. 1–17ᵛ). A conjuration of spirits in a *Clavicula Salomonis* once in the possession of Gabriel Harvey invokes them: 'by the father, the sonn and the holy ghoste, and by hym which shall come to judge the worlde both the quicke and the deade, by fyer; and by the natyvyty and baptisme by the deathe and rysynge agayne of Christe, by the comminge of the holy ghoste our comforter, by holy *Mary*, the mother of our Lord Jhesus Christe, by hir vyrgynnitye, by the 7. giftes of the holy ghoste' (BL Add. MS 36,674, fol. 6ᵛ). Protestant polemicists had a point when they claimed that Roman Catholic rites were no different from conjurations, as the latter had long since appropriated some of the formulae and rhetoric of the former. An adjuration of unclean spirits from a standard book of exorcisms can be practically indistinguishable from a conjuration and may brandish exactly the same divine names and attributes to quell spirits.[16] One of the contests in early modern England over the power of words was in relation to exorcism. The English authorities were battling claims of both Roman Catholic priests and Puritan exorcists to use the power of sacred words to cast out devils.[17]

## IV

The phrase 'metaphysics of magicians' and the use in Faustus' soliloquy up to Wagner's entry of words associated with the metaphysics (miracle, heavenly, omnipotence, deity) allows me to make one more general point. The *OED* records Marlowe's use of the plural in a unique sense: 'used by Marlowe for: occult or magical lore'; although since Marlowe's line is its *only* instance for this sense, it is presumably difficult to be certain. The earliest instance of the English plural to mean 'that branch of speculative inquiry which treats of the first principles of things' is by one of the sixteenth century's most famous magicians, who is alluded to in Marlowe's play. In James Sanford's 1569 translation of Cornelius Agrippa's *Of the Vanitie and Uncertaintie of Artes and Sciences*, chapter 53 is entitled 'Of the Metaphysickes, that is, thinges supernaturall and the Science of them' (fol. 70).

Metaphysics suggests the transcendent that Faustus desires: it really did stretch as far as doth the mind of man. It was not Aristotle himself, but an early editor who gave the title to Aristotle's *Metaphysics* – a work that by tradition was not only dated after (*meta*) the *Physics* but also surpassed it in dignity of subject. 'Metaphysics', because of the nature of this eponymous work of Aristotle's also suggests the systematic. If one were intent on finding irony one could say that this word shows Faustus' unconscious desires merely to replace one economy of knowledge with another. The word would bring to a Renaissance mind the assimilation of Aristotle by Aquinas (who wrote a commentary on the *Metaphysics*, c.1266–72) to produce that vast system of scholastic theology that Faustus finds so unsatisfying.[18] In the play, the 'metaphysics of magicians' will have rules, authorities, books (the Hebrew Psalter and the New Testament turn out to be requisite for conjuring), and the Latin of the tags Faustus parades in his soliloquy will soon produce the ascent of a demon whose first exchanges with the magician include the fine scholastic distinction of causality *per accidens*.

It is difficult to escape from religion in *Doctor Faustus*, even by a flight to magic. A problem for both the play and its protagonist, and for the study of early modern magic period, is the difficulty, perhaps the impossibility, of magic escaping from religion or of finding magic *not* expressed and represented in discourses formed, at least in part, by religious metaphysics and language. The theories and practice of Western magic may be said to rely largely on religion, indeed on Christian metaphysics. The interdependence of religion and magic is differently inflected in the case of each of three discourses about magic this essay will now tease apart: orthodox demonology, high magic, and popular belief. In each of them one may find the others implicated and in each the 'metaphysics', that is the economy of their magical beliefs, is different and often at odds with the others, although and on some subjects high magic and popular understanding are (roughly) on one side, and orthodox opinion on the other. For example, cunning folk used the names of God, parts of Scripture, and appealed to the virtue of Christ's passion and resurrection, as did high magicians, and high magic and popular belief held that spirits might be controlled by magicians. Orthodox demonological opinion condemned both the practice and the belief.

V

Printed demonologies show an orthodox distrust, criticism and condemnation of all magic: theirs are the voices of the Prologue and the Good Angel. These are the primary sources about magic most accessible to us and they are also important sources for the other two discourses although they are generally hostile to them. It is to demonological writings that we turn first when we want to construct a history of magic, annotate *Doctor Faustus* or understand the representation of magic in the Renaissance. They can certainly provide a position from which to view the varieties of early modern magical beliefs and also the play's representations of them, but to assume that this viewpoint is always paramount in the play is to beg all the critical questions and fails to escape from a form of Keefer's 'hermeneutical circle'.

Orthodox Renaissance demonologies[19] are often large, systematic and thorough, and some treatises run to several hundred pages. The Jesuit Martin del Rio's *Disquisitionum Magicarum Libri Sex* (Louvain, 1599–1600), admittedly one of the largest, was printed in three quarto tomes of 374, 373, and 340 pages. These treatises claim to 'discover' an orthodox truth about which there ought to be no dispute and to this end call to their aid God's word, classical, patristic, and (if Catholic) scholastic authorities, more recent writers, common experience, and narratives and reports from the examinations and 'confessions' of witches. Their general desire for system, conformity, uniformity of opinion, and consensus about supernatural matters is explicit in the concluding prayers of Orthodoxus at the end of Deacon and Walker's *A Summarie Answere to al the material points in any of Master Darel his bookes* (1601): 'Well, the Lord make us all wise to his salvation, and so guide us with his gratious spirit, as we may all speake one thing and that there be no dissentions among us: but that wee may all knit soundlie together in one minde, and one judgement' (p. 240). Demonologies define, taxonomise, and condemn magical practices and vigorously identify the ignorance or wilful misunderstanding of certain sorts of misbelievers. They often have in their sights three kinds of infidelity intermittently voiced in *Doctor Faustus*: certain sorts of scepticism and 'Sadducism' ('Come, I think hell's a fable', 1.5.130); the pretensions of learned magicians to control spirits through theurgic operation ('Within this circle is Jehova's name ... By which the spirits are enforced to rise',

1.3.8–13); the errors and 'superstitions' (that is erroneous and pagan beliefs) of the people ('I will teach thee to turn thyself to anything, to a dog, or a cat, or a mouse, or a rat, or anything' (1.4.53–4). Using these works, the major source for ideas about magic we might bring to bear in interpretation, means that it is easy to adopt their orthodox ideology about magic and to assume that must be the play's ideology as well: magic is always sinful, detestable, and diabolic, it is illusory and dangerous and there is no distinction between magician and witch as both operate by either explicit or 'tacit' diabolic pact. For example, King James's *Dæmonologie*, which may well have been written when *Faustus* was written and first performed, gives us in its first book an analysis of a magician's career that it is tempting to employ, because of numerous parallels, as an exegetical tool on *Doctor Faustus*. James charts magicians' careers starting with 'Curiositie in great ingines [ambition in those with great intelligence]' and their 'mounting from degree to degree, vpon the slipperie and vncertain scale [ladder] of curiositie; they are at last entised, that where lawfull artes or sciences failes, to satisfie their restles mindes, even to seeke to that black and vnlawfull science of *Magie*' (1, 10). But to read *Doctor Faustus* through the King's *Dæmonologie* would be automatically to read it within James's unsurprisingly orthodox condemnation of magic. Some critics have assumed an orthodox reading of magic in the play, because it came as part of the ideology of the demonological texts which they understandably used in their discussions of it. In an elision of playwright and critic, Paul Kocher, for whom 'the witchcraft theory expounded by the drama is quite orthodox', says that 'Marlowe's play would successfully pass the scrutiny of such orthodox writers on witchcraft as Bodin and Binsfeld.' Indeed Kocher seems to suggest that whatever the aggregation of magical theories and practices represented in the play, they are ordered and controlled within the framework of orthodox demonology which gives the play intellectual and imaginative coherence.[20] As Warren observes: 'editors and critics constantly reveal their own values, prejudices, and presuppositions about what *Dr. Faustus* is, was, or should be', including a sense of 'Marlowe'.[21] Robert H. West, who cited demonological treatises extensively, too, assumed the 'play's orthodox rationale of magic', although within this orthodox rationale argued for *Faustus* having some theurgic ambitions and pretensions.[22] From here it is a short step to seeing the ironies of the play operating against the play's protagonist. Little wonder, then, that Moelwyn Merchant describes the playwright as 'Marlowe the Orthodox'.[23]

I have chosen to classify the second discourse about magic as 'high magic' as a portmanteau to contain a variety of interests and practices. They range from the high-minded theories of humanists, inspired or influenced by neoplatonism, the cabala and the Hermetic texts, such as Ficino and Pico, through the theurgy of Agrippa and Dee, to the men who made and used the numerous manuscript conjuring books that have survived from the Renaissance. It is the last we know least about. Reginald Scot comments on ceremonial magicians in his *Discoverie of Witchcraft* (1584):

these deale with no inferiour causes; these fetch devils out of hell, and angels out of heaven; these raise up what bodies they list . . . take upon them also the raising of tempests, and earthquakes and to do as much as God himselfe can do. These are no small fooles, they go not to worke with a baggage tode, or cat, as witches do; but with a kind of majestie. (XV.i)

One of the most important claims of high magic is to command spirits: 'for men are nott bownde unto sprites but the sprites are constrayned against their wills to answere men that be clensed or clene, and to fulfill there requestes' (BL Royal MS XVII.A.XLII, fol. 2ᵛ). King James notes, and as an orthodox demonologist rejects, the popular understanding of the difference between witches and magicians:

[*Epistemon*] Surelie, the difference vulgare [the difference ordinarily understood] put betwixt them, is verrie merrie, and in a maner true; for they say, that the Witches ar servantes onelie, and slaues to the Devil; but the Necromanciers are his maisters and commanders . . . but it is [true] onelie *secundum quid:* For it is not by anie power that they can have over him, but *ex pacto* allanerlie [only]: whereby he oblices [obliges] himself in some trifles to them, that he may on the other part obteine the fruition [pleasure of possessing] of their body & soule, which is the onlie thing he huntes for. (*Dæmonologie*, I, 9)

This magic is transitive in its aspirations, its languages are the learned ones of Greek, Latin and Hebrew, and two of its authorities are alluded to in *Doctor Faustus*: Peter of Abano or Apono, and Cornelius Agrippa (1.1.56, 119). In Agrippa we can see what we would now call a theorisation of magic that bestows on it precisely the status of metaphysics: a coherent philosophy that claims transcendence beyond the normal sciences. He did after all call his book on magic 'occult philosophy'.

High magic appears in the early part of the play before the ascent of Mephistophilis. It is to be found in Faustus' early soliloquies, which voice a desire for knowledge and control over nature, and in his conversations with Valdes and Cornelius. His technical preparations for the conjuration, and his behaviour during it and in its immediate aftermath show him confident that words and magical characters might compel spirits. After Faustus agrees to and signs the pact and becomes a diabolic magician, or as the orthodox would see him, a witch, high magic recedes in the play. Theurgists like Agrippa, intent on distancing themselves from diabolic practices and compact, would now join with the orthodox in their condemnation of his magic. The quest of high magic for knowledge flickers briefly in the dry and disappointing dialogue with Mephistophilis about astronomy. In this, one 'metaphysical' question, a commonplace one about angelic intelligences who move the planetary spheres, is answered tersely: '*Faustus*. But tell me, hath every sphere a dominion or *intelligentia*? *Mephistophilis*. Ay'. Another, '[W]ho made the world[?]', is not answered at all (2.3.55–7, 65). So much for Agrippa's hope for the theurgist's ascent through the created world and the angels to some knowledge of God himself.

The last category, a popular understanding of magic, is more difficult to recover, as is always the case with popular culture. Some texts allow a glimpse of it when they represent the confrontation of orthodox understanding and popular belief. The catechistic strategies of English dialogues on witchcraft reveal their desire to propagate their orthodox views, sometimes to 'the simpler sort', and consequently the gaps between orthodox demonology and popular belief and the diversity of opinions in early modern England. In George Giffard's *A Dialogue concerning Witches and Witchcraftes* (1593), Daniel labours to educate villagers. It is not only the simple yeoman Samuel, with his uncomplicated belief in the agency of the witch to cause harm, who is in error, but the schoolmaster M. B. as well, 'a good pretie scholler (they say) in the Latine tongue'.[24] Clearly, many people were ignorant of or indifferent to the niceties of demonological discourse as they were to the technicalities of high magic. Indeed there may have been senses in which magic worried them less than, or at least differently from, the demonologists. In 1590 Henry Holland complained of 'the continuall trafficke and market which the rude people have with witches' and of their riding up to forty miles to go to witches and master conjurers, thinking it not

unlawful in 'their brutish ignoraunce'.[25] Popular and elite understandings of magic and witchcraft could be sharply divergent. A
desire to correct 'vulgar' understanding drives Protestant treatises
like those of King James, Niels Hemmingsen, Lambert Daneau, and
George Giffard. The 'vulgar' are repeatedly told that their conceptions about the difference between witches and magicians, the
magician's power to command the devil, and the automatic efficacy
of words and rituals are wrong. This popular understanding, or lack
of it, might be analogous to what Keith Thomas revealed about
'ignorance and indifference' towards religious doctrines.[26]

Popular ideas of magic might be voiced in *Doctor Faustus'* comic
scenes. It is a critical commonplace that these parody the protagonist's career. Similarly their 'low' comedy is matched by their
representation of 'low' magic and popular beliefs. Act One, Scene
Four, which is an interlude between the conjuration and the pact,
briefly runs a course typical of the devil's first meeting and negotia-
tions with a prospective witch. Wagner approaches Robin, who is
stereotypically poor and needy,[27] and asks for his service,[28] and to be
'bound' to him for seven years. Wagner's threat to turn Robin's lice
into familiars would provide him with the spirits in animal form of
the English witch, who are already feeding on him as familiars as
they suck his blood. We are here in the world of popular belief as the
scene entertains the idea of transformation into animals, rejected by
the orthodox, but clearly held as a popular view.[29] Robin's concerns
are with food, sex and money. The comic scenes are the stuff of
popular stories about magic: garbled demonic names, comic familiarity with devils, accidents with a magician's books.

## VI

Magic then may be plurally understood in the Renaissance. The
matter is complicated further in the *representation* of that plurality in a
Renaissance fictional text, and further again when the text, or texts
in the case of *Doctor Faustus*, are texts for performance or in some
way records of it. In a dramatic fiction magic may not necessarily be
'what is, hath been, or shall be', it may also be differently understood
at different points within it, and also differently in the A- and B-texts
of this particular dramatic fiction. The identification of the three
areas of magical discourse does not answer the question of how some
individual moments of dramatic representation of magic might have

been received by any particular member of the audience in 1594, or thereafter. The plural understandings of magic are more complex when they are represented to the different 'understanders' in the Elizabethan theatre. There will be considerable variety in the sophistication of the understanding of the demonological debates about magic. If Giffard's Essex villagers are at all representative, then some of the finer demonological distinctions of the play (for example the voluntary ascent of demons) will not be familiar to many. Secondly, the case of a play where the esoteric practices of high magic are represented on stage is different from plays like Dekker, Ford and Rowley's *The Witch of Edmonton* or Heywood and Brome's *Late Lancashire Witches*, both of which draw substantially on accounts of English witchcraft cases. And although the case is not as acute as Jonson's *The Alchemist*, where only a few of the audience will understand most of the occult references, it seems likely that many of its early audience will not understand parts of *Doctor Faustus* or will misunderstand them. The play's extensive use of Latin, the language of conjurers, must have been 'Dutch fustian' to many. For example, the Ovidian line in Faustus' last soliloquy sounds like an attempt to cast a spell,[30] and some of the audience may well have heard in Faustus' cry, *O lente, lente currite noctis equi*, another of the magician's Latin conjurations. It is in the imperative mood typical of early modern conjurations, whether in English and Latin, or in the play itself: compare '*Veni, veni, Mephistophile!*' (2.1.29). The popular perception of the line as another conjuration is understandable and in a sense correct, for in a common Elizabethan sense of the word Ovid's lover *is* 'conjuring' (*OED*: 'conjure', *v.* 4b), although vainly, the night to pass slowly. Time cannot be halted by magic, although it can by miracle.

An apt moment at which to consider the plural understandings of magic is one of the play's most intensely magical ones, the early part of the conjuration scene. We may suppose the powerful effect it had on the audience's imagination from such evidence as the illustration on the title-page of the 1619 quarto (B2), and the scare at the Exeter performance where the actors feared there was one devil too many 'as Faustus was busie in his magicall invocations'.[31] Taking my cue from dialogues on magic, I would like to imagine the response of three members of an early audience of *Doctor Faustus* as representatives of the three discourses: Samuel, a countryman up from Essex whose London friends take him to the playhouse; Orthodoxus, a

Cambridge graduate who has been reading some of the demonological works printed in the late sixteenth century, and Master Lordinge, a conjuror with Agrippan leanings.[32]

Samuel hears a largely incomprehensible conjuration in Latin, the language of magicians, the same 'Dutch fustian' as the clowns hear and garble in the comic scenes in B. He catches a strange mixture of holy and diabolic proper names he knows in a general way, or perhaps from the Bible and sermons: Jehova (twice), Lucifer (perhaps),[33] Beelzebub (certainly), Gehenna (probably not).[34] He sees ritual magical gestures which are equivocal as they employ religious but popish practices, such as the sign of the cross and of holy water, and during the conjuration Alleyn may well have worn the 'surplis/ With a crosse upon his brest'[35] thus reinforcing the mixture of the religious and the magical. In the A-text he would also see and hear for a moment that magic works: its practices apparently compel the ascent of Mephistophilis. This is not clearly the case in B which requires the presence of Lucifer and four other devils already at the beginning of the conjuration scene. Samuel's general response to Faustus' conjuration would have been a mixture of incomprehension and 'Blood, he speaks terribly' (4.1.71).

Orthodoxus assumes the emptiness and inefficacy of the circle, its inscriptions and the succeeding conjuration. Words have no efficacy to command spirits.[36] Demons constantly wait on sinful humanity's desires,[37] an understanding reinforced by the entry of the B-text's devils before the conjuration. Orthodoxus understands and is horrified at the mixed invocation of sacred, diabolical and classical powers: the gods of Acheron and Jehova. For him the conjuration is powerless and it is also blasphemous. The orthodox and pious from Augustine onwards express horror and revulsion at what they see as shocking blasphemy in the misuse of the sacred in conjuring.[38] Orthodoxus finds his English Protestant suspicions about popery and magic confirmed by Faustus' use of the cross and holy water.[39]

Master Lordinge finds the conjuration proceeding in the way his books describe. The eclectic mixture of classical gods of the underworld with the name of God, is familiar: in his dialogue, *De Verbo Mirifico*, Johannes Reuchlin had his devout character Capnion invoke God as 'Terror to the shades of gloomy Phlegethon, unparalleled joy of heaven's dwellers, unconquerable dread of the inhabitants of Tartarus'.[40] Equally familiar is the mixture in the conjuration of these with elemental spirits, and the names of demons. The spirit's reluctance to appear and its first ugly apparition are standard prevarications. Faustus addresses the spirit before and after its appearance in the typical imperative mood: 'I charge thee . . . Go . . . I charge thee . . . Speak' (1.3.23, 25, 36, 45). The A-text reinforces Faustus' confidence in his magic: both A and B have the same five lines in which Faustus exults in the power of words, but only A adds two lines where magic's power is further celebrated as a Roman victor's laureation: 'Now, Faustus, thou art conjuror laureate/ That canst command great Mephistopheles.' (A and B, 1.3.27–31; A, 1.1.32–3.) In the A-text, because of this and the absence of devils at the beginning of the scene, Mephistophilis' statement about his voluntary ascent will come as a greater surprise.

VII

The conjuration, like many of the play's words, quotations and passages in Latin, the language of scholars and magicians, is a site of profound equivocation, and also of contestation, particularly over access to and appropriation of different sorts of religious power and language. The ambiguous anagrammatisation of Jehova's name forward and backward (in Hebrew, the sacred Tetragrammaton would have been written 'backward' anyway, HVHI), is an emblem of the tuggings back and forth of the numinous by magic and religion. Even individual moments in the conjuration are ambiguous, for example, *Valeat numen triplex Iehovae.* West rejected the common translation 'away with the triple power of Jehova' and said that it means 'The three-fold power of Jehovah aid me.'[41] It is a typical instance of critical problems in the play. Latin can idiomatically use *valeo* in the subjunctive in a 'formula of scornful dismissal' as when Ovid bids farewell to the lies of poets ('valeant mendacia vatum', *Fasti*, VI, 253), but the sense of *valeat* as 'may it be efficacious' is also possible. It is a typical instance of the play's ambiguities about magic, like the paradox of simultaneous imperiousness and supplication in 'And try if devils will obey thy hest,/ Seeing thou hast prayed and sacrificed to them' (1.3.6–7).

After the conjuration, Mephistophilis' claim to have voluntarily ascended seems to prove the orthodox (both the demonological and critical) right and the heterodox wrong: magic words have no power to compel spirits,[42] the metaphysics of Faustus' magic are fallacious and we have another example of a framing irony that the play operates against its protagonist. What is unsettling here is that the play voices a crucial demonological point through a demon. Mephistophilis' tone is almost pious when he describes the abuse of God's name: 'For when we hear one rack the name of God'. Similarly, when Greene's Friar Bacon repents his magic he recalls: 'The *wresting* [my italics] of the holy name of God/ As Sother, Eloim and Adonai,/ Alpha, Manoth and Tetragrammation' (xiii. 92–4). Mephistophilis concisely gives an orthodox view of magic: it has no power to compel spirits, it brings the danger of damnation and it involves abjuration of God (1.3.46–54). He then provides a series of impeccable theological orthodoxies: the fall of Lucifer through pride, the eternal reprobation and punishment of evil spirits, the loss of God as the greatest punishment of fallen angels (1.3.70–82). Mephistophilis' confirmation of orthodox doctrine makes us uneasy. Demonologists emphasise the devil's subtlety, mendacity and equivocation, quoting his New Testament reputation as the father of lies and his ability to transform himself into an angel of light (John, 8.44; 2 Corinthians, 11.14). As Banquo knew, devils are most to be distrusted when they appear to tell the truth. Demonologists warn against accepting the testimony of any spirit, whether they are spirits raised by conjurors, familiars who pass on information to witches, or possessing demons adjured by exorcists to speak. Most people knew that the devil is a liar and equivocator, and any practiced magician would know conjured spirits are habitual liars who are usually adjured to speak the truth immediately they appear. Ariel's claim. 'Remember I have done thee worthy service,/ Told thee no lies', reminds us that his was unusual behaviour for spirits. Peter of Abano's *Heptameron*, like many surviving manuscript conjuring books, prays to God that spirits may give true answers and 'be understandable to us without any ambiguity' (Agrippa, *De Occulta*, pp. 565, 566). One might even entertain the idea that the demon is lying about the conjuration, that there might have been virtue in Faustus' heavenly words, and this is a demonic trick to hasten on the moment of the pact. Such a reading would make the play a rather different sort of magician's tragedy, although one where irony still operates against Faustus. A demon is even more untrustworthy as a spokesman of orthodoxy than Ferneze in *The Jew of Malta* and Mortimer in *Edward II*.

The play's or plays' contradictory representations of the efficacy or inefficacy of magical words is a synecdoche for other contradictions. Faustus apparently wasn't listening to Mephistophilis' careful demonological exposition, as when he has signed the pact he asks: 'But may I raise up spirits when I please?', and is answered this time: 'Ay, Faustus, and do greater things than these' (2.1.86–7). Later Mephistophilis complains that he has been dragged back from Constantinople by Robin's brief conjuration with its garbled Greek and Latin (A, 3.2.25–33; compare B, 3.3.30–34).[43] 'Ballioll and Belcher' produces and dismisses two devils for Wagner (A, 1.4.45–53; compare B, 1.4.32–9), and with the words 'Belimoth, Argiron, Ashtaroth', Faustus produces devils to torment Benvolio (B, 4.1.148–52). And demonologically, the first clause of the pact ('First, that Faustus may be a spirit in form and substance'), with its increase in scholastic precision on the terms in the *English Faust Book*,[44] is impossible. Only God can change a creature's substance, and so the Evil Angel's line ('Thou art a spirit. God cannot pity thee' [2.3.13]) may be doubly mendacious.

I see no easy way of solving these contradictions, and am reluctant to imitate those critics who, manifesting Stephen Greenblatt's necromantic desire to 'speak with the dead', invoke the ghost of the author.[45] It seems to me that the play mobilises different discourses about magic and sets them at odds. After the conjuration orthodox opinion intervenes but is problematised in that it is voiced by a demon. Jonathan Dollimore took the old arguments in a new direction in a reading of the play which sees *Doctor Faustus* displaying orthodoxy to subvert it and discovering limit to transgress it (Dollimore, pp. 108–19). We have to accept inconsistencies within A and B and between them. To iron them out is to impose that very uniformity so that 'we may all speake one thing and that there be no dissentions among us' that Deacon and Walker's Orthodoxus desired.

Warren warns us of the irrecoverability of the original text of *Doctor Faustus*: 'the compilation or distillation of a single text of any value, let alone authority, from the totality of what is available to *us is not possible*'.[46] Similarly, as a context for *Doctor Faustus* and in place of a coherent metaphysics of magicians, we may have to settle with good grace for the multiple texts of Renaissance magic, their respective attempts to impose orthodox understanding, or escape orthodox policing, to contest and appropriate its discourses and languages, or comically to misunderstand, ignore or resist them. After Giffard's Daniel has patiently acculturated the good people of

Essex, in bursts the unreconstructed voice of popular belief in the rumbustious shape of the Goodwife R. ('she is wilfull indeed', says M. B.), who resists and contests the teaching of the schoolmaster M. B. on whom has fallen Daniel's Socratic mantle. Interestingly she contests it in terms of its own discourse and authorities: 'What tell you me of Gods word? Doth not Gods word say there bee witches, and doe not you thinke God doth suffer bad people? Are you a turne coate? Fare you well, I will no talke no longer with you'.[47] Robin and Wagner's popular beliefs coexist in the same play(s) as Faustus' initial high magic confidence in the power of words and Mephistophilis' impeccable exposition of demonological theory which declares that confidence empty. We must accept a heteroglossic plurality of magical belief and opinion in *Doctor Faustus*, observe the orthodoxy that tries to police and regulate that plurality, and the play's contestations over discourse and language, especially the language of religion. In this the texts of the play world imitate what we take to be the situation in early modern England.

# CHAPTER 5

# Marlowe's 'theatre of cruelty'

## Janet Clare

It is a commonplace of our understanding of Marlowe that he produced a theatre of consistently violent techniques and effects. Confronted with a combination of Renaissance eloquence and extreme acts of aggression, it can be difficult (unless undue emphasis is placed on the fascinating details of the life) to find an appropriate critical vocabulary for Marlowe's dramaturgy. Approaching Marlowe after Shakespeare, there is an understandable yet anachronistic tendency to adapt the critical tools which have served to illuminate Shakespeare's texts. Such difficulties in critical practice are mirrored in the experience of theatre production and performance. Rehearsals for a revival of *Tamburlaine* in 1976 on the new National Theatre stage of the Olivier Theatre convinced actors accustomed to performing Shakespeare that they must discover a new theatrical idiom.[1] Less 'realistic' and more sensational, they found that where there is little humanising of character, acting becomes more stylised; fluidity of movement and symbolic tableaux tend to be substituted for a more localised and intimate use of theatrical space and scenic locale.

In this chapter I want to begin by briefly considering recurrent limitations in the critical reception of Marlowe, before focusing on what I see as the governing aesthetics of Marlowe's theatre of cruelty. In considering the aesthetics of violence developed by Marlowe in the new secular drama of the 1580s, I will argue that we benefit from looking beyond the period to the writings of Antonin Artaud on theatre formulated in a collection of essays published in 1938.[2] Whilst it is generally recognised that Artaud's ideas cannot be decanted into a coherent scheme, his various manifestos help to define what was radically different about aspects and effects of Marlowe's theatre practice.

A preoccupation with readings of Marlowe's plays shaped by what is known and conjectured about the author has, however, over-shadowed interest in theatre aesthetics. Near the end of his brief life and in the immediate aftermath of his violent death, a concern with Marlowe's alleged atheism, iconoclasm, and reckless living tended to displace responses to the plays, producing a series of judgemental allusions to the author. The testimony of the informer Richard Baines gained wide critical currency. Baines's catalogue of Marlowe's blasphemous and heretical thought, together with allusions to his alleged homosexuality, has remained a strong reference point in critical perspectives on the plays and poems. In his indictment of Marlowe's alleged subversions of scriptural authority, Baines en-joined all Christian men 'to endevor that the mouth of so dangerous a member may be stopped'.[3] Despite the notoriety attached to Marlowe's opinions, there is little suggestion that the drama was regarded officially as politically subversive. Curiously enough, while Marlowe was himself to be silenced by the fatal dagger thrust of Ingram Frizer, with the exception of *Doctor Faustus*, there is a lack of any external or bibliographical detail suggesting that his plays were suppressed by censorship. We might say that this is because, in contradistinction to Marlowe's provocative attitudes, the drama does not expressly engage in ideological debate. Transgressive as the life may have been, the plays, with occasional echoes of the residual culture of the morality drama, contrive to appear within the bounds of orthodoxy. As is well known, Shakespeare's *Richard II* suffered censorship for its representation of the King's deposition, but there is no evidence of censorial interference with the scene in which Marlowe's Edward II resigns his crown to the Bishop of Winchester and the Earl of Leicester. Throughout *Tamburlaine*, sovereignty is relentlessly diminished as Tamburlaine defeats and humiliates one monarch after another and treats the symbol of majesty with contempt; yet the dramatic production seems to have gone un-checked. Through the words of the Chorus in *Doctor Faustus*, Mortimer's *de casibus* role, and Tamburlaine's inevitable defeat by mortality, the plays are ultimately contained within traditional patterns. The textual subversions, as I will discuss later, are drama-turgically, not ideologically, inspired.

There remains, however, an underlying assumption that the drama plays out the turbulence and alleged unorthodoxy of the life. Jonathan Goldberg has argued that Baines's note ascribes to Marlowe the same rhetoric as that expressed by his theatrical inventions.[4] Stephen Greenblatt has hinted at subtle connections between the 'cruel, aggressive plays' and a 'dark playfulness in Marlowe's own career' (Greenblatt, p. 220). Yet any reading of the plays in the light of biography would seem to be unreliably premised. Marlowe's construction of the subject, with little deference to either humanist or determinist notions of psychology and agency, excludes traditional 'character'-based criticism and, for the most part, psycho-analytical criticism.[5] There are simply not the same critical perspectives on action and character in Marlowe's *Tamburlaine, Edward II*, and *The Jew of Malta* as there are in the early Shakespearean plays which bear them some resemblance: *Richard III, Richard II*, and *The Merchant of Venice*. We cannot, as in the latter plays and in Shakespeare's early plays, explore how ideology might work to legitimise aggression. History and politics are not intertwined to the extent that they are in Shakespeare. In *Edward II* there is, for example, a relative lack of interest in the historical chronicles; instead, history has become a metaphor for desire.

Displayed throughout the canon there is a reduction of ideology. At an unproblematic level, the interplay of ambition and power allows immediate access to Marlowe's dramaturgy. It is a familiar observation that the Marlovian protagonist is an obsessive, driven by desire for territory, money, knowledge, or love.[6] However, here the genesis or artful operation of power is not explored, but is blatantly portrayed as violence or cruelty, variously expressed in barbaric and tyrannical actions in *Tamburlaine*, dismemberment in *Doctor Faustus*, comic brutality in *The Jew of Malta*, sectarian recrimination and bloodbath in *The Massacre at Paris*, mutilation and torture in *Edward II*, and self-immolation in *Dido, Queen of Carthage*. Undoubtedly, Marlowe was deeply attracted to savage episodes in his sources, but, as in *Dido, Queen of Carthage* and *The Massacre at Paris*, there is often an element of turbulent farce in the theatrical execution of inordinate vehemence and bloodletting. In the latter play, for example, Guise's outrageous heroic ethos, expressed in the soliloquy of Act One, Scene Two, has elements of self-parody. Marlowe expands Guise's role in the St Bartholomew atrocity making him responsible for the murder of the Protestant preacher Loreine (Act One, Scene Six) and, with Anjou, that of the Professor of Logic, Ramus (Act One, Scene Seven), and for the desecration of the Admiral's body in Scene Eleven. As a consequence of Guise's ambition to supplant the Valois and murder the entire Huguenot population of Paris, the stage becomes a bloodbath littered with a score of corpses, and entire scenes are focused on hangings, stabbings, shootings, and poisonings. Court politics sink into criminal atrocity distanced by rhetorical attitudinising.

Recent work on Marlowe, recognising this violence, has been dominated by attempts to draw out the social implications of such cruelty. Viewed from this perspective, the drama can be seen to enact and replicate the aggressions of social behaviour. In regarding the recently established repertory theatre as 'a new place apart, alternative to the church',[7] C. L. Barber has invested the theatre with extraordinary power, as a new organ of consciousness. He argues that Marlowe's plays, and *Tamburlaine*, in particular, emerging from the joint matrix of the Renaissance and the Reformation can be related to the Puritan cult of prophesying, whereby the individual expressed his/her unmediated relationship with God. Further, the violence of the plays is a religious violence. Tamburlaine's exorbitant rhetoric, as 'scourge of God', is animated by a sense of election expressive of the new sense of individuality of Puritan reformers. As Barber suggests with reference to Tamburlaine's burning of the Alcoran, there is a living counterpart in God-fearing men directing their aggression as agents of God's will towards the destruction of his enemies. But for Barber what remains radically innovatory about the play is that cruelty, tyranny, blasphemous defiance, and self-idolatry are presented as unqualifiedly heroic. Poetry and action combine to compel an audience to participate in Tamburlaine's self-aggrandisement. Whereas Barber is right to stress the play's limited moral framework, nevertheless, in its repetition of conquest, its very detachment from its protagonist and the fates of his victims, there is a sense of an appalling routine which in the final stages becomes almost demented. It might also be said that the rhetoric conceals the contradictions within Tamburlaine, an atheist who claims to be God's scourge, a megalomaniac ruler who shows only contempt for kings.

While commenting on the Baines note as illustrative of Marlowe's own estrangement from ideology, Greenblatt has nevertheless positioned Marlovian drama politically, at the specific historic juncture of colonisation (Greenblatt, pp. 193–201). Here, the historical matrix is the acquisitive energies of English merchants who promoted trading companies and of the entrepreneurs who promoted theatrical companies. Following a typically synchronic approach to cultural history and employing an elaborate system of analogues, Greenblatt

has seen in the violent action of Tamburlaine's relentless conquest
the compulsive nature of the Elizabethan merchants in their appropriation of colonial territory. Tamburlaine's land-lust writ large and
Barabas' indomitable quest to recuperate material losses show men
living lives as projects, murderous and self-destructive in their
performance. Thus once more drama is seen to perform the culture
of which it is a product. Greenblatt's analysis of Marlowe's heroes as
alien, divorced from sacramental and blood relations – notably his
comment that the essence of the tragedy lies in the limitations of
rebellion – is a classic study of Marlowe. In his exposition of
Marlowe's stories of tyranny as symbolically, not expressively, representative of the cultural plunder and social acquisitiveness of the
Renaissance, there would seem to be a further endorsement of the
essential point that what we have in the drama is a reduction of
ideology.

Simon Shepherd, at the beginning of his study of Marlowe, draws
attention to the simple point, already here endorsed, that Marlowe's
plays have specific and subtle strategies of their own, and that his
'project' was very different from that of Shakespeare. In examining
not only the plays of Marlowe but also a range of plays performed
contemporaneously, Shepherd explores the political reality of violence and its expression in theatrical terms and thus claims to expose
an ideological function of violence in Marlowe's plays, namely that
of 'making a statement about a political regime' (Shepherd, p. 36).
The disempowering effects of brutality can be seen through an
individual's use of or loss of language. Concomitant with brutality is
the distortion or suppression of speech. When, for example, the
Empress Zabina is incarcerated and subsequently sees the corpse of
her husband, her speech becomes crazed. Speeches such as Tamburlaine's paean to Zenocrate's beauty, which seem in other contexts to
be displays of decorous and courtly rhetoric expressive of inner
feelings, conceal the violence that is the real basis of the speaker's
power. At other times Tamburlaine's triumphal position is demonstrated by the choice of silence at the devastation he has wrought.
Shepherd's analysis of the relationship between language and power
goes some way towards an ideological reading of the play which
incorporates the multidimensional aspects of performance.
However, Shepherd's conclusions do not fully take into account the
limitations in Marlowe's representations of power, shorn in its
reduction to violence of its other attributes.

If the attenuation of ideology, which I am arguing is a fundamental aspect of Marlowe's plays, forecloses any critical engagement
with the operation and enactments of power, what kind of response
does the drama invite? What needs to be stressed is not the failure of
ideology in the plays, but a shift of emphasis to the aesthetic. The
verbal and visual violence essential to all of Marlowe's plays
produces a highly effective idiom of theatre. Marlowe's development
of an aesthetic of cruelty was such as to radicalise the whole nature
and experience of performance. It is clear that the new purpose-built
Elizabethan playhouses were becoming, as Barber has said, places of
social disruption where theatrical aggression could get out of
control. An Elizabethan account of stage spectacle evokes a strong
impression of an institution which was unpredictable and reckless in
its simulation of violence. On 16 November 1587, Philip Gawdy, a
former law student, in one of his letters to his father in Norfolk,
described a recent accident at a performance of a play by the Lord
Admiral's Men:[8]

You shall understand of some accydental newes heare in this towne
thoughe my self no wyttness thereof, yet I may be bold to veryfe it for an
assured troth. My L. Admyrall his men and players, having a devyse in ther
playe to tye one of their fellowes to a poste and so to shoote him to deathe,
having borrowed their callyvers, one of the players handes swerved, his
peece being charged with bullett, missed the fellowe he aymed at and killed
a chyld, and a woman great with chyld forthwith, and hurt an other man in
his head very sore. How they will answere it I do not study unlesse their
profession were better, but in chrystyanity I am very sorry for this chaunce,
but God his judgementes ar not to be searched nor enquired of at mannes
handes. And yet I fynde by this an olde proverbe veryfyed, that never
comes more hurte than comes of fooling.

The stage business reported second-hand by Gawdy is usually taken
as referring to the shooting of the governor of Babylon in the final
act of *Tamburlaine Part II*. Gawdy's account of the performance
betokens a degree of naturalism and of casualness in playing as
distinct from the ritualised or stylised presentation of violence which
is sometimes assumed in discussion of the ferocity of Renaissance
drama. The pistols borrowed for the performance were loaded and
it would appear that nobody bothered to unload them, relying on
the dexterity of the actor to miss the stage target. In so doing, the
two closed worlds of stage and auditorium became one as simulated
violence spilt over into the audience and is easily enacted upon the

spectator herself. The firing of loaded guns suggests the deployment of deliberate shock tactics to provoke audience response. The theatre is no longer a place where an audience can passively assimilate received biblical or moral truths, as in the still contemporaneous interludes; rather it now claims to be recognised as a place of dangerous effects and emotions. Gawdy's trite moral – 'Never comes more hurte than comes of fooling' – underplays the aggression of the early Elizabethan stage on which, partially through the agency of Marlowe, was cultivated an aesthetic of violence, a paroxysmal art with an obsessively violent tone and sensuality of spectacle.

This carnality of spectacle is not executed in a spirit of crude sensationalism, although it is presented with striking moral detachment. In *Tamburlaine* the protagonist's absolutism is exposed in a succession of pitiless acts of cruelty, culminating in Part I with his refusal, once the allotted time of clemency has passed, to change his 'martial observations' and spare either the city of Damascus or the lives of the virgins pleading for mercy. In Part II, the final descent on Babylon and the images of carnage as the walls of one of the seven wonders of the ancient world are destroyed iterate the play's inordinate destructiveness. The aggression is as overwhelming as it is motiveless, but what Tamburlaine's words and gestures convey is the brutal pleasure and the crude eroticism of pure power. The desire to conquer and to kill is represented as a natural drive and a physical need, with all other desires as fleeting impressions. In *Dido, Queen of Carthage* there is experimentation with spectacles of violence and cruelty, enacted through the medium of transposed myth. Adapting Virgil's story, Marlowe first undermines Aeneas' heroism and imperial aspirations, the qualities which made him a figure with whom Elizabeth I could be identified;[9] subsequently, in a bold change of idiom, he amplifies the tragic closure and, as he does in all of the dramatic climaxes, precipitates one action after another. In the last scene of the play, not only does Marlowe represent Dido's self-immolation, but further destructive energy is released in word and gesture as her death is followed by the suicides of Iarbus who has unavailingly loved Dido, and of Anna, who has loved Iarbus. This is far removed from Thomas Lodge's poetic use of myth:[10]

under the person of Aeneas in Virgil the practice of a dilligent captaine is discribed: under the shadow of byrds beastes and trees, the follies of the world were disiphered: you know not that the creation is signified in the image of Prometheus; the fall of pryde in the person of Narcissus; these are toyes because they savour of wisdome which you want. . . . . The vanitie of tales is wonderful, yet if we advisedly look into them they wil seme and prove wise.

For Marlowe, myth has no such moralistic utility.

This viscerally evocative action in the closing scene of *Dido* is repeated in the harrowing murder of Edward II. In enacting Edward's killing as a mirror of sodomy, Marlowe is more than simply repeating Holinshed, indeed he appears to be engaging in the emblematic method of admonitory drama, but to such devastating effect that the audience recoils from it in disgust (see Greenblatt, p. 203). Thus the play provides a conventional moral frame while simultaneously undermining it. If there is ideology here, it is, paradoxically, one of anti-ideology, at least as Marlowe's contemporaries would have seen it. The hideous representation of Edward's death produces a cathartic spectacle in contrast to the savage farce of *The Jew of Malta*. The final scenes of the play intensify the idiom of the grotesque. Barabas' last attempt to play off Christian against Turk produces a semblance of nemesis but one which is scarcely credible. He is the consummate role player, a joker gleefully acting out the audience's sadistic fantasies.[11] As in the case of Richard III, with Barabas there is a cunning mixture of nastiness, humour and irresistible panache. Yet in his disappearance into the scalding cauldron there is no sense of retribution at work; there is no figure analogous to Richmond in the final scenes of *Richard III* to set the whole drama into some kind of relief. The concluding pieties of the play's true Machiavel, the Governor, Ferneze, 'let due praise be given,/ Neither to Fate nor Fortune, but to Heaven' (5.5.130–1) is a wonderfully ironic attribution to God of the casually insensate cruelty we have witnessed.[12]

In focusing upon Marlowe's theatre as essentially one of cruelty, I want to move away from violence analysed in ideological terms and to concentrate on performative violence. Stage violence was hardly innovative, one only has to go back to the image of Herod and the massacre of the innocents in the Townley cycle, but with Marlowe it reaches an onstage, amoral intensity. Elizabethan critics, their aesthetics grounded in didacticism, have little to say about the effects and implications of such violent enactments. In their disquisitions on tragedy, the theoreticians Sidney, Puttenham and Lodge concentrate on the matter of tragedy and its rhetorical style, while striking the familiar moral and instructive note. Philip Sidney's oxymoron, the 'sweet violence'[13] of tragedy comes nearest to suggesting the mixed emotions of horror, fascination, and pleasure which Renaissance tragedy arouses. It could be said that Marlowe's drama is as much a reaction against those, such as Lodge and Sidney who sought to produce a qualified defence of the drama as much as it exemplifies traits abhorred by the anti-theatricalists.

In order to formulate a response to Marlowe's drama, modernist – as opposed to Renaissance – theory and practice are particularly illuminating. Specifically, the writings of Antonin Artaud, who protested at the concept of a theatre that privileged naturalism, psychology, and comfortable morality, would seem to be remarkably instructive. For Artaud, the theatre must distance itself from psychological and social representation and, in so doing, it must employ a rich diversity of materials, including speech, gesture, music, spectacle, mythic, and archetypal situation. Dialogue is only a limited resource: the stage 'is a concrete physical place which asks to be filled, and to be given its own concrete language to speak'.[14] Artaud described his view of theatre as one of cruelty. In several manifestos, he made it clear that by 'cruelty', he did not mean merciless bloodshed and 'gratuitous pursuit of physical suffering', but emotional and sensory violence which is a form of embodied intelligence. Theatre, he argued, must be rebuilt on extreme action pushed beyond all limits; it must inspire with the magnetism of its images while serving as a liberating vent to extreme passions and cultural nightmares. Thought, particularly extraordinary and essential moments of thought, has its place, not in the form of psychological exposition, but illuminated in extraordinary deeds and gestures.[15] In describing Marlowe's dramaturgy from this modernist perspective, I am concerned, then, not only with the excesses of the spectacle but with the sensory assault on the spectator and the violation of any predictable moral or emotional responses. The link with Marlowe is not as tenuous as it might seem, for amongst the eclectic models for a 'true' theatre cited by Artaud was that of the Renaissance. This he recognised as a theatre that excluded placid emotional and moral responses and exteriorised depths of latent cruelty and perverse sensibilities of the mind.

Artaud argued that, for violence to be effective in arousing and challenging the audience's emotional response, its representation must apply pressure to the senses. Spectacle and the use of words for their sensuous emanations are vital. It could be said that Marlowe's 'mighty line', in particular the rhetoric of *Tamburlaine*, corresponds to Artaud's notion of a poetry of the senses. The incantatory nature of the language of the play is illustrated in the scene depicting the crowning of Cosroe where there is the repetition of the famous line 'And ride in triumph through Persepolis' and incremental repetition in Tamburlaine's speech to Techelles: 'Is it not brave to be a king[?]', 'Is it not passing brave to be a king[?]' (*Tamburlaine Part I*: 2.5.51, 53). Again, in Tamburlaine's address to the virgins of Damascus, the use of rhetorical device effectively depersonalises the killing: 'there sits Death; there sits imperious Death'; 'and shew my servant Death'; 'Away with them, I say, and shew them Death' (5.2.48, 54, 57). Rhetoric is certainly employed in *Tamburlaine* but not channelled towards the purposes advocated by contemporary humanist educational projects. Marlowe's representation of Tamburlaine through his 'working words' to some extent exemplifies Puttenham's rhetorical theory: 'the poets were also from the beginning the best perswaders and their eloquence the first Rethoricke of the world. Even so it became that the high mysteries of the gods should be revealed and taught, by a manner of utterance and language of extraordinarie phrase, and briefe and compendious.'[16] Whereas Tamburlaine is made to use rhetoric persuasively, its purpose is also undermined in that persuasion is used not to reveal 'the high mysteries of the gods', but to convince an audience of his own omnipotence.

In approaching the play from an Artaudian aesthetic of total theatre, Marlowe's incantatory language is complemented by the suggestive use of signs and images. The figure of three is prominent in stage tableaux: three tributary kings attend Tamburlaine; Bajazeth is accompanied by the three contributory kings of Fez, Morocco, and Argier; in *Part II*, Tamburlaine's rivals are commanded by three contributory chieftains; Zenocrate has three sons and she is surrounded by three physicians when she is dying.[17] Tamburlaine's conquests are presented in strong visual images, notably his ascending the throne on the back of the Emperor Bajazeth and the drawing of a chariot by defeated kings harnessed '*with bits in their mouths*' (*Tamburlaine Part II*: [stage directions], 4.3). Marlowe's dual exploitation of word and image is again clear in the incident described by Gawdy in which Tamburlaine's two surviving sons and the monarchs who have accompanied him on his dizzying ascent to power are ordered to shoot the governor of Babylon hanging in chains. That done, in language which supercharges the visual image, the governor is likened to the wall of Babylon: 'So, now he hangs like Bagdet's governor,/ Having as many bullets in his flesh/ As there be breaches in her batter'd wall' (*Tamburlaine Part II*: 5.1.157–9). The language here sustains the physical violence, just as, elsewhere in *Tamburlaine*, verbal and stage images are integrated so that the poetry operates to sustain conquest and make events happen.[18] While Tamburlaine is still in the garments of the Scythian shepherd, his boast to the captured Zenocrate that he and his supporters will bear empires on their spears is rapidly realised.

Artaud held that the true theatre was not one that dealt with individual psychology, the representation of well-dissected character and feeling, but one that dealt with archetypes. Members of the audience are not meant to identify with what happens on the stage. In 'No More Masterpieces', Artaud condemns the theatre of psychology and attributes the valorising of psychology to the influence of Shakespeare:[19]

It is because we have been accustomed for four hundred years, that is since the Renaissance, to a purely descriptive theatre – storytelling psychology it is because every possible ingenuity has been exerted in bringing to life on the stage plausible but detached beings, with the spectacle on one side, the public on the other – and because the public is no longer shown anything but a mirror of itself.

The attack on social and psychological representation through the image of the mirror has particular resonances for Elizabethan drama. Mirrors were, of course, commonplace metaphors for dramatic representation and social and moral reflection. The Tudor interlude writers regularly employed the image and saw their work in the words of Lodge and Greene as 'a looking glass for London and England'.[20] Shakespeare has Hamlet accept unquestioningly the moral and psychological implications of art when he describes the purpose of acting, 'at the first and now' as holding 'the mirror up to nature, to show virtue her own feature, scorn her own image, and the very age and body of the time his form and pressure' (*Hamlet*: Act 3, Scene 2). But Marlowe in the late 1580s self-consciously distorted the familiar image in the prologue to *Tamburlaine* and invited a more radical audience response: 'View but his picture in this tragic glass,/ And then applaud his fortunes as you please' (*Part I*: [Prologue], 7–8). What the audience will not see in Tamburlaine is a moral exemplum, nor will they discover an empathic figure. At no point in the play does Tamburlaine invite identification or engagement from the audience. It is not that Marlowe is practising a prototype of an alienation technique, but simply that by surrendering the ethical to the aesthetic spectators are expected to complete Marlowe's text, that is to formulate their own responses.

The prologue to *The Jew of Malta* has a similar de-stabilising effect when Machevill requests the audience not to form an *a priori* judgement of Barabas: 'I crave but this – grace him as he deserves,/ And let him not be entertain'd the worse/ Because he favours me' ([Prologue], 33–5). The audience's disconcertion continues in the drama with the dehumanisation of Barabas, notably at the point in the play when he expounds to Ithamore on his acts of villainy: 'I walk abroad a-nights,/ And kill sick people groaning under walls./ Sometimes I go about and poison wells' (2.3.179–81). There is nothing that we see or hear elsewhere in the play which corroborates Barabas' enumerated acts of vengeful cruelty. Granted that Barabas later goes on to poison an entire nunnery with contaminated porridge, the speech is dramatically redundant, but highly significant theatrically as contributing to the overarching brutality of a play in which there is no moral hierarchy for Jews, Christians or Muslims. Here, again, Artaud's theories are illuminating. Despite his emphasis on the physical, plastic, nature of theatre, Artaud insisted that it was not a matter of suppressing speech, but of changing its role, that is 'considering it as something else than a means of conducting human characters to their external ends'.[21] *The Jew of Malta* is confined within the excesses of its language to convey the enormities of its conflicts and, thus, speech breaks with any sense of actuality.

In chronological approaches to Renaissance drama, *Edward II* is seen as the play of Marlowe's that is most bound by psychology and, as such, influential on Shakespeare's *Richard II*. But to consider *Edward II* and *Richard II* within the same compass reveals more striking dissimilarities in dramatic dynamics than parallels. In *Edward II* emotions are rawly exposed as the play explores the tragic manifestations and effects of infatuation. As in the violence of Dido's passion, there is extremity in this love: 'Ere my sweet Gaveston shall part from me,/ This isle shall fleet upon the ocean,/ And wander to the unfrequented Inde' (1.4.48–50). The tumultuousness of Edward's passions brings to mind Artaud's admiration for a further representation of taboo violation and libido in late Renaissance drama, that of Giovanni for his sister Anabella in *'Tis Pity She's a Whore*.[22]

Similarly, Marlowe succeeds in displaying passion, rebellion, and, in
the cruel excesses of Edward's murder, latent human cruelty. In what
seems to be a firm refusal to engage with human psychology, there is
no self-reflection, mental growth or development in the play as there
quite patently is in *Richard II*. Actions are grounded on unmediated
impulse. Like Zenocrate's profession of love for Tamburlaine, Isabella's defection from Edward to Mortimer is abrupt with slight
indication in the text of the flow of feelings. This is perhaps what
Artaud would recognise as the 'untimely transition', the theatrical
realisation of the objective unforeseen.

The destruction of theatrical and dramatic norms can be understood in relation to polemic against, and defences of the theatre. In
his re-examination of Puritan anti-theatricalism, Jonathan Crewe
makes the point that Marlowe began his career in a milieu precondi-
tioned by anti-theatricalism.[23] Indeed, most of the pamphleteering
opposed to or defending the stage preceded the more provocative
Elizabethan drama. William Rankins' attack on the theatre, *A Mirrour
of Monsters* (1587), is not quite, as Crewe has suggested, an equation
of transgression with new and alien personae represented on the
stage, but more an eccentric polemic about the corrupting power of
the stage. Rankins inveighs against the players, 'what men are these?
(naie rather monsters) that thus corrupt so sweete a soile: such are
they, as in outward shew seeme painted sepulchres' (fol. 2) and,
employing common rhetoric against the actors' art of impersonation,
accuses them of sacrilege and blasphemy. Yet Rankins' indictment of
the players and their roles does evoke, as Crewe has suggested, the
Marlovian protagonist:

> when they take upon them the persons of Heathen men, imagining
> themselves (to vainglory in the wrath of God) to be the men whose persons
> they present, wherein, by calling on Mahomet, by swearing by the Temples
> of Idolatry dedicate to Fools, by calling on Jupiter, Mars, Venus, and other
> such petty Gods, they do most wickedly robbe God of his honour, and
> blaspheme the vertue of his heavenly power. (fol. 21ᵛ)

Although Crewe seems to have contracted the meanings of mon-
strosity implied in Rankins' diatribe, it is possible to see that in
*Tamburlaine*, at least, Marlowe aggressively renegotiates the relationship of what is monstrously transgressive with the assumed norms.
To see Marlowe's plays in the light of an implicit dialogue with
Rankins, as Crewe does, is an arresting idea and one which might be
extended to include not only anti-theatrical discourse, but the moral

and didactic defences of the theatre which Marlowe also challenges. In his *Defence of Poetry*, a reply to the Puritan stage critic Stephen Gosson, Lodge goes so far as to say that Gosson's argument against the theatre would have been more cogent if he had held up as example those poets, including the sometime playwright Gosson who, according to Lodge, abused their art:[24]

And surely if I may speak my minde I think we shal find but few poets, if it were exactly wayd, what they oughte to be: your Muscovian straungers, your Scithian monsters wonderful, by one Eurus brought upon one stage in ships made of sheepe skins, wyll not prove you a poet, nether your life alow you to bee of that learning. If you had wisely wayed the abuse of poetry, if you had reprehended the foolish fantasies of our Poets *nomine non re* which they bring forth on stage, my self would have liked of you and allowed your labor . . . but most blessed were we, if we might find a judge that severely would amende the abuses of Tragedies.

Lodge's allusion to dramatic malpractice in the representation of 'Scithian monsters' curiously anticipates Marlowe's Tamburlaine. His not uncommon disapproval of what is alien and fantastic in the drama prefigures what were to become, in Marlowe's use of myth and legend, preoccupations of Marlovian drama.

In conclusion, it is not primarily the subject matter nor its ideology which makes Marlowe's drama so relentlessly subversive. Marlowe represents famous personages and concentrates on the same subjects of atrocious crimes and superhuman devotions as his contemporaries. What is so disconcerting about his plays is that he does not orientate the audience through the moral perspective of an innocent victim or psychologically developed character. In its defiant severance of violent effects from moral paradigms, myth and history are disturbingly transmuted. The myths which he utilises, as in *Dido* and *Doctor Faustus*, are not merely represented but revitalised by the recognition of the compulsive passion and conflicts constituted within them. Such techniques preclude a placid or predictable audience response and make of theatre a dangerous and intimidating experience. Marlowe's dramaturgy works through an assault on the audience's sensory perceptions and the release of extreme conflicts, ambitions and passions. Such techniques approach a theatrical aesthetic which centuries later Artaud wished to recover for the theatre of his time.

# CHAPTER 6

# Marlowe onstage: the deaths of the author

## Lois Potter

It is hardly surprising that the quatercentenary of Marlowe's death inspired more interest than that of his birth; a playwright born in 1564 is like a child whose birthday falls on Christmas Day. Indeed, many Marlowe revivals have depended for their justification on a comparison with Shakespeare. The most important ones of the 1960s were explicit Marlowe-Shakespeare pairings: Clifford Williams' *Jew of Malta* in Stratford (1965–6) featured Eric Porter as both Barabas and Shylock; in 1969–70 Ian McKellen, touring with Prospect Theatre Company, played Edward II alongside Richard II. The 1986 opening of the Swan Theatre in Stratford-upon-Avon, with its special mandate to perform Shakespeare's contemporaries, offered perhaps the first opportunity since the age of William Poel to separate Marlowe from his Siamese twin. Even so, the RSC began its series of Marlowe revivals, in 1987, by setting *The Jew of Malta* in the Swan opposite *The Merchant of Venice* in the main house. The fact (possibly fortuitous) that Antony Sher played Shylock but not Barabas did, however, make it easier for the earlier play to be judged on its own terms, and the subsequent Swan performances of *Doctor Faustus* (1989–90), *Edward II* (1990–1) and *Tamburlaine* (1992–3) were not paired with Shakespeare plays.

The plays at the Swan will make a useful stopping-point for this chapter. As a starting-point, I should like briefly to look at a curious episode 100 years before the Swan's first Marlowe production. In 1889, two years after the publication of Havelock Ellis' Mermaid edition of Marlowe,[1] the newly created Oxford University Drama Society asked, and received, permission to perform *The Jew of Malta* – the Oxford Vice-Chancellor, Benjamin Jowett, had originally insisted that the society should do only Shakespeare. The play was carefully revised (by Courtney) 'in such a manner as not to offend the moral sensibilities of an Oxford public'.[2] The production never took place, because Robert Browning died in 1889 and the OUDS decided to perform his *Strafford* in place of the Marlowe play. The first modern production of *The Jew of Malta* would instead take place at Williams College, Massachusetts, in 1907, and OUDS did its first Marlowe play, *Doctor Faustus*, only in 1934.

The incident shows the importance of editors to performance history (a subject discussed by Richard Proudfoot elsewhere in this volume). But it also shows the power of Marlowe's life – or rather, his death – and indeed suggests that Oxford students may have been more fascinated by the deaths of authors than by their works. Nor were they the only ones with this macabre taste: the earliest previous English treatment of Marlowe's life, by R. H. Horne, is called *The Death of Marlowe*.[3] Courtney himself went on to write *Kit Marlowe's Death*, privately performed in London in 1890 and 1892.[4] Like Horne's play, it is heavily indebted to the pre-Hotson tradition, especially the forged ballad by Collier which made Marlowe an actor as well as a victim of 'lewd love'. Horne's Marlowe was in love with a courtesan, but Courtney's – 'that handsome, careless, devil-may-care Kit Marlowe, with his saucy manners and his sparkling eyes, who hath taken the whole town by storm' – is much more innocent. The action is about equally divided between the hero's literary life and his romantic one. Marlowe has just become bored with *Dido*, handed it over to Nashe for completion, and is now writing *Titus Andronicus*. For want of anything better to do, he flirts with the simple adoring servant Nan; the innkeeper Archer, who loves her himself, stabs him in a frenzy of jealousy. Marlowe dies quoting from his own works and someone moralises, 'Cut is the branch that might have grown full straight', thereby ensuring the identification of the author with his most famous character that has been implicit throughout the play.[5]

It is hardly surprising that most Marlowe revivals (those of *Tamburlaine* and *Dido* in particular) have taken place in academic or experimental contexts. William Poel's Elizabethan Stage Society inaugurated its series of Marlowe productions in 1896 with *Doctor Faustus* and performed *Edward II* in 1903 – a brave decision, in view of the Oscar Wilde trial in 1895. The first *Tamburlaine*, at Yale University in 1919, conflated the two parts. The next was Nevill Coghill's in Worcester College gardens in 1933, which confined itself to *Part II*.[6] Of the other productions listed by J. S. Cunningham in his Revels edition of 1981, about half were given at universities.[7]

Both Oxford and Cambridge have a tradition of professional directors and (sometimes) visiting professional actors, that has enabled them to mount productions which the professional theatre could not do. Thus, the two most significant early revivals of *Edward II* were at Cambridge: John Barton directed Toby Robertson in 1951 and Robertson himself directed Derek Jacobi in 1958; both productions went on to successful London runs. None of the Oxford revivals has been as influential, though the appearance of Richard Burton and Elizabeth Taylor in Coghill's *Doctor Faustus* of 1965, later filmed, did more for Marlowe's fame than any other event this century. *Faustus* also became briefly famous when Orson Welles directed it in New York in 1937; the production used actors in Roosevelt's WPA and attracted an untypically diverse theatre audience.[8] Of the four major plays, *Faustus* seems likely to remain the most frequently produced, and it will be apparent from this essay that it is virtually impossible to generalise about its history. The others, however, have been strongly affected by extra-dramatic factors.

Marlowe's first great success, *Tamburlaine*, is always likely to be something of a rarity. It is generally considered impossible to perform in its entirety,[9] and conflation always involves over-simplification and distortion. The 1919 Yale production, clearly under the influence of the Havelock Ellis concept of Marlowe, emphasised the author's youthfulness. In the immediate aftermath of a war which had destroyed so many young lives, an undergraduate cast and a heavily cut and adapted text apparently created a sympathetic 'Mongolian Robin Hood, ridding Persia of its lamentable cankers'.[10] Since World War II, Tamburlaine has been more easily identifiable with the military leaders whose ambition kills civilians and soldiers alike. The barbaric, frightening, and increasingly insane hero played by Donald Wolfit in the Tyrone Guthrie *Tamburlaine* (1951) has been shown to derive from a 1948 adaptation by Basil Ashmore, who obviously had Hitler's career in mind.[11] Keith Hack's 1972 production for the Assembly Hall at Edinburgh and the Glasgow Citizens' Theatre took the stylisation and cruelty still farther, with a striking set that featured corpses on gallows and wheels, and a central platform, striped in white, red, and black, that was also Tamburlaine's chariot. It seemed lit mainly by torchlight, often reflecting off the gold on the costumes; the lights were brought up, non-naturalistically, when Tamburlaine showed Theridamas his heap of treasure. The action took place all over the theatre (Zenocrate and Zabina insulted each other from opposite balconies) and the emphasis was on the play's heavily stylised theatricality. The playing of Tamburlaine by three actors in succession (Rupert Frazer, Jeremy Kissoon and Mike Gwilym) defused the 'star-as-hero' element which had been so important in the Wolfit performance.

Peter Hall's 1976 *Tamburlaine* for the National Theatre's Olivier auditorium was still more a company production, despite Albert Finney's highly praised performance in the title role. It surprised one reviewer because of its relative absence of 'frightening moments' – a result of Hall's intellectual approach and the visual patterning, which drew attention to the work as an artefact.[12] Doubling was also a significant part of the patterning, as when Dennis Quilley (Bajazet in the first half) returned in the second as his son Callapine.[13] In an extended review, J. S. Cunningham and Roger Warren praised Hall's effective use of the play's colour-coding, his clarity of detail, and his unexpected but never gratuitous humour. This humour, sometimes resulting from a joke shared with the audience, made the action more tolerable but also reinforced the cruelty by discouraging emotional identification with the victims. Hall became convinced, in the course of rehearsal, that the play was atheistic,[14] but the crucial point, Tamburlaine's sudden illness, following almost immediately on his challenge to Mahomet (*Part II*, 5.1.216), was played so ambiguously that spectators differed as to how to interpret the silence that fell after Tamburlaine's challenge and his later upward glance, 'as if to acknowledge Mahomet's intervention'.[15] On the one hand, the production offered visual equivalents for the splendour of Marlowe's language; on the other, it allowed that splendour to be undercut.[16]

Probably because of its relationship to Shakespeare's *Merchant of Venice*, *The Jew of Malta* is unlike Marlowe's other plays in that it has never depended on academic productions for its continued existence. Of the eight post-World War II productions listed by N. W. Bawcutt, only one (by the Marlowe Players of Reading University in 1954) was university-based. A production at Drury Lane in 1818, starring Edmund Kean, was the only commercial revival of a Marlowe play before the twentieth century. Kean's first great successes had been as Shylock and Richard III, so it is natural that he should have been attracted to a role that seemed to combine the two. His biographer, F. W. Hawkins, later felt it necessary to deny that the production's opening in the week of Passover had been intended as an insult, 'as was supposed at the time', adding that the play had been carefully altered to remove 'much of the rancour against the Jews that sully [sic] Marlowe's pages'.[17] The following year, it should be noted, saw the publication of Scott's *Ivanhoe*, with its highly influential portrayal of Isaac of York and his daughter Rebecca.

Several reviewers of the Kean production note the audience's particular enthusiasm for the scene where Barabas impersonates a French musician, and its request for an encore. This reaction, and the disapprobation which some critics seem to have felt, suggest that confusion over the play's genre existed then as now.[18] A similar polarisation can be seen in the casting of Clifford Williams' RSC production of 1964–5: in the London season, Barabas was Clive Revill, the original Fagin in the musical *Oliver Twist*; Eric Porter, best known as a tragic actor, took over the part when the production moved to Stratford.[19] Throughout the play, Barabas was in fact both clown and tragedian, capable of arousing emotion, then openly undercutting it, until by the end the audience showed well-justified suspicions every time he appealed to them directly, and felt some relief when his trickery was aimed at someone else – as when, having invited the carpenters to 'drink your fill' in his cellar, he added the two-word aside, 'and die' (5.5.10).

The production highlighted the speed and economy of Marlowe's text: for example, the second half opened with the rapid entry of a Turkish ambassador and the assembled Knights of Malta, whose terse exchange, summing up as it did the world of the play, took one's breath away:

FERNEZE: Welcome, great Basso; how fares Calymath?
    What wind drives you thus into Malta-road?
BASSO: The wind that bloweth all the world besides,
    Desire of gold.                                        (3.5.1–4)

So much unabashed and obvious greed and hypocrisy was almost reassuring; it shone like the sun-drenched white slabs – whited sepulchres? – that made up the set. As James L. Smith has noted, Williams' production fitted easily into a recognised genre of the 1960s, black comedy.[20] In the midst of this corruption, the white-robed Turks, especially Calymath, seemed figures from a simpler and better world; Calymath's hiss of horror at the end, when he realised that he had been betrayed by Ferneze as well as Barabas, was followed by a final anti-Christian effect, as the Christians solemnly lifted their swords and inverted them to make the shape of the cross as they processed offstage.

Despite some controversy over Heywood's possible involvement in *The Jew of Malta*, its text is remarkably free of problems. On the other hand, the lack of consensus about the text of *Faustus* means that every production is likely to differ from the previous one. Post-1960 productions often specify and justify the edition used – which, despite the current scholarly consensus in favour of the B-text, is more likely than not to be A. The assumption that the comic scenes are not part of Marlowe's original conception has often encouraged cutting and rearrangement; in 1974, John Barton also added some lines from the Faustbook and a love scene between the hero and the Duchess of Vanholt. Recent productions are less likely to ignore the comedy, but the directorial problem is recognised: a production which sees Faustus as romantic and tragic will be embarrassed by the comic scenes, but one which treats him simply as a fool risks boring and alienating the audience.[21]

The subject matter of *Faustus*, with its focus on magic and the supernatural, also imposes decisions about spectacle. Everyone who hears it for the first time is stunned by Mephostophilis' great line, 'Why, this is hell, nor am I out of it' (1.3.76),[22] the idea that hell (and everthing else) might be mental has inspired a number of austere, small-cast productions. In Barton's 1974 version, Ian McKellen ventriloquised the lines of two puppets representing the good and evil angels, and, in the original plan, was to have played Mephosto-philis as well.[23] However, much of the play's success in its own time probably depended on non-verbal elements such as the conjuring tricks and the spectacle of foreign courts. The most successful productions have been those which were not afraid of the comedy and which also gratified the desire for spectacle.

Michael Benthall's *Faustus* of 1961, a success both at the Edinburgh Festival and the Old Vic, changed the order of the central scenes so that they culminated at the court of Rome; the episode at the papal court was genuinely funny and at the same time was played to show that Faustus was using farce to distract himself from his own approaching fate. The scene in which the friars curse those who have disturbed the papal feast was a case in point: a friar who had just been intoning the curse was slapped by a still-playful Faustus and burst out with a heartfelt 'Cursed be he that struck Friar Sandalo a blow on the pate' (3.3.101).[24] Faustus laughed, but, at the end of the scene, his laughter became hysterical: the inept cursing, 'Backward and forward, to curse Faustus to hell' was, he realised, bringing coals to Newcastle. There have been other funny and grotesque court scenes: 'a trick sausage that sprang off the pontiff's fork at Faustus' command';[25] custard pies in many versions, often to the annoyance of the critics.

Ever since the early anecdotes about real devils appearing among the cast of *Faustus*, there has been a tendency to confuse illusion and reality in this play. It is strange how often the theatre has, at the moment of Helen's entrance, lost its nerve on the subject of theatre magic, seeking to find an equivalent for the most beautiful woman in the world. William Poel's 1896 revival used 'a model in a dampened, clinging dress'; we never saw the face that launched a thousand ships save through the eyes of Faustus.[26] In the OUDS production of 1934, directed by Gyles Isham, Helen was played by the 'deb of the year', whose picture appeared in the *Tatler* several times during the production.[27] Even Williams, who depicted the other devils as they 'really' were, had Helen played by an attractive naked actress, a fact which got more advance publicity than anything else in the production. More recently, she has been visibly a construct, a puppet or a doll dressed up before our eyes; in one production she was produced from a bucket, 'a shrunken head with wet red hair'; she was 'yards of white silk' in York (1977) and vanished 'as smoke blew into his eyes'; she has descended in a shower of gold (Manchester, 1981), or has been nothing but 'wind pouring through a red tunnel'. She was Eartha Kitt in Orson Welles's Paris production of 1950, Elizabeth Taylor in Coghill's of 1965.[28] In a number of recent productions, Helen has been played by a man. There have also been all-male productions – not out of antiquarian interest in boy actors, but in order to exploit the extra-dramatic 'knowledge' about Marlowe. A production in the chapel of Jesus College, Cambridge, in October 1980, began with a reading of the Baines note.[29]

The inherent fascination of the *Faustus* story has made it available to every kind of theatre. In 1977 alone – to choose a year at random – a Victorian version at Perth (directed by Andrew McKinnon) made the Chorus an elderly lady telling a cautionary tale; Barry Smith's Puppet Theatre performed a largely farcical version; and a ninety-minute *Shorter Faustus* with a cast of five, by the York Theatre

Royal (directed by Alan Drury), divided the hero into his past and present selves, the latter 'a confirmed but enforced alcoholic, drinking red wine all evening'. Feeling no need to turn it into an organic whole, the Jesus College production accentuated its disjunctions. The Medieval Players' *Doctor Faustus*, though criticised as too 'lightweight', showed that it can be effective to focus on, instead of avoiding, the low comedy and conjuring. Faustus, a bumbling academic (Neil Salvage), was easily distracted by the spectacular musical, fire-eating, stilt-walking tricks of the rest of the cast. But his ending was striking and sobering. There was no diabolical reaction at the end of his final speech. He nodded grimly, realising what the silence meant ('*this* is hell'), went inside the inner stage, and drew the curtains. A few moments later, the scholars opened them, to reveal him hanging from a noose.[30]

*Edward II* is the Marlowe play for which performance history has been most drastically affected by outside events, particularly the disappearance of pre-performance censorship in 1968. Toby Robertson, who directed it in both 1958 and 1969, recalled that on the first occasion 'it seemed extraordinary that you should actually do this on the stage at all', while the second production could show Edward and Gaveston kissing.[31] Even so, the production aroused controversy in Edinburgh and McKellen (already scheduled for Richard II) got the part because, when the actor originally cast was obliged to drop out, 'no other actor was prepared to play the homosexual king'.[32] Since that time, productions have become so explicit about both the hero's homosexuality and the nature of his death that it is hard to believe that the play was once able to make its effect in any other way. No production of *Edward II* has failed to respect the tragic intensity of Edward's passion for Gaveston, but the treatment of the other characters has varied considerably. William Poel's 1903 production treated Gaveston as a 'quite delightful stage character'; it was his impudence and frivolity that made him a threat to the barons. The horrors of the king's (offstage) murder were suggested by Lightborn's putting on his gloves as he re-entered.[33] Glynne Wickham's 1964 production for the Bristol Old Vic Drama School used simple patterning to make a poignant contrast between Edward's capacity for affection and that of the men for whom he cared most. For instance, when Edward had been forced by the barons to send Gaveston to exile in Ireland, the two men exchanged portraits; Edward carefully placed the precious object round his neck, while Gaveston almost instinctively held it so as to estimate its likely weight and value. In the final prison scene, as Edward repented his suspicions of Lightborn, he burst out with his offer of the one jewel still remaining to him: it was the portrait of Gaveston. Interpretative questions about whether Gaveston, Spencer, and Baldock reciprocate Edward's love often disappear when the production is concerned simply to show them in bed together. There was a time when Mortimer could be sympathetically portrayed, at least in the early scenes and in his final defiances, and Isabella could be seen as the victim of her husband's self-fulfilling prophecies, finally embracing the adultery of which she has so often been accused (see Joanna Gibbs's chapter, pp. 164–70). When the play is paired with *Richard II*, as in the 1969 Robertson production, the cross-casting of Mortimer with Bolingbroke can make him a powerful alternative as well as an antagonist. Timothy West's performance brought out not only the character's strength but also his pettiness, as in his complaints to his father about the way in which Edward and Gaveston make fun of the unfashionably dressed barons, and his no-nonsense attitude: after the King's Champion had challenged all comers at the coronation of young Edward III, he cut short the pageantry with the brusque 'None comes'. The emotional intensity of Ian McKellen's Edward, who, in his interpretation, did not become cruel until after the murder of Gaveston, was something which the barons were comically – and tragically – incapable of understanding.

Despite the sprinkling of productions which surrounded the quatercentenary of Marlowe's birth in 1964, Clifford Leech commented in the 1970s on the discrepancy between the high place the playwright is usually given in English literary history and the scarcity of opportunities for seeing his plays.[34] By contrast, as the anniversary of his death approached, a *Times* journalist claimed that the country had been gripped by a 'Marlowe mania'.[35] It culminated, on the day itself, in Ian McKellen's unveiling of a memorial at the Marlowe Theatre in Canterbury.[36] The Swan at Stratford produced all four major plays in the run-up to that event. Despite the obvious differences resulting from three different directors, the productions shared some stylistic features: for instance, the exploitation (in all except *Edward II*) of the unusual height of the new theatre. Barry Kyle's *Jew of Malta* opened spectacularly, as Machevil shot from below the stage up to the gallery level. His *Doctor Faustus* featured an

enormous spiral stairway that spanned heaven and hell; Faustus
(Gerard Murphy) climbed it at the end in a desperate attempt to
escape, but it descended through the stage,[37] much like the trapeze
bar on which Barabas had been dropped through the floor at the
end of the previous production. The most often mentioned moment
in Terry Hands's *Tamburlaine* came when Antony Sher climbed a
rope and spoke a soliloquy while hanging upside down, thirty feet
above the stage, then slid down head-first, 'still declaiming'.[38]
Earlier Marlowe productions had also been excitingly staged, but
usually without such a strong sense of danger to the actors themselves. They were on the whole intellectually detached; the word
'Brechtian' was often used of them.

By contrast, the Marlowe of the 1980s was very much present in
his works. The exception was perhaps Barry Kyle's 1988 *Jew of Malta*
– like Clifford Williams' in its emphasis on comedy, but given an
eclectic mixture of periods and styles rather than a recognisable
setting. Alun Armstrong's Barabas was closer to Clive Revill's than
Eric Porter's, a music-hall comedian with a nice line in ad-libs.
These had become even better by the time the production reached
London in 1988: Michael Billington 'liked his cry of "Don't go" to
the sole member of the audience who got the point of his reference
to Agamemnon and Iphigenia', also his banjo and straw hat in the
French musician impersonation, and the fez he wore when the Turks
had conquered Malta.[39] But there were reminders of darker things:
the appearance of Abigail with a battered suitcase, after the Jews
had been expelled from their home, immediately evoked 'the
unmistakable pathetic figure of the late thirties queuing up on [a]
platform station on the way to all hell'.[40] The production was very
much a product of its time in that the Turks, so glamorous and
comparatively pure in the Clifford Williams version of 1964–5, were
now dangerous thugs; several reviewers noted the resemblance
between Calymath and Yasser Arafat.[41] The terrorism associated
with religious conflict, in Ireland as well as the Middle East, gave
Marlowe's fantastic plot a new relation to real life, which could be
counted on to undercut its comedy.

Kyle had already directed *The Merchant of Venice* in Israel and
'couldn't bear the idea of Marlowe's play seeming to be an anti-
semitic piece of work'.[42] Where, as in Barabas' catalogue of his evil
past, there seemed no way of avoiding apparent anti-semitism, he
had Alun Armstrong play it, as Kean apparently did, as if he merely

wished 'to try Ithamore's disposition'.[43] Mainly, the play emphasised
the evil of the Christians – for instance, by doubling Machevil with
Ferneze, a smooth, totally corrupt figure in a white suit (John
Carlisle). Even though Carlisle, one of the most recognisable of RSC
performers, dropped back into Machiavelli's accent for the last
words of Ferneze's closing speech, the point may not have been clear
to those unfamiliar with the play, and they probably did not realise
that Ferneze had also been 'trying to do a deal with Del Bosco over
Barabas's gold'.[44] Still, David Nathan, in *The Jewish Chronicle*, wrote:
'it is no use going to see it and then complaining that it is anti-
semitic. It is. It is also anti-Christian and anti-Moslem. Indeed, it is
anti-everything except . . . a good laugh'.[45] Others compared its
attitude of 'we are all as bad as one another, ho ho' to that of high-
powered traders in the City, a world already made familiar by Caryl
Churchill's *Serious Money*.[46]

The *Doctor Faustus* of Barry Kyle and the *Edward II* of Gerald
Murphy were directed as the works of a homosexual dramatist. The
AIDS epidemic of the 1980s, like the Holocaust, was the sort of
event that seems to make certain kinds of humour impossible. Even
though the overt references to homosexuality in the Baines note
have no apparent connection with the dramatist's death, a sense of
impending doom, linked with a wistfulness about close male relationships, casts its shadow over many productions of Marlowe.
Kyle's austere, all-male *Faustus* seemed haunted by more than the
fear that the clock would strike. Peter J. Smith drew attention to a
characteristic effect at the end: 'Mephostopheles [*sic*] mysteriously
extends his arm to the disappearing Faustus; whether an attempt to
pull him back from the brink of Hell or to push him on, the
production did not say.'[47] When Kyle's Faustus, Gerald Murphy,
went on to direct *Edward II* in 1990 with Simon Russell Beale as the
King, the production doubled Gaveston the lover with Lightborn the
killer – a familiar practice by now, but significant nevertheless. As in
Nicholas Hytner's production at the Manchester Royal Exchange
(1986), and in the Jarman film of 1991, the play became an apologia
for homosexuality in general rather than the story of a particular
king in a particular historical situation (see Lawrence Normand's
essay, pp. 177–93). While Edward's cruelty toward others was not
exactly ignored, the horrifying playing of his sufferings made
everything else fade into insignificance. Like Jarman's film, the
production demonised Isabella and Mortimer (Katy Behean and

Ciaran Hinds) – the latter actually had hair and moustache like Hitler's, in case anyone should be in doubt as to what to think of him.

The Swan's *Tamburlaine*, the last of its sequence of Marlowe revivals, was the production that actually coincided with the anniversary of Marlowe's death and Terry Hands, who directed it, was generally praised for his willingness to come to terms with the unpleasant side of the play. As nearly all reviewers noted, the basic imagery was that of the jungle. The characters ate and drank like animals, blood was everywhere, always in danger of sloshing on to spectators in the front rows. Martin Wiggins (quoting Martin Buzacott's *Death of the Actor*), called it 'theatrical terrorism',[48] perhaps intensified by the intimacy of the small Swan theatre. One example: Antony Sher's Tamburlaine 'rubs his fingers in the defeated Emperor Bajazet's sweaty hair, licks it greedily, and gives it to his mistress to smell'.[49] There were some strong gut reactions: Michael Billington argued that this 'repellent masterpiece' was worth reviving *only* 'as a prefiguration of the madness of modern tyranny'.[50] Perhaps Hands was trying to avoid the kind of response that shocked Eric Bentley when Guthrie's *Tamburlaine* played in New York in 1956: 'cries of Bravo when the Governor [of Babylon] was hoisted in the air and transfixed with arrows'.[51] The cries may have registered only admiration at the production's technical skill,[52] but Bentley clearly found them indistinguishable from sadistic delight in cruelty. At least, Hands left the audience in no doubt that, as Irving Wardle said, 'applauding [Tamburlaine] is like applauding National Front graffiti'.[53] Yet even this production softened some aspects of the play. Tamburlaine's unheroic son Calyphas chooses to sit out a battle and play at dice in his tent with his companion, Perdicas; by transforming Perdicas into the female Perdica, Hands avoided charges of homophobia. He also undercut the triumphalism of the play's final moments by ending with Tamburlaine's recognition of the unfinished state of his conquests ('And shall I die, and this unconquered?').

Intentionally or not, this line links the play with its author's early death and thus with Peter Whelan's *The School of Night*, which opened at The Other Place in Stratford a few months after *Tamburlaine*. Like W. L. Courtney's play 100 years earlier, it is inspired by the poet's death, but also draws on information about the Elizabethan secret service, not available to Courtney, and on a vast literature of speculation – for instance, about the 'School' of the title, which may never have existed. Though Calvin Hoffman's work is acknowledged in the published text, it is used only as a starting-point. The final scene is supposed to be the rehearsal for the fake death hypothesised by Hoffman, but the poet becomes increasingly suspicious that the elaborate scheme conceals a real murder plot. By tauntingly revealing his suspicions to Ingram Frizer, the man who is to pretend to kill him, he virtually ensures that he will die in earnest. But the plot allows one to believe in any one of a number of hands behind Ingram's. He is patronised – perhaps loved – by Audry Walsingham, who resents her husband's former homosexual relationship with Marlowe.[54] Ralegh, once a member of the School of Night, may be prepared to kill Marlowe to keep him from revealing his involvement. If one were to replace Catholicism with Communism, the plot's multiple double-crosses, and its emphasis on the association between Cambridge and espionage, might be those of a Le Carré novel. Also topical, in Thatcher's 1980s when Whelan first wrote the play,[55] is the implication that the real enemy is a powerful female (the always-offstage Elizabeth I, or fanatical, philistine Audry Walsingham). Whelan even suggests, through the depiction of his rival, Thomas Kyd, and his murderer, Ingram Frizer, that Marlowe may destroy himself by his contempt for others. Though he dreams of a republic on the lines of Venice, he avoids the public theatres, preferring his private theatricals in the houses of aristocrats. Evidence against him is drawn (under torture, admittedly) from Kyd, whom he has consistently humiliated; Frizer, described early in the play as 'well aware that he is excluded', may kill, at last, simply out of anger.

Most intriguing of all is the question of the responsibility of the actor Tom Stone. He consistently claims to admire Marlowe but he later admits that he is in the pay of the queen; he also admits that his real name is Shakespeare. Marlowe is not sure whether to believe him. The possibility that Shakespeare may not really be Shakespeare, comic in the context of literary history and pseudo-history, is understandable in this world of double-agents; although 'Stone' claims to want to help Marlowe, nothing in his enigmatic behaviour is incompatible with the idea that he is preparing, however reluctantly, to betray him. In Courtney's earlier play, Shakespeare never appears but Marlowe speaks (apparently without envy) in his praise, though 'he is but in the first blush of his spring, and mayhap none of us shall see his summer'.[56] Whelan's depiction of their relationship is far more problematic. Marlowe's fear of being destroyed by 'Stone' is based less on his rival's possible intentions than on the extraordinary fluency and productivity, which contrast so sharply with his own failure to live up to his early promise.[57]

Like Horne and Courtney, though in a far more sophisticated postmodern fashion, Whelan finally makes Marlowe's life merge with his works. The scene of Marlowe's murder derives its suspense from the eerie sense that it has all happened before, in the imaginations of dramatists of the period, including Marlowe himself. While the Audry Walsingham theory is one of many about the ultimate responsibility for the poet's death, her relationship with Ingram repeats that of Isabella and Mortimer in *Edward II*. The rehearsal for a fake death which turns out to be real is a familiar dramatic device, and Marlowe and Shakespeare have already talked about Kyd's Hamlet play with its buttoned and unbuttoned foils. Marlowe's repeated visions of the room in which he will finally die always include the smell of water. He himself recognises the possible pun on Ralegh's name (Walter/Water). But the prophecy 'that by water I should die' actually occurs in the one play that Shakespeare is supposed to have written at this point: *Harry the Sixth*, now called *Henry VI, Part Two*; the Duke of Suffolk recognises, too late, the meaning of the words when he dies at sea, by the hand of a pirate named Walter Whitmore. So perhaps Marlowe foresees his death because it has already been scripted by Shakespeare. Essentially a postmodern device, which explains a historical event in literary terms (and thus does not explain it at all), Whelan's subtle intertextuality plays intriguingly with most of the trends in current Marlowe criticism and production; perhaps it even critiques their solipsism and misogyny. Despite its biographical focus, Whelan's great merit is that it releases Marlowe from the role of victim and martyr, making the playwright's work, after all, more interesting than his death.

# CHAPTER 7

# A bit of ruff: criticism, fantasy, Marlowe

## Simon Shepherd

Although interpretation of his plays may change with critical fashion, two things about Marlowe's life remain consistently known. He was accused, rightly or wrongly, of making favourable remarks about sodomy – this immediately sets him apart from, say, Jonson or Shakespeare, in that sexuality, with handy simplicity, becomes a defining feature. And he died in mysterious and violent circumstances in a pub in a suburb, a rumble ungraced by the stroppy machismo of Jonson's duel: aborted without the well-heeled poise of Shakespeare's retirement. Marlowe's name, in short, means, before anything else, sex and violence.

*I pushed the bolt across the door. Underneath our feet the floor was wet with piss. We manoeuvred so that he was standing with his legs either side of the lavatory bowl. Then, leaning towards the cistern, the king began to undo his jeans.*

### PROLEGOMENA TO THE QUESTION

In his account of *The Jew of Malta*, one of the modern fashion designers of Renaissance criticism, Stephen Greenblatt, suggests that the play makes the audience complicit in its work of dismantling moral values. By way of example Greenblatt tells how the 'audience at the Royal Shakespeare Company's brilliant 1964 production roared with delight when the poisoned nuns came tumbling out of the house' (Greenblatt, p. 204). It is characteristic of Greenblatt's anecdotal method that he should attend to, and use, the 'evidence' of a real-life audience. The evidence then becomes an illustration of basic human feeling. That anecdote, far from being a diversion from critical discourse, is to be understood as the irruption into it of the real. As such the effect of reality doesn't amount to a deepening engagement with the historically real (like asking who the RSC audience was in 1964) but is instead a rhetorical device which enacts criticism's respect for its notion of the real.

The militant sensitivity to the effects of 'real' theatre works to establish Greenblatt's distance from an older, more traditional, distrust of theatre. Such distrust is spoken by N. W. Bawcutt's edition of the *Jew*: 'I would suggest to producers that Abigail should be played as realistically and sympathetically as possible; if she is guyed, one dimension of the play is lost'.[1] The suspicion is that theatre-workers, dealing as they do with live audiences, are always drawn to an instant way of pleasing, and thus theatrical performance threatens to diminish the thing over which the editor is the guardian, the verbal text. This is particularly the case with a play such as the *Jew*, where there is a problem in 'maintaining the right balance of the "ludicrous" and the "terrible"'.[2] But these warnings acknowledge that performance, however unbalanced, is rather better at being ludicrous and terrible, however it fancies, than is the printed play. Creaking on its hinges here, the stage door later swings wide open when modern editing accepts that the theatre can't be kept out of the play. To this end, the general editor of the 1980s Oxford Shakespeare, after appropriate agonies, permitted the editorial insertion of stage directions 'with the aim of assisting the reader to imagine a performance in a theatre of Shakespeare's time'.[3] Which is a nifty move, because it eschews Bawcutt's stuffiness while it also ensures responsible – historically proper – imaginings: not, presumably, assisting in the conception of tumbling nuns.

But it is only by skewing the balance of ludicrous and terrible that the nuns can draw from the audience laughter at what they normally wouldn't find funny, and at that moment we hear something very dear to Greenblatt and his followers, the sound of transgression. This is a key element, we might say an essence, of the fashionable approach to Renaissance drama which strode the conference-circuit catwalks from the mid-1980s onwards. From their association with transgression all the other critical buzz words draw their energy. Thus Renaissance drama is seen to be part of an organic popular culture that also comprises bear-baiting and clowning, languages and forms outside the dominant, heteroglot plurality: keyword *carnival.* The theatres in which the plays were done are described as being geographically, and culturally, outside the jurisdiction limits of the City of London, in areas for which the technical term was 'liberties' – which produces very satisfying double-meanings:

keyword *marginal*. Situated in these 'liberties', theatres found themselves alongside institutions that housed others whose bodies and
lives had to be excluded from the proprieties of dominant culture,
the leper-houses and brothels, whose inmates were clearly deeply
implicated in the life of the city without being approved by it:
keyword *liminal*. In the theatres, people who had the legal status of
vagabonds dressed up as, and imitated, bishops and kings; young
male actors, men doing their craft apprenticeship, put on the clothes
and behaviours of women: keyword *transvestite*. For the duration of
the play, dressed-up people may be seriously treated as the thing
which, socially and biologically, they are not: '[t]he stage thus
presented classed and gendered identity as problematic rather than
given and fixed . . . it also exposed and troubled the very concept of
autonomous individual identity' (Kastan and Stallybrass, p. 9):
keywords *unfixed identity*. And with those keywords we find out why
Renaissance drama became so attractive to all the denizens of Eng.
Lit. who, in the turmoil to update their subject, wanted to demonstrate not only that they had embraced post-structuralism but also
that its tenets were already (presumably always) inscribed in the
most conservative heart of the national canon, the drama of the
golden age. The sacred cow of English letters was diagnosed with
BSE.

But the diagnostic vets aren't quite the people they claim to be.
The search for transgression in Renaissance drama is not so much a
disinterested science as a rage against literary fuddy-duddies and
English nationalism; not vets, then, but animal rights activists
disguised in lab coats and rubber gloves. For the claims about
transgression don't always follow dispassionate logic. Take this one:
'the transgressive cross-dressing on the streets of London was of
course the very essence of the English Renaissance theater' (Kastan
and Stallybrass, p. 9). With the same rhetorical shape we could say
that the transgressive body-piercing on the streets of London is the
very essence of late twentieth-century English theatre. Apart from
being untrue, the claim erects a minority practice into something
apparently major, which is ideologically authenticated by the image
of essence. That same logic derived from essence also seems to
inhabit the claim that any spaces deemed liminal will at the same
time be automatically transgressive. As Mick Wallis says, our own
out-of-town liminal spaces are occupied by large buildings called
'Homebase' and 'Toys "Я" Us'. These, though, are not 'liberties':

but then liberties, we might say, have been taken with liberties. One of the liberties was Blackfriars, very close to the respectable heart of the City of London, without a brothel in sight. But even where the brothels were close, how did they link up with theatres? For instance, the Royal National Theatre at Waterloo is pretty close to what was the Shell building, and made out of a similar coloured fabric: sitting in its auditoria was one imbued inevitably by the ethos of the petroleum industry? Presumably that's not what Jonathan Goldberg means by saying the 'theater was permitted to rehearse the dark side of Elizabethan culture';[4] but then, how much of the dark side of Blair's Britain is rehearsed by *Cats*? Maybe a keyword such as *liminal* should just be ditched (going the way of the 1960s preoccupation with the subliminal): the theatres on the south bank of the Thames could just as appositely be described as 'littoral'.

*He dropped his jeans just far enough to reveal an arse that was slim, well-shaped and shaved clean of hair. Next to the damp bog-roll on the cistern was his crown and a bottle of poppers. He steadied himself with his hands against the stained walls and bent over further.*

If people find regrettable the passing of liminal, marginal, carnival then something extra needs to be said about the vets who aren't vets but activists in lab coats. It is that the wearing of rubber-gloved costume can have pleasures of its own. There's quite a lot of fun in writing literary analysis that conjures up TRANS-GRESSION: in the familiar space of one's study being able to focus imaginatively on the sorts of bodies which are always elsewhere, seeing the shape of a beautiful risky physique, much as if the computer had generated, shall we say, Helen of Troy. . . . Have you ever wondered why academics *like* to speak quotations from literary texts? Have you ever watched their bodies when they enter the domain of the quotation? . . .

## MARLOWE AS VIOLENCE

Through the focus on transgression the way is opened into a fantasy of a lost popular culture, all those clowns and whores and cross-dressed boys and maddened bears rubbing shoulders with each other and nary a karaoke machine in view. Reinforcing this fun-loving mêlée there is the theatre, institutionally enshrining co-operative method: '[t]he company commissioned the play, usually stipulated the subject, often provided the plot, often parcelled it out, scene by scene, to several playwrights . . . the text belonged to the company, and the authority represented by the text . . . is that of the company, the owners, not that of the playwright, the author'.[5] This picture has particular attraction for those in lit. crit. who oppose author-centred criticism, and in general it sustains a rosy ambivalence about the 'company', triggering associations with 'company of players' rather than Merchant Taylors, sharing not share-holding, buskins not Boots plc. These companies succeeded precisely because they had a sharp eye for the specific skills that could generate profit: as prized as a good navigator or a good metal worker, a good writer. Writers not only had skills that differed from those of actors, but they sometimes had personal reputations and idiosyncratic styles – which then contributed to the development of theatrical product identities in what was a highly competitive market.

But what also lurks in this radical picture of the author's unimportance is a sense that theatre is rather cavalier with text. As Alan Sinfield puts it, with abrasive glee: '[m]ost professional stage productions are, in fact, cunning manipulations of the texts, together with conventionally permitted stage business'.[6] The main thrust of Sinfield's argument suggests that it is not only necessary to treat the verbal text with informed irreverence but also, more importantly, that the verbal text owes its continued canonical status to such 'manipulations'. But the phrasing here is also marked, in a binary intimacy, by that which it polemicises against. Thus, in the hands of the cunning men that injured innocent the text is not only distorted but jostled by the addition of that which is both hack and, tellingly, business. This prospect isn't a long way distant from Bawcutt's alarm about Abigail's fate in the theatre. For him too these cunning men have Sinfield's 'licence', the 'wider freedom that theater directors are customarily allowed' (Sinfield, p. 16). A freedom wider than whose? Presumably the literary critics, who, like them or loathe them, dutifully stand guard over the proper text, looking on with worldly resignation at the licentious tricks of the cunning men, much as a good angel contemplating Mephostophilis.

The cunning man is as much a fantasy as the sharing company, and it is even more conspicuously an inversion of the real state of affairs. For literary criticism finds for itself the freedom to come up with steadily more arcane 'readings' of texts, keeping its hands clean of the ideological muck that attaches to any interpretation that seems commonly understood; while by contrast the freedom of theatre directors has institutional and discursive constraints upon it, forced to follow the rules of specific modes of practice, even of genre, putting bums on seats to survive. And modern Renaissance criticism isn't really taking the part of the angel. For there is something all too attractive about the activities of the cunning men. After all, they make hilarious dying nuns. This sort of effect works upon us, suggests Thomas Cartelli, because, 'freed of normative constraints by the dependence on theatrical convention, the playgoer is able to turn the occasion of someone else's suffering into an occasion of pleasure' (Cartelli, p. 35).

That was Stephen Gosson's complaint in the 1590s: but the licensed wider freedom infects those who have not even gone to the play, who evoke in imagination both the performance and its spectators. In these conditions the grasp on the distinction between theatre and life begins to weaken. For by James Shapiro's account when Pedringano faces death in *The Spanish Tragedy*, 'neither the actor to be executed nor the spectators who witness the execution can be entirely sure that the violence is not real'.[7] At the risk of being a little dour, one might say that the actor had a pretty shrewd idea about the reality of the violence. Indeed, even within a Stanislavskian performance, the emotional reality mobilised at that point by the performer would not be the same reality as that which extinguishes life. But Shapiro is by this stage well deep into an imagined conflation of pretend and real violence, prodded by a single anecdote on to new heights:[8]

[w]hat would have happened to our conception of theatrical representation, one is tempted to ask [ah – wicked temptation], if a cutpurse had been caught and dragged onstage at that moment in a production of *The Spanish Tragedy* when Pedringano was bound to 'the stake' . . . ? Would the actor have been cut down and the cutpurse put up in his place? . . . What distinguishes the punishment of an actor playing a criminal from the punishment of a criminal brought onstage and turned into a kind of actor? For that matter, when actors punish cutpurses onstage, is it still theater?

With the briefest of pauses to remark that slide from 'if' to 'when', we can add: would people who were paid to act feel free to stop acting? Would the narrative have so little hold that the audience would scrap it? Would a stage trying to define its space tolerate confusion of it? Is this literary criticism succumbing to the devils – tempted not only to take pleasure in violence but to insist that it really is violence, not an actor pretending to be dismembered but actually coming apart?

Once we are in the domain of the cunning men, beyond the norms of the Text and sacred book, we are in fantasy space. And that space, called Renaissance theatre, is inhabited by bodies that are sold, diseased, tortured, killed. The proximity to those whores, lepers and criminals becomes an identity with them. And, as the concepts of performance, convention and theatre evaporate, so the audience's relation to these bodies turns into a moral struggle of Manichæan simplicity. That struggle is described in a set of key pairs: succumbing versus perception; Cartelli's 'appeal' versus 'normative persuasion'; engagement versus resistance; illusion versus demystification. The last pair might recall the rigours of Brecht, but that too is an illusion – for Brecht is conflated with the Elizabethan Gosson, sharing a distrust of theatre's treachery: so the issue really is only a moral one. Greenblatt summarises it in another anecdote: in Naples once he saw a pickpocket at work: '[t]he thief spotted me watching but did not run away – instead he winked, and I was frozen in mute complicity. The audience's conventional silence becomes in *The Jew of Malta* the silence of the passive accomplice, winked at by his fellow criminal' (Greenblatt, p. 216). The play itself, an artwork, is anecdotally reconceived as a criminal, a person.

This anthropomorphism is particularly characteristic of writings about Marlowe, who is portrayed as personally inhabiting his fictions. Thus for example, 'Gaveston shares with Marlowe the desire to make a place for himself in the world through his creative resources' (Cartelli, p. 131) – both like boys, both die violently. Cartelli's opinion here can be taken back to the authority on self-fashioning, so to speak, Greenblatt, who asserts that 'Marlowe is deeply implicated in his heroes . . . the one true goal of all these heroes is to be characters in Marlowe's plays' (Greenblatt, pp. 220–1). And this innovatory insight from 1980 can be taken back, almost a century, to J. A. Symonds in 1887: 'Marlowe's dramas are mostly series of scenes held together by the poetic energy of his own dominating personality. He is his own hero, and the sanguinary Scythian utters the deepest secrets of the artist's heart'.[9] When dealing with Marlowe, it seems, all those developments since Symonds – questions about the identity of author with text, debates about what precisely 'character' might be – don't really need to apply. Lit. crit. can have characters where it wants them, on the couch.

Marlowe has brought it on himself. When he is compared with Shakespeare as a producer of transgressive fantasy, 'Marlowe does not generally offer his audiences', says Cartelli, 'as balanced a disposition of his fantasy material as does Shakespeare' (Cartelli, p. 27). Pause if you will to treasure the fantasy of a fantasy that observes balance: and return to Marlowe. In that his control of the material is inadequate, we are dealing not with a craftsman but with a fantasist. At the same time it is by being unbalanced that Marlowe achieves individuality. Thus in their 'lavish pictorial biography', reissued to coincide with the 1993 death celebrations, the authors of *In Search of Christopher Marlowe* focus on him 'as an individual' rather than as precursor of Shakespeare: 'Marlowe's life is the antithesis of dullness. The photographs recreate the world in which he moved and are a delight in themselves.' It is not so much that Marlowe is playwright as player: his 'turbulent 29 years were filled with drama, mystery and romance'.[10] The figure of the unbalanced Marlowe totters through modern plays, novels, biography; even lit. crit. busily writes its script for a violent Marlowe drama. Thus Greenblatt's Marlowe, 'whose life suggests the very opposite of that "peculiar equilibrium" that distinguishes Montaigne, rushes to embrace the tragic'. Left there, Greenblatt's remark looks like a dispassionate restatement of the unbalanced Marlowe, not the stuff of what I have called fantasy. But he doesn't stop there. Marlowe rushes to embrace the tragic – here it comes – 'with a strange eagerness' (Greenblatt, p. 219).

Without wishing to conflate author and text, I am arrested by the strange eagerness. Whose is it? Where has it come from? It is not Greenblatt's alone, since Marlowe study is merely a heightened instance of that approach to Renaissance drama which insists on carnival, liminal, marginal, etc. The approach downplays profession, artifice, rhetoric, blurring the fictive and the real, so that eventually 'real life' takes over in the form of genuine criminals instead of actors, the 'essence' of transvestism instead of role-playing, real disease and violence instead of performance . . . Marlowe instead of his characters. The aim here is to write a literary criticism which shows itself to be serious because it is concerned, however vicariously, with that which is not arty but 'real', dealing with the dark side.

*Sweat was running down between his shoulder blades. He fumbled in his pocket for a tube of lubricant. I pulled on a rubber glove.*

The case of Marlowe proves itself so amenable because, while

Shakespeare has to be treated primarily as a consummate artist,
Marlowe's work can't keep out the signs of an illicit sexuality and a
violence that is about to happen, really. But what precisely is this
'real'? Greenblatt's story of the laughter at poisoned nuns tells us
that what is 'real' is the transgressive pleasure produced by
Marlowe's play. So insistent is Greenblatt on this reality that he
doesn't stop to point out that Marlowe never wrote a scene showing
the nuns dying. It might be of interest to ask why such a scene was
not scripted. But that question leads into a different real. In order
for the fantasy about carnival-complicity-transgression to stay in
place, as real, questions about artifice must be suspended. In
approaches to 'Renaissance drama', the praxis of theatre must be,
we might say, unreal.

## MARLOWE AS SEX

It is not a surprise, then, to find that in fashionable criticism
something like Greenblatt's version of the nuns seems to have
displaced Marlowe's. In her 1993 book, *Spectacles of Strangeness*, Emily
Bartels remarks of Abigail's death, 'the fact that she is killed along
with a convent full of nuns . . . turns the tragedy into farce, our
sympathy into laughter. The thinness of her characterization, like
that of the friars [and the other victims] create a distance between
their interests and ours, their victimization and our sympathy'
(Bartels, p. 21). In this way the play estranges the viewers from their
world and thus prompts them to question assumed 'categories of
meaning'. That strategy, Bartels argues, makes Marlowe's plays both
important and subversive in that they undercut the certainties that
make self securely different from other.

The basic outline of the old radical Marlowe is recognisable here
– it has been around since at least the time that *Faustus* was first seen
as pastiche Morality. But by colouring in the outline with the
vocabulary and concepts of otherness and imperialism, differences
mapped across race and sexuality (though not, of course, class),
Bartels has both re-costumed radical Marlowe for the 1990s and
demonstrated, once again, that literary criticism is organised by the
serious agenda of its times. Given this high mission it feels somewhat
underhand to point out that in the play I think Marlowe wrote the
references to the dying nuns take up about three lines, placed either
end of a scene. In between Abigail enters, makes a confession which

incriminates her father, and dies. The comedy is located in the two friars, Jacomo and Barnardine, who open the scene, worried that the deaths will screw up, as it were, their appointments to 'confess' with the nuns. Barnardine repeats the joke when Abigail dies. Against the comedy the dramaturgy sets the confession sequence. This is made both intimate and emotionally engaging in that one of the men is removed before Abigail enters, she is already dying and she needs urgently to confess, the scandalous truth she hands over is to be kept secret by the person it is handed to. This is not just a woman woven into male practices, it is a suffering person looking for peace, needing to share something private, and because she uses the only means at her disposal, institutionally and ideologically, she also compromises herself and the one person she wants to protect. The dialectical dramaturgy doesn't depend for its operation on character-isation, thin or thick: you only need to grasp the contradiction within the need and process of confession. This contradiction, embodied within the physical gestures of terminal suffering, is not so much trivialised as deepened by satirical laughter at religion. Which means that the dramaturgy is offering something a touch more complex than the choice between sympathy and laughter. But there's no need for me to describe what you can read for yourself.

What interests me here is that, once we have got rid of Green-blatt's nuns, we are left with a dramaturgy that doesn't unarguably put the audience where Bartels' hypothesis wants them to be. To get the straightforwardly estranged audience, who are thereby amenable to familiar(ised) 1990s concerns about self and other, Marlowe's dramaturgy has been simplified or adapted. In order to address ourselves properly to serious real-life issues, it seems, we must be careful how far we rely on the drama. Alan Bray warns about this when he comments on the Elizabethan image of friendship, 'which will be very familiar to students of Elizabethan poetry and drama . . . but the image there is misleading, for when we see how it was used in the tumble of daily life we see something more immediately practical than the literary images at first glance reveal'. It is Bray's job as a historian to keep a very tidy grip on the tumble of daily life as he disentangles friendship from sodomy. Spurning the efforts of those who confuse culture with daily life he points out that what the literary images in *Edward II* actually reveal, to those beyond the first glance, is that the embraces between Gaveston and Edward work within the conventions of Elizabethan friendship 'without being signs of a sodomitical relationship'. If you want signs of overt sexuality you have to look to Edward's 'determination to marry Gaveston to his niece', which is like – says Bray – Henry Howard having Robert Carr marry his grandniece Frances.[11]

This compliantly neat 'parallel' with the tumble of daily life is something to which Bray is a little more sensitive than Marlowe, who of course isn't a historian. For Marlowe doesn't give a great deal of stage space to the marriage. He also sets up a fairly pointed visual parallel: this is Gaveston reading a letter from Edward: 'Ah, words that make me surfeit with delight!' (1.1.3); and this the niece with a letter from Gaveston: 'This argues the entire love of my lord' (2.1.62). Quite apart from the contrast of 'surfeit' and 'argue', the scripted sigh is something which us drama folk (also not historians) might attend to. The niece, far from connecting Gaveston and Edward, presents Edward with the two men, Spenser and Baldock, who will become Gaveston substitutes. That substitution is staged by Edward in response to Gaveston's death: 'in this place of honour and of trust,/ Spenser, sweet Spenser, I adopt thee here' (3.2.146–7). What might this be a sign of? Defiance, yes, but articulated as an insistence on a man in the Gaveston role. A sign of friendship – or of sodomitical relationship? Again there is something dialectical about the dramaturgy which threatens to be intractable. Bray, however, is not to be side-tracked by the specificity of the medium: in the higher work of defining sodomy a play is to be treated as representation, something with 'signs' and 'accurate' pictures of the tumble of Elizabethan life.

This higher work has its own name, alluded to in the title of the book which incorporates Bray's (reprinted) essay. *Queering the Renaissance* has about it a specific 90s flavour, tastier than formulations such as 'blacking the Renaissance'. Queer Theory, as Bruce Smith defines it, aims to 'deconstruct the textual record', locating contradictions and forcing them open with the polemical intention of exposing 'the arbitrariness with which social absolutes are set in place and maintained' (Smith, p. x). When it deals with the Renaissance, QT, as we might call it, finds in Marlowe an amenable example. This is not as obvious as it might seem: for if QT is committed to forcing open the fractures, it could perhaps try its hand on, say, domestic conduct books, or the terms of employment of apprentices. By being drawn to people like Marlowe it shows a sentimental attachment to those of its own kind, ye olde friendes of

Dorothy, spotting them before the matter of sexuality has been problematised or put up for grabs. Marlowe is someone on whom you do QT, the Statute of Artificers mainly isn't.

This choice of vehicle has as much to do with pursuing current debates as with prising Renaissance cracks. Thus, in *Edward II*, where a culture apparently has no concept of homosexual identity (as is claimed for the Renaissance), how might Edward be defined? What do his barons object to? Are his relations with Gaveston to be seen as sodomy or friendship? Is the problem class rather than sodomy? What are the relations between personal and public within the political domain? To what extent is homoeroticism a threat to dominant order? How may the accusation of sodomy be exploited as a political weapon? Is homoeroticism sodomy? Do nice gay men like back-room bars? Are homosexuals in high places likely to be radicals? Are they even homosexuals? Does shit sex constitute a radical gesture?

*Outside the door a couple of lads were gossiping. One was combing his hair in the mirror. Someone else was crouched on the floor near the urinal. From inside the cubicle came the sound of gentle moaning, and the hiss of water on a red-hot spit.*

For Gregory Bredbeck, a strength of *Edward II* is its use of Mortimer, whose 'recognition of the role of homoeroticism in political construction enables him to efface his own agency' (Bredbeck, p. 72). For Smith, who places himself outside the Queer Theory practised by Bredbeck, Marlowe's strength here comes from 'his ability to see character from the inside as well as the outside' (Smith, p. 214) – Gaveston's opening soliloquy is so ingenuous that we sympathise. Clearly these two, both interested in Renaissance sodomy, are doing different things: Smith seeing how characters create emotional responses, Bredbeck focusing on character as a proposition about sodomy's relation to order. Both, however, have a notion of staged character as something that can be 'ingenuous', or 'recognise' concepts. It's a post-naturalist version of character. It doesn't, however, guarantee that either QT or Smith's 'cultural poetics' manages to put much pressure on the specific texture of the artwork, the cracks in the form. Indeed, although all the gay critics mention, with a shudder, the red-hot spit death, they are all concerned only with its meaning – an allegorical gesture, a statement of sodomitical sin, a literal branding with sodomy. The rest of that scene, and that which is sensual but not always meaningful, vanish in importance before this act of inscription. As if, under threat of the spit, the cracks close up.

And that spit, as Stephen Orgel so sensibly points out, is a critical fantasy. By the elegantly simple device of quoting from Marlowe's play, Orgel informs us that 'Edward is pressed to death.' He goes on to ask why modern commentators fantasise the use of the very object that Marlowe's text abjures: 'we want the murder to be precisely what Marlowe refuses to make it . . . the mirror of Edward's unspeakable vice'.[12] The dramaturgy as it stands could be said, by contrast, to problematise, if not foreground, exactly that which is critically taken for granted – the audience's relationship to the representation or, to coin a phrase, what the spectator wants. Lightborn, momentarily alone, holding a light, has given orders for his equipment and now announces that a king is about to be 'finely handled'. The scene has both finesse and handling. Verbally it is organised not just to 'express' character but to enact the decorums of tragedy. Snatches of stychomythic exchange, the set-piece 'tale', the verbalisation of 'heart break': all are sketched in, enough to be recognisable, not sufficient to be satisfying. Furthermore, Edward's attempt to produce pity and Lightborn's performance of it are both ploys, necessary steps in getting the victim appropriately ready but also not the real thing. Visually there is a movement towards stillness, with the Edward performer acting a numbed body and Lightborn taking the role of responder. Yet this stillness, the relaxation of vigilance, is felt to be both dangerous for Edward and an illusion, since violence is on its way. On the other hand, Edward's spasms of activity are difficult. His summoning of the gestures and stance of kingship are out of place, mistaken, incomplete; his hell of grief is abrupt, like a reflex, with over-large gestures. These spasms are simultaneously expressive and embarrassing. The Edward actor is set up to occupy the narrative and theatrical centre, to be what is focused on. Yet the body doesn't give back to the spectators the usual pleasure derived from centredness, for that body shakes and trembles. And the longer it is at the centre the more frustratingly tangential that body becomes, as it moves from being upright to lying on a bed. Upright it occupies a pastiche tragic role, on the bed it is dissatisfyingly flattened to the view. Yet the dramaturgy makes us *want* the real, fully centred, thing – the killing.

Lightborn's fine handling consists of a scrupulous respect for the body of the king. Partly he is pretending tenderness to produce trust in his victim; partly he is enacting a reverent insistence that the royal body be unblemished. These attitudes tie in with contemporary political myths about the monarch's body, which in its carefully staged perfection, its processions and portraits, assimilates and satisfies desires about nation, state and order. Marlowe's dramaturgy sustains the reverence, but focuses it narrowly onto the fleshly body, dislocating it from the other ideas with which it is meant to be imbricated. The reverence is made cruel. This is done through a repeated emphasis on the activity of looking and seeing. Edward suggests that how he looks – pathetic, royal – will move Lightborn. We know that this belief and his postures are ineffectual. Edward also thinks that he can maintain control by anticipating what will happen, seeing the stroke before it comes. He is encouraged to yield up this control by closing his eyes in rest. The audience, knowing what is at stake, watches the more attentively when the performer acts a man who can't keep his eyes open. The audience is determined to see what Edward dreads seeing, wanting to have everything fully known at last. They await the moment at which the dissatisfying feints at tragic decorum, royal posing, fidgety stillness give way to the busy-ness and apparatus that have been ready all the while to fill the stage. At that moment the tyrannical centredness of a royal body, radiating control and mystique, can be pressed back in on; that which has power in its wholeness can be touched all over, wholly, so hard that it dies. The overdue authentic action happens at last, a satisfying cruelty meticulously observed.

*He began to pull his hand out of that meticulously shaven arse. The grease-covered glove shone on the knuckles over which it was stretched. Waiting outside the door I wondered if they had both come or if I would get a chance with the king.*

A criticism that confines this scene to being a gesture of homosexual inscription is one preoccupied with Marlowe as sex. As with the attitude to violence, there is a preference for not engaging with the specifically sensual complexity of the stage. Instead there is, on one hand, a recitation of concerned sentiments about illicit sex and, on the other, a fantasy staging of bodily transgression. It is as if Marlowe were being constructed in imagination by Lightborn or Faustus. At least, that's how I want it to end.

# CHAPTER 8

# 'Writ in blood': Marlowe and the new historicists

## Richard Wilson

When Marlowe's Machevill proclaims the maxim that 'laws were then most sure/ When, like the Draco's, they were writ in blood' (*Jew of Malta*: (prologue), 20–1), he exactly anticipates the belief of those critics who sought to monopolise the study of his creator in the 1980s, and this pre-modern philosopher is uncannily represented as a post-structuralist. Though it has become obvious that, as Terry Eagleton says, 'Shakespeare was familiar with Hegel, Marx, Nietzsche, Freud, Wittgenstein and Derrida',[1] it took New Historicists to infer that when Marlowe pretended to be reading from Niccolò Machiavelli, he was in fact quoting Michel Foucault. Marked for life by discourses scored into their flesh and blood, Marlowe's characters might have been devised to display how, as Foucault exulted, 'power relations have a hold upon the body, they invest it, train it, torture it, force it to carry out tasks, to perform ceremonies, to emit signs'.[2] So it is hardly surprising that a dramatist who showed how 'Might first made kings' (*Jew*: (prologue), 20), should be identified from the day of its inception with a movement that took to heart Foucault's axiom that 'Power is everywhere, because it comes from everything';[3] or that a criticism which concluded its reading of Renaissance drama with *soixante-huitard* fatalism that 'There is subversion, no end of subversion, only not for us',[4] should have recognised its own disillusion in the trajectory of Marlowe's Icarian protagonist: 'Oh, I'll leap up to my God: who pulls me down?' (*Faustus*: 5.2.155). Though Shakespeare came to be the template on which New Historicism played out its game of subversion and containment with language and the body, it was Marlowe who prompted its Foucauldian lament that 'limit and transgression depend upon each other',[5] and that if power is inscribed in signs, there can be no escape from the prison-house of words. And it was Marlowe who first incited New Historicism to panic at the compression of such 'Infinite riches in a little room' (*Jew*: 1.1.37).

A date, as Foucault admits of the classical Age of Confinement, can be a watershed, but few intellectual upheavals can be placed with such precision as the New Historicism that would transform the study of English literature in the America of Ronald Reagan. For the birth of New Historicism commenced at 1.45 p.m. on Friday, 3 September 1976, and was effectively completed by 11.00 a.m. the following morning. The occasion was a seminar on Marlowe held at the conference of the English Institute at Johns Hopkins University, Baltimore, and dedicated to the memory of William K. Wimsatt, the godfather of the hitherto hegemonic New Criticism. It was Wimsatt's doctrine that there is nothing outside the text which primed the conference for the textualism of what Geoffrey Hartmann saluted as its 'French connection', and the debt of the newest criticism to the old orthodoxy was paid when Margery Garber opened proceedings with an imaginary 'conversation with W. K. Wimsatt' on 'the labyrinth as an icon of human society'.[6] Under the influence of linguistics, French theory had redefined the labyrinth as a model not of transcendence, but of the symbolic order, from which maze no free agent ever emerged,[7] and Garber's lecture methodically applied this claustrophobic figure to Marlovian drama, which thus became a Piranesian architecture of incarceration, designed to repeat over and over 'the inevitable trajectory between aspiration and limitation'. For Garber, therefore, Dido's cave, Barabas' counting-house, Edward's arbour, Tamburlaine's chariot, and Faustus' study are all stage settings that manifest the characters' 'attempts to imprison and wall up one another, while maintaining the fiction of breaking barriers down' in a carceral dramaturgy where *enclosure equals power*. In every case, Garber observes, the bondage fantasy ends with a binder bound, as 'those who would transcend limits are remanded to a place that "hath no limits, nor is circumscribed"', and 'play after play finds closure in enclosure': Dido's pyre, Barabas' cauldron, Edward's dungeon, Tamburlaine's coffin, or Faustus' hell. Falling from a figurative into a literal prison, each Marlovian hero thus enacts the entrapment of language itself:[8]

The list of enclosures is striking and consistent, [and suggests] another kind of enclosure, one equally germane to the nature and possibility of power. I refer to the limit represented by language – by the power of speech and silence. Manifestly, however great its power, language is ultimately an enclosure. Once uttered, a phrase is unutterable and unrecapturable, and conveys the speaker into the power of his hearers, whether on or off the stage.

'Once uttered, speech enters the service of power': whether or not she had had advance notice of Roland Barthes's famous Inaugural Lecture at the College de France, which he was to deliver on 17 January 1977, Garber's critique of Marlowe was almost a paraphrase of his theory that 'all language is fascist' because 'fascism does not prevent speech, speech is what it compels'.[9] And her analysis of those acts whereby Marlovian heroes plot escape only to find themselves for ever enthralled – such as Faustus' conjuration of Mephostophilis into his magic circle – perfectly illustrated Barthes' conclusion that: 'If we call freedom not only the capacity to escape power, but to subjugate no one, freedom exists only outside language. Unfortunately, language has no exterior: there is no exit from words.' So it was in a Marlowe seminar that New Historicist alarm at the trammels of linguisticity was first heard, and that Barthes' theme (for which he thanked Foucault), that '[t]he object in which power is inscribed for all eternity is the language we speak and write', was first applied to Elizabethan words.[10] Here the grotto designed by Dido to lure Aeneas, as Venus netted Mars, became a paradigm of all those claustral constructs in Marlowe's drama which trap their own makers, like the letters returned to sender from Mortimer and the Duchess of Guise; the 'dainty gallery' of 'cranes and pulleys' that hurls Barabas into the pit (5.5.35, 2); the map that becomes Tamburlaine's *memento mori*; and Faustus' 'anagrammatized' signs (1.3.9). For Garber, with each of these ironic reversals, when 'the artisan becomes not the encloser, but the enclosed', we confront a legend 'at the heart of the Renaissance' (Garber, ' "Infinite Riches" ', p. 16). This is the story of death and the labyrinth, and what it tells is that power will capture even those, like the artist, who imagine they can fly, because (in Barthes' terms) it 'creeps in everywhere . . . in the State, in classrooms, entertainment, family . . . and even in the forces of liberation themselves'.[11] Marlowe's Icarus fixation was nothing less, on this view, than a premonition of the theory of the Death of the Author in Renaissance guise:

The error made by these Icarian figures is to imagine they are not Icaruses, but Daedaluses. It was of course just such a misconstruction that brought grief to their mythic forbear; in Marlowe it produces tragedy from enclosure. Daedalus, the master craftsman, was celebrated not only for his waxen wings, but also for the maze he built to hold the Minotaur, a maze that is the prototype of all enclosing artefacts . . . In each of Marlowe's plays there is an artefact similarly designed to be the craftsman's master-work . . . Fittingly, these encapsulated and encapsulating artefacts usually appear near the closure of the play: in each case, the enclosure victimises its maker, and becomes, not a Daedalian maze, but a Pandora's box. (Garber, ' "Infinite Riches" ', p. 18)

Two mythic spaces dominate the Western imagination, wrote Foucault in *Death and the Labyrinth,* his only book of literary criticism: the carceral enclosure of the labyrinth and the transgressive void of metamorphosis, which is the space in which the self transcends the manacles of power.[12] By the time he came to America, however, the abortive 'Events' of 1968 had darkened Foucault's philosophy of power and resistance, and it was significant that the 1976 seminar should have applauded Garber's pronouncement that it is when Marlowe's protagonists seem to be liberated that they are in fact most circumscribed, since 'no end is limited to damned souls' (*Faustus*: 5.2.181). For it was in California over the summer of 1975 that Foucault had begun his attack on the 'repressive hypothesis' – the illusion of personal liberation – and outlined his contrary theory that, far from repressing desire, power *produces* it to fabricate the self.[13] No wonder, then, that the only earlier study acknowledged at the conference was Harry Levin's *Christopher Marlowe: The Overreacher,* which prepared for this Foucauldian turn by presenting the plays as variations on hyperbole, the Icarian trope of those, like the Guise, who 'mount the top . . . with aspiring wings,/Although . . . downfall be the deepest hell' (*Massacre at Paris*: 1.2.46–7). Levin had proposed that their 'Icarus complex' predestined Marlowe's characters to self-destruction, as Dido prayed for 'wings of wax, like Icarus' to melt, rather than soar to freedom (5.1.243).[14] When Foucault spoke at Berkeley there were many, then, already sceptical enough of the ruse of emancipation to respond to his report, soon published as the first volume of *The History of Sexuality,* of how, when he had set out to research the history of liberation, he discovered that 'far from undergoing a process of restriction', our desires have been incited the better to subject us.[15] One of those evidently most impressed, in any event, was the Berkeley professor, Stephen Greenblatt, whose lecture to the Baltimore conference imitated Foucault by arguing that in Marlowe's plays 'all objects of desire are illusions' fashioned by characters who are themselves mere fictions.[16]

'I intended to explore the role of human autonomy in the construction of identity', Greenblatt echoed Foucault in *Renaissance Self-Fashioning*, the 1980 book in which his paper was eventually collected, 'but as my work progressed, I perceived there were no moments of pure unfettered subjectivity: indeed, the human subject came to seem remarkably unfree, the ideological product of the relations of power in a particular society' (Greenblatt, p. 256). A student of Wimsatt, Greenblatt would make much of his defection from the latter's formalism, without admitting that his encounter with Foucault had given him the means to reduce the whole of history to a cultural text.[17] However, it was on the flight out of the Baltimore conference that he claimed to have suffered acrophobia at the thought that he too might be one whose 'waxen wings' of self-conceit did 'mount above his reach,/ And melting . . . conspired his overthrow' (*Faustus*: (prologue) 21–2), and his Marlowe paper had been vertiginous with the sensation that 'to abandon the craving for freedom, to let go of one's stubborn hold upon selfhood, was to die' (Greenblatt, p. 257). For in the plays, he suggested, fear of falling into endless space propels not just Faustus' 'demonic flights', but the 'transcendental homelessness' of Aeneas, Barabas, Edward, and Tamburlaine, as they 'ceaselessly traverse the stage' in the endeavour to represent 'physical movement within the narrow confines of the theatre' (Greenblatt, 'Marlowe and Renaissance Self-Fashioning', pp. 42–4). Where Garber had fixated on the claustrophobia of those trapped inside the Marlovian labyrinth of language, therefore, Greenblatt imagined the horror of the vacuum outside: the 'anguished perception of time and space as abstract, neutral and unresponsive'. Like the critic's own fear of flying, Faustus' consternation that 'The stars move still, time runs, the clock will strike' (5.2.153) was caused, on this view, by realisation that the void is 'profoundly indifferent to human longing'; but the reaction of the Marlovian hero to this 'vacancy of theatrical space' was simply to repeat, Greenblatt asserted, the mantra of the self:

Self-naming is the major enterprise of these plays, repeated over and over as if the hero continues to exist only by constantly renewed acts of will . . . In the neutrality of time and space this constructive power must exist within the hero himself; if it should fail for an instant, he would fall into nothingness. Hence the hero's tragic compulsion to repeat his name . . . and to fashion lines that echo in the void, that echo in the void more powerfully because there is nothing but a void. (Greenblatt, 'Marlowe and Renaissance Self-Fashioning', pp. 45–6, 49, 56)

If Greenblatt's Californian paranoia at being a victim of 'some device secreted on board the plane that would blow us all to pieces' detonated his trepidation at the fragility of his own identity (Greenblatt, p. 256), the text he carried on the flight from Baltimore was a truly deconstructive bomb. For his Marlowe talk was both resumé of the un-American heresy that the self is determined by language, and brazen demonstration that identity is thereby 'something *appropriated, seized from others*'. Like the wandering Jew he made of Barabas, Greenblatt's own self was 'exceedingly unstable' in his 1976 lecture, being compacted of a volatile mix of 'all the neatly packaged nastiness of his [postmodernist] society'. So, though it seemed 'virtually autochthonous', and was acclaimed as if the 'man was author of himself' as well as a whole new way of reading literature (Greenblatt, 'Marlowe and Renaissance Self-Fashioning', pp. 55–7, 60; cf. *Coriolanus*: 5.3.36), Greenblatt's self-fashioning, with its flourish of Flaubert and Nietzsche, reads today like a translation of the Lacanian theory of the de-centred self as meditated by Foucault. In particular, his phenomenological method, with its discussion of time, space, and language as 'a vast system of repetitions in which men learn what they desire', could have been quoted from a book such as *Death and the Labyrinth*, where Foucault had characterised the suicidal writer Raymond Roussel in identical terms. Greenblatt actually attributed to Gilles Deleuze the notion that desire is the 'absurd' effort to leap the 'tragic epistemological distance' between words and things, though this ontology of self and void, being and non-being, and becoming and annihilation was common to all those postwar French intellectuals who embraced Hegelian and Heideggerian thought (Greenblatt, 'Marlowe and Renaissance Self-Fashioning', pp. 54, 60, 63).[18] But since it was he who had had the luck to introduce this philosophy of anxiety into Elizabethan criticism, and in obedience to his premise that the hero repeats himself to exist, Greenblatt would reprint his Marlowe lecture in numerous versions, so that its revisions came to be the best witness of its own theme: that men invent themselves out of the language of others, each time *representing* themselves as if their words and identities 'were given by no one but themselves' (Greenblatt, 'Marlowe and Renaissance Self-Fashioning', p. 56).

Much of the impact of Greenblatt's criticism sprang from the

inconsistencies that made it almost a diary of the Vietnam generation, and these were typified by his reluctance to discard the
Marxism he had absorbed, he said, from Raymond Williams at
Cambridge.[19] So in his Baltimore paper his new Foucauldian
awareness that those, like Barabas and Faustus, who 'imagine
themselves set in opposition to society simply reverse its paradigms'
and 'remain embedded in orthodoxy', was still referred back to
Marx's dialectical formula that 'Men and women make their own
history, but not in circumstances of their own making' (Greenblatt,
'Marlowe and Renaissance Self-Fashioning', p. 54). It was not until
1978 that Williams' student was able to decry Marx's 'relentless
pursuit of emancipation', and submit literature to the force of
Foucault's demolition of the repressive hypothesis. 'Marlowe, Marx
and Anti-Semitism' was ostensibly a commentary on *The Jew of
Malta*, but in fact an intensely personal assault on Marxism's
'greatest illusion . . . that human emancipation can be achieved'.[20]
Those who branded New Historicism 'a kind of Marxism'[21] can
hardly have read this article, therefore, since its starting-point was
an acid Foucauldian critique of Marx's surrender, in stereotyping
Judaism as the essence of capitalism, to the anti-semitism which he
had himself endured. Marx's socialist utopia was nothing less, on
this view, than a society purged of Jews, and thus the most
catastrophic of all those snares by which intellectuals, dreaming of
liberation, have locked us all in chains. Conflation of socialism with
*national socialism* was, of course, a Cold War cliché, and Greenblatt's
relief that while 'Marx envisaged liberation, Marlowe cannot', has to
be set beside the attacks on 'left-wing anti-semitism' launched at this
time by French Foucauldians such as Bernard-Henri Levy, who
likewise traced culpability for the Holocaust to Marx's Enlightenment 'concern for purity, justice and good'.[22] As Jewish intellectuals
who each foreswore the revolution for the media, Greenblatt and
Levy would in fact share the same disdain for the 'great hopes' of
1968, and the ending of the new Marlowe essay might have been
written by either of these apostates from Marx: '*The Jew of Malta*
diverges most crucially from Marx at the point at which the latter
invokes what [the Marxist philosopher] Ernst Bloch calls *the principle
of hope*. In Marx there is the principle of hope without the will to
play; in Marlowe, the will to play without the principle of hope'.[23]

What did Greenblatt mean by the phrase, 'the will to play', which
would provide a final title for his Marlowe piece and a slogan for his

work? If it was Lacan who cued the idea of the Marlovian hero as a split subject wandering for ever through a maze of empty signifiers, the notion that what Marlowe stages with this libidinous 'playfulness' is not therefore hope, but 'hostility to transcendence and the whole metaphysics of presence', had analogies with the post-modernity of Jean-François Lyotard, who in 1974 likewise signalled incredulity towards Marxism by subsuming politics into play. Indeed, when Greenblatt honoured Barabas' 'progress towards the boiling caul-dron' over Marx's goal of liberation, he came very close to Lyotard's provocation that the victims of capitalism 'were overjoyed by the hysterical exhaustion and masochism of *staying* in the mines, in the foundaries, in hell'. The *jouissance* of capitalism, Lyotard asserts, lies precisely in its 'insane destruction of personal identity';[24] and Green-blatt was now comparably thrilled by the 'cruel humour, murderous practical jokes [and] radical insensitivity to human suffering' in the libidinal economy of the Jew's purposeless and self-destructive games. Where New Historicism differed from mere historicism, it was understood, lay in spurning any 'grand narrative' of truth or freedom, a disavowal that found a precedent, therefore, in Marlowe's universal *contempt*. Like Lyotard, Greenblatt would come to query the ethical distinction between criticism and fiction, and his own storytelling was clearly spurred by the amorality of *The Jew of Malta*, where 'to lie and to know one is lying seems more attractive . . . than to lie and believe one is telling the truth'. If we are all caught in the web of falsehood, this ludic reading suggested, then we must 'guffaw at hypocritical sententiousness', like the audience that 'roared with delight' at the Jew's mendacity, Greenblatt recalled, during the RSC's 'brilliant production' at 'the National Theatre': a professional impossibility which simply served to prove his point, that in the labyrinth of language the only exit will be through 'the power to deceive'.[25]

As 'Marlowe and Renaissance Self-Fashioning' mutated through the bitter 1978 essay and into its final composite version, 'Marlowe and the Will to Absolute Play', Greenblatt's timely amendments shadowed Foucault's efforts during these Berkeley years to rethink the relations of language and power, 'so those caught in them might escape by acts of rebellion and resistance'.[26] Whereas Marlowe's drama had seemed a crucible for the dissolution of selfhood, therefore, by 1980 the plays needed to accommodate a shift back towards agency, with Greenblatt's discovery of the resilience of those who 'struggle against the social construction of identity' (Greenblatt, p. 209). So, while his interpretation had originally colluded with carceral society by stigmatising Marlowe's life as 'violent, sordid and short', the very first change to the revised text instead affirmed political correctness by valorising '[t]hose who threatened order, on whose nature nurture could never stick: the traitor, vagabond, homosexual, and thief' (Greenblatt, 'Marlowe and Renaissance Self-Fashioning', p. 64; cf. Greenblatt, p. 201). This was a dossier of deviants that might have been compiled by any of the faddish French *nouveaux philosophes* of the late 1970s, and what it signified was renewed faith that disciplinary power might yet meet its 'limit or counterstroke' in what Foucault called 'the "plebs": a certain plebeian quality in bodies, souls, energies, and individuals'.[27] So, just as the *nouveaux philosophes* began at this time to romanticise the marginalised ' "rabble" made up of criminals, hippies, immigrants, and homosexuals',[28] Greenblatt now envisioned Tamburlaine not in thrall to the will to power, but 'in radical opposition to hierarchy, legitimacy, the whole established order' (Greenblatt, pp. 210–11). If there was irony in this co-option of the Scythian juggernaut to a trend partly inspired by Solzenhitsyn's denunciation of the Gulag, it was lost on Foucault, who saluted the 1980 book as an 'interesting analysis' of the techniques by which the enslaved assert their freedom,[29] like that of the 'pleb' to whom Greenblatt compared the 'endless resourcefulness' of Marlowe's heroes: 'Years ago, in Naples, I watched a deft pickpocket lifting a camera from a tourist's shoulder-bag and replacing it instantaneously with a rock of equal weight. The thief spotted me watching but did not run away – instead, he winked, and I was frozen in mute complicity. The audience's silence becomes [in Marlowe] the silence of such a passive accomplice, winked at by his fellow criminal' (Greenblatt, p. 216).

Greenblatt's re-reading of Marlowe initiated a decade of so-called 'political criticism' that interpreted Renaissance literature through just such a disingenuous identification with 'the marginalised voices of the ruled, exploited, oppressed, and excluded', or what Deleuze acutely anathematised as 'a martyrology feeding on corpses'.[30] The bad faith of this 'mime . . . in which intellectuals who occupy the place of master identify with the persecuted',[31] had been discernible in Greenblatt's original paper, which compared West African slaves with Tamburlaine's hostages; but it was transparent when the 1980 text recorded with a satisfied Foucauldian *frisson* that those who go cursing to the scaffold, such as 'the illiterate visionary condemned to death for claiming to be Christ come in judgement upon the queen', are yet 'bound by the orthodoxy against which they revolt' (Greenblatt, pp. 209–12). With its chorus of 'plebs' from Tyburn, Naples and Sierra Leone, the celebrity of *Renaissance Self-Fashioning* confirmed its author's intuition that 'Americans like porous borders and think access should be easy';[32] but the real cause of its success was undoubtedly the audacity with which it soared above such victims, 'tragically bounded by the dominant ideology against which they vainly struggle', into the enfranchisement of 'aesthetic experience'. There it was the 'recklessly courageous' artist who created the 'only truly radical alternative . . . to God or state', because he 'exceeded his peers in the power to deceive'. So, instead of consigning the Elizabethan renegade to the squalid dungeon of his days, Greenblatt crowned his definitive book with an apotheosis of the literary genius 'surmounting' the iron bars of the Clink through 'the creation of enduring works of art' (Greenblatt, pp. 210–11, 214–15, 221). There was a discursive precedent for this mystification of the artist as trickster and escapologist, of course, in the final aestheticism of Barthes, whose Inaugural had similarly concluded by floating the concept of *jouissance* which was to provide such a vital escape-route for postmodern theoreticians: 'We can get out [of language] only at the price of the impossible . . . But for us, who are neither saints nor superman, the only remaining alternative is to cheat with speech, to cheat speech. This salutary trick, this evasion, this grand imposture which allows us to understand speech *outside the bounds of power,* in the splendour of a permanent revolution of language, I for one call *literature.*'[33]

Greenblatt's successive alterations to his Marlowe essay articulated all the contradictions that made New Historicism so convenient for an academy conflicted between leftist *miserabilism* and elitist nostalgia for the literary canon. In particular, his vision of the dramatist as some Till Eulenspiegel, outwitting the thought police with a 'dark playfulness' that 'embraces what culture finds loathsome or frightening', elided not only his own discomfiture at Marlowe's sexuality, but the tension between irresistible French theories of collective meaning and the American ideology of the individual, nowhere more imperative than in the academic star system. It was the Californian cult of self-invention which licensed Foucault's taste

for San Francisco leather bars; and *Renaissance Self-Fashioning* proposed a similar commentary as *The Care of the Self* and *The Use of
Pleasure* on the paradox that whenever human beings discover
freedom, 'they do not do so as they please', but flaunting their own
chains (Greenblatt, p. 210). As Frank Lentricchia observed, this was
a type of liberation theology with a special appeal to 'our colleagues
in literary study who take pleasure in describing themselves as
powerless', for what it legitimated was exemption from 'the central
commitment of historicism: to the self as a product of forces over
which we can exercise no control'. According to this objection, the
hidden agenda of New Historicism has been 'to avoid the consequences of that commitment, to free us from a world in which we
are forced to become what we do not want to become';[34] and it was
therefore no accident that Greenblatt should turn to a poet whose
games with human helplessness were played with such consummate
artistic control: 'Even as a bird, which in our hands we wring,/ Forth
plungeth, and oft flutters with her wing' (*Hero and Leander*. II.
289–91). Earlier critics had been repelled by Marlowe's 'cynical
laughter of belittlement' at old men 'Kneeling for mercy to a
Greekish lad,/ Who with steel pole-axes dash'd out their brains'
(*Dido*: 2.1.198–9) but it was precisely this sadistic 'taste for humiliation' (Steane, p. 360) that tickled New Historicism's fantasy of
aesthetic domination:[35]

There is a self-subversive tug in New Historicist discourse – a need to
ensure some secret hiding place where we do not feel ourselves to be just
entities of vast, impersonal systems . . . Hating a world that we never
made, we settle for a holiday from reality, a safely sealed space for the
expression of aesthetic anarchy, a long weekend that defuses the radical
implications of our unhappiness.

'Would it not be marvellous', wondered the Foucault who came to
California, 'to have the power, at any hour of the day and night, to
enter a place equipped with all the pleasures and possibilities that
one might imagine . . . and to "desubjugate" oneself through a kind
of plunge beneath the water?'[36] and for the New Historicists he
taught there it was the drama of Marlowe which satisfied this
craving for aesthetic extremity. There, in the dungeon where
Edward is sodomised to death, and Bajazet is kennelled like a dog,
the rituals of freedom and imprisonment, of mastery and slavery,
that the philosopher enacted in the bath-houses were re-imagined by
critics as symbolic solutions to the impasse of their own institutional

entrapment. For while Greenblatt's exhilaration at the playwright's 'murderous, playful courage . . . delight in role-playing, entire absorption in the game, and indifference to what lies outside its boundaries' (Greenblatt, p. 220) left readers baffled as to his own sympathies, by substituting his new term 'playful' for the original accolade 'magnificent' in his ultimate tribute to Marlowe, he aligned Renaissance studies with one of the most effective of all postmodern ploys to de-politicise history: the ethnographic metaphor of society as sport and critique as itself 'Just Gaming' by the way.[37] Futile 'shadow play' is how the historian Raphael Samuel has characterised the sense of history of Greenblatt's entire *Representations* school of critics, with their ludic model of the past as 'vacant space';[38] and the implications of this shift from 'the will to power' to 'the will to play' were spelled out by Garber when she returned to Marlowe in 1984 with a revised interpretation of the author as *homo ludens*, which did indeed reduce his entire dramaturgy to 'the trope of writing and unwriting', or shadows in the cave:[39]

Patterns of intertextual reference, texts 'deconstructing' or undoing other texts, and authors asserting competing authority recur throughout Marlowe's plays. This drama of the word is played out in *Tamburlaine* with reference to the Koran and the conqueror's map of the world; in *Faustus*, with reference to the Eucharistic testament and the sorcerer's 'deed of gift' to Lucifer. In *Edward II* a letter serves as the material embodiment of the concept of countertext as counterplot. In all these instances, the act of writing or signing conveys, not just a struggle between contending characters, but a struggle for mastery of stage and text between the playwright and his inscribed characters.

Seldom can what Umberto Eco mocked as 'the frenchified affectation of inscribing everything and seeing everything inscribed'[40] have been so exhaustively paraded as in Garber's revisiting of Marlowe. Here the Foucauldian fascination with discipline and constraint was concentrated on those textual shackles which, according to Garber, *literally* prescribe and circumscribe the lives and bodies of Marlowe's characters. ' "Here's Nothing Writ": Scribe, Script, and Circumscription in Marlowe's Plays' thereby demonstrated how much New Historicism shared the postmodern obsession with the primacy of the signifier and the ways in which 'the signifier is distinguished not only by its own laws, but prevails over the signified on which it imposed them'.[41] Garber found the *locus classicus* for this Lacanian knot, of course, in Faustus' 'bill', conveying his 'body and soul, flesh, blood or goods' to Lucifer (1.5.112–23), but equally crucial for his discussion was the instrument that countermands this deed: 'But what is this inscription on mine arm?/ *Homo fuge!* Whither should I flie?' (1.5.75–6). For the scholar who begins 'enraptured by the idea of becoming author of himself' through his command 'Lines, circles, scenes, letters and characters' (1.1.50) ends instead as parchment on which the battle for textual authority is waged, his very flesh made word in diabolic inversion of the Word made Flesh. 'Written in blood, substituting blood for ink', Faustus' contract had been drafted to 'superscribe Christ's own testament of body and blood', yet, as his scarification instantly signifies, this sacrifice merely *sub*scribes him, body and soul, in a palimpsest of 'writing and unwriting' that unscrolls for ever, 'Forward and backward, to curse Faustus to hell' (3.3.94). As 'Christ's blood streams in the firmament' (5.2.156) so this man of books is therefore doomed to remain 'a figure, a representation, a terminable fiction', like the writing on his skin, to be 'deconstructed' and re-signed, until, washed by the tide of his discourse, 'Here's nothing writ'.[42]

When Garber prefaced her new essay with an epigraph from *The Jew of Malta*, 'The meaning has a meaning' (4.4.105), she confirmed the aptness of re-evaluating Marlowe's stage machinery – with its archives, inventories, despatches, contracts, maps, and will – by the light of post-structuralist theory, as a metacritical theatre of the all-conquering word. In this hermeneutic drama, where language materialises and congeals as flesh and blood, the human body had never seemed more like the tattooed text Foucault made of it, nor the self more like a figure of speech. At the close of *The Order of Things*, the philosopher had famously predicted that 'man' will soon be 'effaced, like a face drawn in sand at the edge of the seas',[43] and in Garber's analysis this was exactly the extinction Marlowe staged, with the dismemberment and disappearance of all those characters, from Tamburlaine to Mortimer, who live and die, not by the sword, but by pen, book and speech. So Faustus is finally 'nothing' in this account, being composed, like some Arcimboldo portrait, out of the hell of other people's words, and the claustrophobia of such a reading would be even more asphyxiating than that of Garber's earlier essay, were it not for her conviction that just as the fictional character is wiped from the slate, his annulment testifies that 'someone else is present here – the poet Marlowe, who absent-present becomes all-powerful . . . precisely because of his absence from the limits of the stage'. Here again, then, is the surprising corollary of New Historicism's fetishising of the text: even as the human subject is obliterated from history, '*Someone* intervenes, inscribing Faustus' arm.' For Garber, as for Greenblatt, this 'someone' whose invisible hand generates and terminates meaning can only be the godlike author, the Marlowe whose signature is 'the haunted, disembodied final line of *Doctor Faustus*, "*Terminat hora diem; terminat Author opus*"': 'Faustus is incarnated as a dramatic character, not an autonomous author, and as Marlowe's written supplement to his play declares, the author, not the self-inscribed character, ends the work: *terminat Author opus*. Marlowe signs his own writ, which must be executed, "and Faustus must be damned"' (Garber, '"Here's Nothing Writ"', p. 318).

'The poet survives his poems' in Garber's account; and in Greenblatt's, too, the dramatist 'surmounts' the fate of his own protagonists by being 'far more intelligent and self-aware . . . For the one true goal of these heroes is to be characters in Marlowe's plays' (Greenblatt, pp. 220–1). The revival of the author was to be the most unexpected consequence of New Historicism's aesthetic turn. To be sure, the author who returned in Garber's re-reading was not the autonomous maker Faustus aspires to be, but the creation of his favourite texts, which he plundered for plots and playthings 'In the library of Corpus Christi, endowed with Archbishop Parker's magnificent bequest of books and manuscripts' (Garber, '"Here's Nothing Writ"', p. 314). But for all their evasiveness about the autonomy of art and authorship, Garber and Greenblatt effectively laid down the parameters within which Marlowe criticism, and New Historicism as a whole, would develop for the last quarter of the century. If modernist critics had read Marlowe's work through his biography, postmodernists interpreted his life through the plays, as the struggle of the subversive author to break from the glasshouse of incarcerating words. As Thomas Dabbs remarks, the paradox of this theoretical twist was that the Marlowe these critics presented, 'the artist bravely forging human values in the face of an impersonal abysmal universe' was not far removed from the romantic outcast of Victorian letters. From Levin's 'disillusioned nihilist' to Greenblatt's courageous 'aficionado of aesthetic transcendence', Dabbs suggests, postmodern Marlowe criticism has simply repeated the nineteenth century's 'evolutionary' interpretation of the dramatist as Shakespeare's doomed precursor (Dabbs, pp. 136–8). Thus the Barthesian aestheticism that promised an exit from the confinement of the symbolic order turned out, when applied to the Elizabethan writer, to be the *fin-de-siècle* revisited. And never was this impression of *déjà vu* stronger than when New Historicism's biographical slant took critics back to the question of Marlowe's homosexuality.

If Marlowe provided the ideal testing-ground for Foucault's ideas about the hermeneutics of the self, it was inevitable that New Historicists would follow him in reformulating the problem of sexual identity, and their attempts to do so comprised a coda to Renaissance studies at the end of the millennium. It had been at Berkeley in 1983 that Foucault explained how it had proved impossible to discuss the genealogy of the modern subject without considering sex,[44] and Jonathan Goldberg's 1984 essay, 'Sodomy and Society: The Case of Christopher Marlowe', established how deeply under the sway of Foucault's histories of sexuality his American epigones would fall. The philosopher overshadowed the essay most oppressively in its thesis that Marlowe's identity as dramatist, sexual dissident, and spy was constructed by the discourses not of revolt, but of Elizabethan empire itself. On this view, the sodomy which defined the play-wright's seditious status should be seen not as a positive act, but as a rebellion licensed by authority to be its defining ground. Like the counterfeit coining with which he was also indicted, or the histrio-nics of his heroes, Marlowe's pederasty was thus merely the reverse of the official stamp. This was an analysis that applied a recurring New Historicist theme – that the Elizabethan playhouse was toler-ated, like Renaissance carnival, as a safety-valve, where 'counter-voices were acted out' – to forward the dismal prospectus that opposition is never spontaneous, but is always produced by power as its foil. Comparing the fates of Marlowe and Oscar Wilde, therefore, Goldberg ended his essay doubting 'whether we can ever find an authenticity not capable of being crushed by the society in which we exist'; and his telling misreading of Greenblatt's 'void' as a figure not of emptiness, but entrapment, showed how grimly critics would be gripped by the dystopian vision of the individual lost in the labyrinth of signs:[45]

Like the heroes he created, Marlowe lived and died in the impossible project of the marginalized, negativized existence permitted him. Marlowe and his heroes, Stephen Greenblatt says, live lives in the recognition of the void, in the realization that rebellion never manages to find its own space, but always acts in the space that society has created for it. To play there is to be nowhere and to recognize that the solidity of discourse carries with it the very negations in which such play can occur.

Goldberg's 1984 essay marked the pessimistic depth to which gloom about 'the solidity of discourse' would plunge the humanities in the age of AIDS and Star Wars; but a decade after interpreting Marlowe's sexual delinquence as mere shadow-play, he returned to the history of sodomy with a revived sense of its potential to subvert the systems of gender and power. His discussions of Marlovian theatre in *Sodometries*, a book on male homosexuality in Anglo-American culture, was no longer straitjacketed by the Foucauldian obsession with inescapable discourse, but actually took issue with other critics, such as Simon Shepherd, for allegedly reproducing homophobic stereotypes with a scenario of effeminised lovers, such as Edward, Henry III or Mycetes, dominated by macho men. By contrast, Goldberg presented *Dido, Queen of Carthage* as a problemati-sation (written to be performed entirely by boys) of institutions – the school, army, and playhouse – which were themselves constructed upon covert sodomy, the 'unmentionable sin' that unravels every order, including the empire of which it is the 'dirty secret truth'.[46] When Aeneas deserts Dido, therefore, he rejects not only the effeminisation of warriors by women, but heterosexuality itself. The colonialism of Drake and Ralegh was an enterprise that depended, we infer, on the sodomy with which Marlowe opens his play with Jupiter '*dandling* GANYMEDE *upon his knee*', and which is then simulated by successive boys. In words quoted from William Empson, Marlowe's earliest play thus 'insists that the illicit is the proper thing to do', and the radical effect is to deconstruct the discourses that separate the 'masculine' state from an 'effeminate' stage. Goldberg's 1992 conclusion thus cleanly contradicted his earlier one, and challenged Renaissance studies with a far more liberating perspec-tive on language and resistance:[47]

It has been my assumption that Marlowe's radical rethinking of the possibility of being a sodomite was not widely shared in his time, that the deconstructive energies he bequeaths are not assimilable to the subsequent discourses of sexual difference . . . Marlowe's singularity [lies] in the value he attached to what his culture so vehemently opposed. Hence, it is possible, imperative, to recognise in Marlowe a site of political resistance. To recognise too that this could have literary consequences. A rereading of Elizabethan drama through what Marlowe makes available might be undertaken, and even Shakespeare would be implicated.

Like the painter Caravaggio or the film director Pasolini, whom he resembled so much in the sensational manner of his life and death, Marlowe came to be an icon of sexual dissidence for popular culture in the 1990s. But Derek Jarman's Marlowe drew unconsciously on a generation of re-reading by academic critics, who in the aftermath of 1968 envisioned the dramatist in their own self-image, simultaneously captivated by, and emancipated from, the shackles of subjection. If there was conflict between Garber's construction of Marlowe as a concentration camp commandant and Goldberg's construction of Marlowe as a pioneer of gay liberation, then that expressed the tensions of both postmodern politics and Marlovian theatre. For there was no question in the minds of these commentators of the elective affinity between the works of the secret 'ENGLISH AGENT' (*Massacre*: 5.5.56) and a post-structuralism that held that '[t]here is no binary opposition between rulers and ruled . . . hence no single locus of rebellion. Instead there is a plurality of resistances: some that are savage, solitary, or violent; others that are quick to compromise, interested, or sacrificial.'[48] While critics had once idealised the Marlovian hero as the prototypical Renaissance man, insurgent against medieval authority, New Historicists therefore countered that it is the very limits imposed by orthodoxy that produce transgression, and which suspend the plays in an endless oscillation between power and subversion. Thus, the Marlowe who was restored to the labyrinth of his texts came to seem strangely like the academic in the contemporary university: 'wilful, masochistic, and defiant',[49] but an Icarus, rather than a Daedalus. Marlowe the high-flyer may have been an invention of the 1890s, but the fallen angel of the 1990s was as much the projection of this 'mercenary drudge' on campus: 'the man that in his study sits' 'graced with Doctor's name', and 'glutted . . . with learning's golden gifts', yet for all his 'cunning . . . self-conceit' for ever the 'servile and illiberal' 'subject of the institute'. So, if its function had indeed been to mediate between European theories of the de-centred self and the American ideology of individualism, then New Historicism had found a perfect pretext, it seemed, in this 'boy falling out of the sky', whose writing constituted such 'an important failure', but whose body – like that depicted in Breughel's *Icarus* – was immaterial to the power that, having crushed it, 'Had somewhere to get to and sailed calmly on'.[50]

# CHAPTER 9

# 'Hero and Leander': the arbitrariness of desire

## Claude J. Summers

*Hero and Leander* is a remarkable achievement, principally because of its curious tone, an unusual blend of apparently affectionate but actually scathingly unsentimental comedy and iconoclastic realism in its depiction of love. If Marlowe's critics can no longer be neatly divided between those who labour mightily to discover (or to impose) a moralistic point to the comedy and those who aver that the comedy is its own reward,[1] that is all to the good. The moralistic critics are not very convincing, for Marlowe does not simply disregard conventional morality in *Hero and Leander*, he also positively flouts it. The poem, in fact, mocks received ideas about sexuality and morality. On the other hand, descriptions of the work as merely iconoclastic or simply an exuberant celebration of Eros for its own sake are also dubious. The poem is more complex than either of the polarised responses allows; it demands readings that acknowledge its lively irreverence, wicked wit, savage irony, and affecting seriousness. *Hero and Leander* takes as its theme the utter arbitrariness of desire, a perspective that is pointedly at variance with the conventional morality of Marlowe's society and its dominant constructions of sexuality and that has tragic as well as comic potential. In retelling the familiar story of star-crossed lovers, Marlowe destabilises his society's ideas about sexuality by refusing to idealise love or to endorse hegemonic notions of eroticism. In so doing, he demonstrates the inequities of a gender system that commodifies women and illustrates particularly the cost such a system exacts of desiring women. In transforming the tragic tale of Hero and Leander into a sexual comedy, Marlowe burlesques the literary tradition that he exploits; yet even as the poet spares his characters the *liebestode* they are traditionally assigned, he nevertheless envelops them within a penumbra of tragedy.[2] *Hero and Leander* is as unsettling as it is amusing.

Marlowe's project of destabilisation may be seen most clearly in his treatment of homosexuality, a matter of particular interest since Marlowe represents homoerotic situations and incidents in his plays and poems more frequently and more variously than any other major figure of his day.[3] A writer deeply immersed in both religion and classics, he characteristically reflects in his work the tension between Christian culture's condemnation and classical culture's acceptance of homoerotics. What is most noteworthy about Marlowe's depiction of same-sex relations is that his posture is consistently oppositional *vis-à-vis* his society's official condemnation of homosexuality as sodomitical even as that condemnation inevitably and powerfully shapes his varied representations. The construal of same-sex relations as sodomitical – i.e., conceived in terms of the biblical prohibition that justified the destruction of the Cities of the Plain and related to a whole host of social, sexual, and political transgressions – has been overemphasised by recent historians and critics who have tended to neglect the competing classical construction, which treated same-sex relations with more equanimity. Still, the force of sodomitical discourse in early modern England ought not to be underestimated. The deep horror expressed about homosexuality in the period's moral and legal thought constitutes a reality that impinges on the coexistent and often contradictory poetic discourse that is indebted to classical ideas about same-sex relations.[4] Thus, the depiction of homosexuality in even a work as self-consciously classical as *Hero and Leander* must be seen in the context of Christian ideas about sexuality. These ideas constitute a presence even by virtue of their conspicuous absence in the poem.

Homoeroticism pervades *Hero and Leander*, but it is seen most fully in the sensuous blazon devoted to Leander and in the farcical encounter between the beautiful young man and a love-smitten Neptune. These passages are infected by the sodomitical construct even as they are literally and defiantly Ovidian. That is, these comic scenes derive their power to shock and titillate from the satiric view of homosexuality that they delightfully mock. For example, the enthusiastic celebration of Leander's beauty, figured forth in a proliferation of homoerotic classical myths, itself constitutes a challenge to the Christian strictures against sodomy. In describing 'Amorous *Leander*, beautiful and young', whose 'body was as straight as Circe's wand,/ Jove might have sipp'd out nectar from his hand', Marlowe not only compares Leander with Ganymede, the classical figure who functioned in the Renaissance as the very byword for homosexuality; but he also calls particular attention to 'That heavenly path with many a curious dint,/ That runs along his back' (I. 51, 61–2, 68–9), only to confess the inability of his 'rude pen' to do justice to the shapeliness of the youth's buttocks.[5] Clearly, this homoerotic catalogue that culminates in the very site of sodomy is exuberantly defiant. Part of the effect of the extravagant celebration of Leander's nude body results from its contrast with the blazon devoted to Hero, which focuses not on her body but on her clothing. Indeed, as Gregory Bredbeck has suggested, Marlowe's employing the blazon technique to fetishise the masculine subject has the effect of interrogating the naturalness of desire itself, including especially heterosexual desire.[6] The blazon establishes Leander as sexual object as well as subject; moreover, the objectification of Leander is complemented by the poem's blithe assumption of a universal homoerotic impulse, which similarly interrogates dominant cultural assumptions. Leander's beauty is 'all that men desire' (I. 84); it moves alike both the 'rudest peasant' and the 'barbarous Thracian soldier' (I. 79, 81). This universalising of homoerotic response questions Renaissance gender constructions and challenges the period's moral discourse that denounces homoerotics as filthy and depraved. The very playfulness of Marlowe's subversiveness here and throughout the epyllion might be seen as a version of what Judith Butler describes as 'necessary drag'; it functions to destabilise the seriousness and 'naturalness' of hegemonic constructions of gender and sexuality.[7] However self-contained they may seem, Marlowe's daring adaptations of classical homoeroticism are in-scribed within a conservative cultural context that can never be escaped but which can be – and is – resisted.

Resistance to the massive condemnation of homosexuality in Renaissance England is also at the heart of Marlowe's account of Neptune's infatuation with Leander, who is 'made for amorous play' (I. 88). When the 'sapphire-visag'd god' sees Leander in the sea (II. 155), Neptune concludes that he must be Ganymede. He pulls the young man down to the splendours of the pearlstrewn, goldheaped seabottom where the mermaids sport. In this spectacular and amorous setting, 'The lusty god embrac'd him, call'd him love, / And swore he never should return to Jove' (II. 167–8). Only when the mortal youth is almost drowned does Neptune realise that he is not Jove's beautiful cupbearer. He releases him and gives him safe passage through the sea, but not before caressing and attempting to seduce him:

> He clapp'd his plump cheeks, with his tresses play'd,
> And smiling wantonly, his love bewray'd.
> He watch'd his arms, and as they open'd wide,
> At every stroke, betwixt them would he slide,
> And steal a kiss, and then run out and dance,
> And as he turn'd, cast many a lustful glance,
> And threw him gaudy toys to please his eye,
> And dive into the water, and there pry
> Upon his breast, his thighs, and every limb,
> And up again, and close beside him swim,
> And talk of love.                    (II. 181–91)

When the shocked Leander protests in exasperation, 'You are deceiv'd, I am no woman, I' (II. 192), Neptune merely smiles and begins to tell him a homoerotic tale of shepherds and satyrs, evocative of Theocritus' *Idylls*.

Marlowe's joke in this farcical episode turns out to be not only on the passionate god, who mistakes a beautiful mortal for Ganymede, but also – and more trenchantly – on the naïve youth, who can imagine only heterosexual desire and who so indignantly rejects for himself the role of sexual object. As Bredbeck observes, the tale that Neptune begins reciting is designed to suggest 'an alternative world existing beyond the limits of Leander's narrow perspective' (Bredbeck, p. 132). Significantly, the point of the episode – quite apart from its considerable titillation-value and its foregrounding of the awkward heterosexual lovemaking of Hero and Leander that follows and which, as M. Morgan Holmes points out, inversely echoes the Neptune–Leander encounter[8] – is not the unimaginableness of homoeroticism but the essential likeness of same-sex and other-sex attraction and emotion. Reconciled, the deity and the mortal are united in their common emotional state despite their differences in sexual object-choices. As the narrator concludes, 'In gentle breasts,/ Relenting thoughts, remorse and pity rests./ And who have hard hearts, and obdurate minds,/ But vicious, harebrain'd, and illit'rate hinds?' (II. 215–18.) Surely, the hardhearted, harebrained hinds indicted here include those censorious souls in Marlowe's society who were unable to conceive of homoeroticism as other than sodomitical. And, surely, the epithet 'illit'rate' constitutes important evidence that Marlowe's own construction of homosexuality is, to an extraordinary degree, literary and, more specifically, classical, a construction at variance with and in opposition to that promulgated in his age's sodomitical discourse.

But Marlowe's deconstruction of his age's received ideas about same-sex relationships is not merely an isolated expression of a particular *idée fixe*. Rather, it is but one piece of the poem's larger, elaborately orchestrated strategy to interrogate conventional ideas about and idealisations of love. The homoeroticism that looms large in *Hero and Leander* is simply one manifestation of a polymorphous perversity that characterises the entire world of the poem and is manifested in the arbitrariness of desire itself. Not only would even 'wild Hippolytus' have been enamoured of Leander's beauty (I. 77), but Hero's beauty also similarly moves 'all that view'd her' (I. 118). Most significantly, Marlowe's comic account of the tragic couple's mutual seduction and fulfilment takes place against a truly astounding backdrop of transgressive sexuality. Hero and Leander first glimpse each other in Venus' temple, whose marvellously wrought crystal pavement depicts the loves of the gods in salaciously comic detail:

> There might you see the gods in sundry shapes,
> Committing heady riots, incest, rapes:
> For know, that underneath this radiant floor
> Was Danae's statue in a brazen tower,
> Jove slyly stealing from his sister's bed,
> To dally with Idalian Ganymede,
> Or for his love Europa bellowing loud,
> Or tumbling with the Rainbow in a cloud;
> Blood-quaffing Mars, heaving the iron net
> Which limping Vulcan and his Cyclops set;
> Love kindling fire, to burn such towns as Troy;
> Sylvanus weeping for the lovely boy
> That now is turned into a cypress tree,
> Under whose shade the wood-gods love to be.     (1.143–56)

Riots, incests, rapes, pederasty, bestiality, adultery, sexual metamorphoses, and the passion that precipitates devastating war: these are the loves of the gods commemorated in Venus' temple, a commemoration that itself partakes of the voyeurism that is emphasised again and again in the poem and in which we as readers also necessarily (and greedily) indulge. What is so fascinating about Marlowe's evocation of these events from classical myth is that he betrays knowledge of their frequently tragic consequences even as he represents them jocularly as mere peccadilloes. In rehearsing the loves of the gods not in the tones of the *Ovid moralise* so familiar to the Renaissance but, more startlingly, in the comic accents of an unmoralised, unallegorised, unrelentingly literal-minded Ovid, Marlowe mocks his culture's dominant practice of co-opting and Christianising classical myth and literature (including, in fact, the story of Hero and Leander, which was sometimes read as a Neoplatonic allegory of the soul's union with God).[9] At the same time, however, by acknowledging the tragic dimensions of experience that he presents as comic, he establishes the crucial point that the comic and the tragic, the farcical and the serious, are not mutually exclusive.

The unconventional escapades of the gods that Marlowe so gleefully recounts here and alludes to throughout the epyllion constitute both an alternative sexual norm to that sanctioned by Christian culture and a challenge to prevailing notions of sexual morality. As Clifford Leech observed some time ago, 'Marlowe takes the emptied Protestant universe . . . and refills it with his pagan deities', but he does so not merely, as Leech suggested, to make fun of 'the supernatural order that men once fashioned for themselves out of nature'.[10] Rather, he uses his deliciously potted history of the ancient religion (and his extended network of religious allusions) to attack indirectly the supernatural order of his own day by turning it on its head. Not only does he imagine a sophisticated world unfettered by constricting morality, but he also implies that the examples set by the amoral classical deities more accurately reflect human nature than do the expectations and prohibitions of Christian culture. After all, one of the most practical uses of myth is to justify the mortal desires of human beings. This equivalence between humans and the deities is reflected in the poem's reciprocal tendencies to mythologise the human characters and to humanise the immortal ones. Indeed, these tendencies link particular characters in interesting ways, as when Neptune's pursuit of Leander is recapitulated in Leander's pursuit of Hero, or when Hero is identified with Venus to such an extent that Cupid is said to mistake the young mortal for his goddess mother, or when Leander assaulting Hero strongly resembles Mercury in his greedy lust for the country maid. Most importantly, the transgressive (and frequently destructive) sexuality of the gods functions as a pattern for the human sexuality into which the protagonists of the poem are so entertainingly yet disturbingly initiated.

The world of *Hero and Leander* is one in which sexual licence is sanctioned even by religion and where the conventional sexual morality of Christian culture is flouted and rapes and riots are figured as comic. Yet Marlowe's poem is not, therefore, a defiant brief for the delights of free love. Its perspective is more complicated and enigmatic than that. In fact, even as *Hero and Leander* impishly revels in the variety and perversity of classical eroticism, it is also acutely aware of the pain of tyrannical desire and of the complexity of human attitudes toward sex, as well as the particular absurdities and inequities of early modern gender systems. But unlike other love poets of his age, who were also fully cognisant of the frustrations and disappointments of desire, Marlowe refuses to romanticise the paradoxes of love or to subsume them within a transcendent vision of Eros. Rejecting Petrarchan and Neoplatonic idealisations, he opts instead for a disconcerting materialist perspective, creating in the process what Joanne Altieri has termed 'the most fully idealized anti-idealistic poem of the late sixteenth century and a perfect counter to Petrarchism in being so, for what is idealized is the material'.[11] In fact, love and beauty are quite literally commodified in the poem, repeatedly compared to treasure and jewels and material wealth generally. Marlowe's refusal to place love within a transcendent vision is analogous to his refusal in *Edward II* to embrace a providential view of English history; just as he declines to moralise English politics, so he resolutely fails to spiritualise sexuality. As the principals of *Hero and Leander* come to learn, 'Love is not full of pity (as men say)/ But deaf and cruel where he means to prey' (II. 287–8).

The cruelty of love is, indeed, at the very heart of the poem's meaning and of its unsentimental comedy. This cruelty is suggested by the amorous history of the gods and symbolised by the stains on Hero's kirtle, somewhat extravagantly attributed to 'the blood of wretched lovers slain' (I. 16), but more likely the blood of turtle-doves sacrificed to Venus. It is suggested as well by the pattern of disappointment in love that stretches from the humiliation of Venus, who 'in her naked glory strove/ To please the careless and disdainful eyes/ Of proud Adonis' (I. 12–14), mentioned at the outset of the poem, to Neptune's rejection by Leander and, finally, to the anticlimax of Hero's guilty disillusionment the morning after her lovemaking with Leander. This pattern is buttressed by repeated allusions to such mythical embodiments of frustration as Narcissus,

Ixion, Tantalus, and Sisyphus. The pattern of frustration and disappointment is emphasised as well by the fact that the solemn Feast of Adonis over which the aloof Hero presides is not only in honour of an uncaring and unresponsive lover, but is also itself a cruel exercise in frustration. Hero's beauty enchants all who gaze on her, but her prideful disdain entails the disappointments (and possibly even deaths) of rejected suitors. Appropriately, the cruelty of love is crystallised in the dance of desire at the centre of the poem, especially in the initiation – or, rather, victimisation – of Hero herself. In Marlowe's poem, even the fulfilment of desire partakes of frustration and disappointment, an outcome attributable largely to early modern England's deep-seated ambivalence about feminine sexuality.

As William Keach has pointed out, the irony of Hero's status as 'Venus' nun' (I. 45) is made apparent by reference to Marlowe's chief source, Musaeus' Greek poem, which explains Hero's puzzling choice of serving Aphrodite by dedicating herself to a life of chastity (Keach, p. 89). As Musaeus makes clear, Hero is motivated by her fear of Love's 'quiver's dreaded fire'. Hero's worship of Venus through the practice of abstinence may at first seem merely preposterous or ironic in the extreme, but it reveals, in addition to her naïveté, the young woman's divided impulses, her simultaneous attraction to and repulsion from sexual experience. The action of Marlowe's poem traces Hero's surrender to the very fate that she most dreaded and literally vowed to avoid. She ultimately accedes to Leander's sophistical blandishments and her own desire, but not without an internal struggle and not without a legacy of guilt and shame. Unlike in Musaeus' poem, in Marlowe's *Hero and Leander* the triumph of sexuality is not an unmixed blessing. In fact, in Marlowe's work desire's triumph consists of the defeat and humiliation of Hero.

Hero's ineffectual struggle against her own desire is the source of much of the comedy of the poem. As Keach has pointed out, Musaeus dramatises Hero's fluctuating emotional states, but Marlowe develops the conflicts to a far greater extent than his Greek source (Keach, p. 98). Although ambivalence toward desire is seen elsewhere in the poem, including especially in the Mercury episode, Hero is the character most poignantly (and comically) torn between conflicting emotions. After the stock *carpe diem* speeches of Leander, 'like to a bold sharp sophister' (I. 197), attacking virginity, Hero weeps, then dissembles, then wavers. She is moved not by Leander's arguments, which are hardly novel or particularly compelling, but by her own sexual response to him and by her resistance to that response. She is described as

> like a planet, moving several ways
> And one self instant, she poor soul assays,
> Loving, not to love at all, and every part
> Strove to resist the motions of her heart.        (I. 361–4)

It is at this point that Cupid intervenes:

> Cupid beats down her prayers with his wings,
> Her vows above the empty air he flings;
> All deep enrag'd, his sinewy bow he bent,
> And shot a shaft that burning from him went,
> Wherewith she strooken, look'd so dolefully,
> As made Love sigh, to see his tyranny.        (I.369–74)

The comedy here at Hero's expense is not without poetic justice, for the disdainful virgin who has so unconcernedly stirred the passions of others without being moved herself has finally become subject to desire. Yet what is usually elided in discussions of the poem is the utter arbitrariness of her passion and the role of Cupid in sealing it.

Cupid's role in *Hero and Leander* is similar to the role he plays in *Dido, Queen of Carthage*, where he pricks both Dido and the old nurse. As a result of Cupid's intervention, Dido is transformed from a dignified and self-confident queen to an indecisive schoolgirl who gushes forth her love for Aeneas, but, again, not without a fierce and protracted internal struggle that has elements of both pathos and farce. The nurse's reaction to Cupid's arrow sting is the source of even crueller comedy, as she berates herself for her inappropriate response: 'Blush, blush for shame! why shouldst thou think of love?/ A grave, and not a lover, fits thy age' (4.5.29–30). In *Dido*, Cupid acts at the behest of his mother, using his power to inspire erotic longing as a means to effect Venus' ambitions for Aeneas, unconcerned that his actions will have tragic consequences for both mortal women. The play laments the limitation of human power – including power over human sexual response – in a world controlled by arbitrary, often perverse deities.

In *Hero and Leander*, Marlowe is also concerned with the limits of human power, though here the limits are imposed by the nature of human sexuality rather than by the manipulation of the gods for some grand purpose. While Cupid is specifically credited with inspiring the infatuation of Leander, Hero's initial response is to the amorousness of Leander rather than to any action of Cupid, who acts to confirm rather than to inspire her attraction toward Leander. Cupid here is not presented as a tool of the gods so much as a personification of sexual desire itself and of its contingency. Thus, he may be seen more simply as an objectification of the erotic longings already present within the lovers. It is significant, however, that after he shoots his shaft and observes Hero's reaction to his arrow, he immediately regrets his intervention, demonstrating his own ambivalence toward the effects of passion. He appeals to the Destinies that Hero and Leander be blessed in love, but this plea is ineffectual, for the Fates despise Cupid for his role in the Mercury episode, which Marlowe interjects to explain not only the poverty of scholars but also to offer yet another example of the power and destructiveness of desire. In a pithy explanation of the rejection of Cupid's request, Marlowe alludes to the tragedy of Hero and Leander and couples it to the frustration of the Fates' love for Mercury: 'Then muse not Cupid's suit no better sped,/ Seeing in their loves the Fates were injured' (I. 483–4).

What is most noteworthy about desire in *Hero and Leander* is that it is utterly arbitrary. Immediately following the release of Cupid's arrow that inspires Leander's amorousness for Hero, the narrator reflects on the illogicality and irresistibility of desire:

> It lies not in our power to love, or hate,
> For will in us is over-rul'd by fate.
> When two are stripp'd, long ere the course begin,
> We wish that one should lose, the other win;
> And one especially do we affect
> Of two gold ingots like in each respect.
> The reason no man knows: let it suffice
> What we behold is censur'd by our eyes.
> Where both deliberate, the love is slight;
> Who ever lov'd, that lov'd not at first sight.          (I.167–76)

The significance of these lines is that they so plainly delineate the mystery of human sexual response and the arbitrariness of sexual object-choice that the poem dramatises. Marlowe's point is simply that human sexual response is irrational and involuntary, a thesis that Shakespeare will explore as well in *A Midsummer Night's Dream* and *As You Like It*. 'Will' in the Renaissance means not merely volition, but also sexual desire itself. Sexual response to other individuals, Marlowe insists, is the result not of careful deliberation or calculation, but of a fate that is arbitrary and inscrutable. Behind such a perspective on desire is, of course, the ancient dictum that love is blind, an idea that is expressed iconographically in the art of the Renaissance through the depiction of Cupid as blindfolded and that may be related to the poem's own progression from an emphasis on sight to an emphasis on touch.[12] At the same time, however, the idea of love as irrational directly challenges such dominant Renaissance theories of love as Neoplatonism and Petrarchism, both of which attempt to ground sexual attraction in reason and virtue.[13] In presenting his lovers as victims of arbitrary passion, and in emphasising the physical and material and corporeal rather than the allegorical or theoretical or mystical aspects of desire, Marlowe rejects Renaissance idealisations of human sexuality and removes sexual desire from the arena of morality.

In so far as *Hero and Leander* is a social comedy, its comedy flows from its exposure of the sexual hypocrisy that informs the courting rituals of the lovers and from its betrayal of early modern England's deep-seated anxieties regarding sex, especially feminine sexuality. The lovers' courtship indeed illustrates, in Brian Morris' analysis, 'the absurdity of young love',[14] though that is not all it illustrates. As Keach has observed, the poem's two principals are contrasted in terms of innocence and experience: Hero's pose as chaste nun disguises her ascendant sexual curiosity while Leander's pose as rhetorician of love disguises his lack of experience (Keach, p. 101). Leander may be 'made for amorous play' (I. 88), but, 'being a novice' (II. 13), his knowledge of love is more bookish than first-hand; exposed as a better talker than lover, he is actually 'rude in love, and raw' (II. 61). The naïveté apparent in his encounter with Neptune is true as well in his courtship of Hero. When she 'offers up herself a sacrifice' (II. 48), he has no idea what to do with her: 'Like Aesop's cock, this jewel he enjoyed,/ And as a brother with his sister toyed,/ Supposing nothing else was to be done,/ Now he her favour and good will had won' (II. 51–4). Only Hero's artful struggle revives 'a gentle pleasing heat' that 'taught him all that elder lovers know' (II. 68–9). But if Leander's inexperience and ineptness as a lover makes him the object of laughter, the plight of Hero is both funnier and far more poignant.

The poignancy of Hero's predicament results from her particular vulnerability as a sexually responsive woman in a patriarchal society that applies a sexual double standard. Marlowe is acutely aware of the fact that the sexual attitudes of his society are thoroughly gendered, and even as he hilariously and scathingly exposes the absurdities of the sexual conventions of his day, he evinces considerable sympathy for Hero's position. Leander may appear foolish because he is far less experienced sexually than he pretends to be, but the comedy at his expense – rooted in the cultural expectation of male sexual knowledge – is quite different from the comedy at Hero's expense and arouses much less empathy. Hero's comic dilemma is that she feels the social need to conceal her sexual responsiveness even as she also must signal it ever more blatantly to convey her acquiescence to her clumsy and unobservant lover. The comedy thus proceeds from the way experience is gendered: sexual ignorance in men arouses laughter, but sexual knowledge in women has the potential to excite scorn and derision. The conflicting emotions about sexuality so apparent in Hero thus reflect not merely her personal ambivalence about sex and her fear of experience, but also her knowledge of her society's anxiety about female sexuality and infidelity. Indeed, Hero's inability to speak directly of her desire is a consequence of her shame and anguish and, as David Lee Miller notes, is indicative of the social 'taboo that bars her access to the *active* position of desiring subject' in a world where to be 'masculine' is to be the subject of desire and speech, while to be 'feminine' is to be their object.[15] If the plot of the poem is, finally, the humiliation of Hero, the transformation of her from universal icon into a comic victim of her own desire and, finally, into Leander's personal toy, the process of humiliation is less revealing of any personal failure on her part than of the deficiencies of an erotic economy that valorises women as trophies of male virility but devalues and even despises expressions of their own desire.

One of Marlowe's most significant departures from his source facilitates his interest in exposing the consequences of his society's highly gendered sexual conventions. In Musaeus' poem, Hero has strict parents who virtually imprison her; Hero's fear of her parents' wrath explains why the affair with Leander must be kept secret.[16] Marlowe, however, eliminates the parents, and thus presents Hero's obsession with her reputation as motivated less by a specific impediment than by a more general awareness of the negative social consequences for women of being counted light. As J. B. Steane observes, the poem focuses constantly on the 'partly comic tension between Hero's official and private selves, between natural "will" and the conscientious sense of propriety inculcated by society and religion'.[17] But this tension is not merely evidence of Hero's sexual hypocrisy or duplicity; the proprieties urged by society and religion are themselves products of the widespread fear of female sexuality. Moreover, by robbing the religious prohibitions against extramarital expressions of sexuality of any credence, Marlowe reduces Hero's sexual fears from religious to social concerns. Indeed, in Leander's admittedly self-interested appeal, she is but a 'holy idiot' (I. 303) whose vow of chastity is actually misdevotion. Still, Hero's fear of exposure is well founded. In a society that practises a double standard, the consequences of sexual dalliance are minor for men, but potentially grave for women. Tellingly, Leander evinces very little concern for maintaining the secrecy of his infatuation with Hero. As the narrator comments after their first encounter, 'what the secret trusty night conceal'd/ Leander's amorous habit soone reveal'd' (II. 103–4), donning as he does Cupid's myrtle in his hat, Hero's ribbon on his arms, and her 'sacred ring' on his finger (II. 109). Not surprisingly, Leander's father immediately recognises the youth's amorousness and realises the nature of his relationship with Hero, 'and for the same mildly rebuk't his sonne' (II. 137), the mildness of the rebuke functioning as a form of masculinist approval. In contrast, Hero is at considerable pains to preserve the secrecy of her passion throughout the courtship. Like the maid pursued by Mercury, Hero strives to disguise her desire and to preserve her virginity, an 'inestimable gem' (II. 78) highly prized by Leander even as he mounts a concerted attack against it. The cost of exposure is obvious in the poem's final tableau, when the de-virginised Hero is literally exposed to the commodifying gaze of Leander.

As Werner von Koppenfels has recently pointed out, Marlowe pioneers by staging the 'first and, arguably, greatest Elizabethan "bed-scene"'[18] at the end of *Hero and Leander*. By actually depicting the consummation of a love affair, the poet mocks the ethos of denial at the heart of Petrarchism. But Marlowe's brilliantly comic love scene is itself much less than blissful. Dominated by images of warfare and other kinds of violence, reminiscent in fact of the 'heady riots, incest, rapes' of the depictions in Venus' glass, the scene is shadowed by a sense of foreboding. At her very moment of surrender, for example, Hero is compared to a captured bird in a particularly unsettling image: 'Even as a bird, which in our hands we wring,/ Forth plungeth, and oft flutters with her wing,/ She trembling strove' (II. 289–91). That the couple's vigorous lovemaking culminates in mutual pleasure may itself be part of Marlowe's project of de-spiritualising sex; but, despite the physical satisfaction, Hero's surrender to desire also yields guilt and shame.

The lovers at the end of the poem are not the same as they were at the beginning. The conclusion features a reduced Hero and an inflated Leander. Marlowe emphasises the change in relative status that follows the consummation. Hero, attempting to steal away from the bed she has shared with Leander, is tripped by him. Recovering from the prat-fall, the naked young woman is exposed, blushing and embarrassed, to her lover's coolly calculating eyes:

> So Hero's ruddy cheek Hero betray'd,
> And her all naked to his sight display'd,
> Whence his admiring eyes more pleasure took
> Than Dis, on heaps of gold fixing his look.        (II.323–6)

Her blush betraying her own (arbitrary) passion, Hero displays here far more than her physical nakedness: she exhibits at once both her desire and her shame. In the gaze of pleasure-taking Leander, she finds herself utterly objectified. She has become his trophy, merely a valuable possession and the sign of his sexual success. She is the ultimate commodity in this poem about the commodification of love. This tableau also, of course, exposes Leander, whose conquest of Hero has been described in terms not far removed from rape.[19] Here, the comparison with Dis, the god of wealth and of Hades, reveals him as appropriately grasping and possessive. But if the lovers are each exposed in the final tableau, they are not on that account made equal. Indeed, the tableau reveals the inequalities inherent in the Elizabethan sexual system that privileges female sexual innocence and male sexual experience.

The poem ends on a distinctly sour note (or rather, thud). A rising masculine sun sneers at a fleeing feminine Night: 'Till she, o'ercome with anguish, shame, and rage,/ Dang'd down to hell her loathsome carriage' (II. 333–4). Night's predicament as an exposed and mocked woman, overcome with anguish, shame, and rage, mirrors not merely the particular plight of Hero, but also, more generally, the fate of desiring women in early modern England.

Marlowe's comic depiction of the tragic couple provides him the opportunity to ridicule sexual conventions and hypocrisies. He destabilises the dominant constructions of sexuality of his day and resolutely refuses to idealise or moralise sexuality. While he arouses sympathy for the plight of Hero, he does so in order to expose the inequities and contradictions of the sex-gender system rather than to sentimentalise her or to point a moral about her loss of innocence. *Hero and Leander*'s project of demystification marks it as a pivotal work in the literary representation of sex.[20] The poem had an enormous influence on love poetry of the late Renaissance by initiating the transition from Petrarchan to Ovidian attitudes toward love and by criticising the Elizabethan sex-gender system. Yet the greater freedom and realism in the representation of sex pioneered by *Hero and Leander* led not, as one might have anticipated, to celebrations of sexual contentment. Instead, the influence of the poem also embraces the surprisingly large number of poems in the period that express post-coital *tristesse* and other reactions against sexual satiety. Central to its insights into the complexity of human sexuality is its apprehension of the arbitrariness of desire.

CHAPTER 10

# Gender and voice in 'Hero and Leander'

*Georgia E. Brown*

Claude J. Summers identifies *Hero and Leander* as an agent of destabilisation which exposes the self-contradictions and deceptions in hegemonic constructions of gender and sexuality (see pp. 133–47). By applying the resources of queer theory and feminism, he demonstrates that Marlowe's theme is 'the arbitrariness of desire', and he describes the ways in which the poem interrogates conventional ideas about love and gender by emphasising 'the essential likeness of same-sex and other-sex attraction'. The 'arbitrariness of desire', and its potential for creation or destruction is the subject of Ovid's *Metamorphoses*, but Marlowe resists his culture's 'dominant practice of co-opting and Christianising classical myth and literature', by refusing to moralise or allegorise the Ovidian narrative. For Professor Summers, Marlowe's particular reading of Ovid challenges the supernatural order of his day. He calls this reading a 'literal-minded' use of Ovid because it focuses on the irrational events of the story and its simultaneous potential for comedy and tragedy.

My reading of *Hero and Leander* also identifies the poem as an agent of destabilisation, but I place Marlowe's poem in the context of the aesthetic and literary debates of the 1590s. Thus the poem not only interrogates gender assumptions, it also interrogates the very notion of the aesthetic and the nature of the canon. The desire the text describes is not proper. It cannot be summed up, simplified, made stable, and made one. It is most accurately described by ambiguity, by 'polymorphous perversity', to echo Summers' reworking of Freud. However, this 'polymorphous perversity' has repercussions on the formal level that can be seen, for example, in the poem's refusal to end, and it is the formal elements of the poem that will be my focus. Marlowe's attack on aesthetic conventions exists in complicated interrelationship with his attack on gender relations.

148

I read *Hero and Leander* in the context of the epyllion craze that
swept England in the 1590s. The epyllion is a genre that effeminises
its author, not only because it deals with feminine subjects, such as
love and emotion, but also because it identifies itself as a form that is
marginal to epic. The epyllion, or little epic, is a reduction of epic
that elaborates precisely the sort of private, recreative and feminised
matter that is peripheral to epic. Thus, while the authors of the
epyllion define new concepts of literary value and exalt the creative
personality by exploiting its particular generic resources, the radical
kind of authorship so defined is also an effeminate kind of authorship. I contend that the Marlowe of *Hero and Leander* is really
Marlowe in drag. The crudity of this assertion invites correction, but
*Hero and Leander* does explore a feminised form of authorship and
does acknowledge an analogy between the aesthetic and the feminine. This analogy is the focus of my essay as I explore how *Hero and
Leander* figures desire and its relationship to authority, aesthetic
activity, and the issues of authorship.

In some ways painfully, perhaps even dangerously, old-fashioned,
my chapter threatens to bypass the critical developments of the last
twenty years, namely New Historicism and Cultural Materialism,
and return to New Criticism with its prettification and dandification
of the text viewed outside history.[1] In fact I propose a deliberately
perverse reading of *Hero and Leander*, one which resists the kind of
contextualisation promoted by New Historicism. Thus my literary
focus needs some defence, but my reading is not an ahistorical one. I
argue that the 1590s were not only characterised by the expansion of
literary activity and rising standards, but also by important conceptual changes that run the risk of being downplayed by an exclusively
interdisciplinary approach. Prior to the 1590s, writers tended to
defend literature in Humanist terms, by arguing that literature held
a serious kernel of political or moral truth. Yet, as some writers came
to realise, this was a pyrrhic victory for authors, because such
defences did not recognise advantages that were specific to literature,
as the didactic and allegorical character of a text was seen to be
more important than its fictional or poetic qualities.[2] The questions
raised in the 1590s as to whether literature was a political, civic, and
moral activity, or whether it was, in some sense, a thing apart, are
echoed in current debates over New Historicism. My response to
such questions is that literary discourse is both a form of social
praxis and a thing apart – a specialised form of discourse that is not

exactly equivalent to other social discourses, although it shares many points of contact with them, and probably more similarities than we might care to admit. New Historicism is a practice that acknowledges and analyses the social and political work done by texts and in this way it aligns itself with Humanist orthodoxy.[3] Like the Humanists, New Historicism looks for a text's impact on, and interrelationships with, areas other than the purely literary, and while Marlowe would share and understand this kind of reading, he was also in the process of discovering and elaborating purely aesthetic institutions and traditions.

*Hero and Leander* does do political work, as Professor Summers demonstrates. Even if one takes the narrowest definition of political, it resists the legitimising myth of virginity surrounding Elizabeth I and the sublimated eroticism that fashioned political transactions in her court. Such resistance is conveyed through burlesque when, for example, Leander, the erstwhile sexual ingenue, adopts the resources of the *carpe diem* tradition in order to seduce Hero:[4]

> This idoll which you terme *Virginitie*,
> Is neither essence subiect to the eie,
> No, nor to any one exterior sence,
> Nor hath it any place of residence,
> Nor is't of earth or mold celestiall,
> Or capable of any forme at all.
> Of that which hath no being, doe not boast,
> Things that are not at all, are never lost.          (269–76)

However, *Hero and Leander* also develops a new kind of defence of literature, one which does not deny the traditional association of literature with the trivial and peripheral, but capitalises upon it, and uncovers the paradoxical value of marginality, error, and game. By drawing attention to its weaknesses, to its effeminised, errant, and shameful contents, *Hero and Leander* does serious work in extending the authorial role. In this way it constructs a self-consciously literary text out of the attributes that Humanism dismisses as trivial, and generates a *literary* canon from non-canonical texts. *Hero and Leander* is not simply a serious trifle, it is important *because* it is a trifle, because its fictional and recreative status enables Marlowe to think the unthinkable, to challenge sexual, gender and aesthetic conventions, by exploiting its licence.

The poem proclaims its allegiance to the more questionable elements of classical culture. As Gordon Braden has pointed out,

Musaeus' version of the myth of Hero and Leander is not wholly respectable. It exploits bathos, digression and a volatile emotional field, and exposes 'the meretriciousness of all rhetoric'.[5] While subsequent re-workings of Musaeus tended to soften its stylistic and narrative 'meretriciousness', Marlowe's version bypasses this sobering tendency. Then of course there is Ovid. In the 1590s the *Metamorphoses* came to epitomise literary creativity through its association with the metamorphic power of wit as writers acknowledged a parallel between transformation and the processes of imagination. For the authors of the 1590s, who sought to defend writing against restrictive and formulaic criticism, Ovid became an important model which valorised authorial individuality, flexibility and technical skill. Ovid's compendious epic suggested ways in which competing values could be brought together to challenge existing conceptions of literature, and its luxuriant wantonness challenged the simplicity of conventional moral judgements based on the denial of sensual experience, by insinuating a connection between poetic creativity and sexual desire which made literary morality a chimerical goal and helped free literature from the necessity to be didactic.[6] Moreover, metamorphosis functions like paradox and generic mixture as it breaks down existing categories and offers structures of thought through which new ideas can be conceptualised. In Clark Hulse's words, 'the metamorphic [image] is integral, minimising differences. It may suggest the ecstasy or terror of the flesh made free to move across the categories of substance, and of the mind to move across the categories of thought. Indeed, it may call into question our ability to categorise experience at all.'[7]

It is the combination of a powerful imagination with licentiousness that forms the focus of reinterpretations of Ovid in genres such as the epyllion and writers like Thomas Nashe.[8] One of the more extreme instances of wanton Ovidianism is Nashe's *Choise of Valentines* where pornographic wit is used to mock a variety of popular forms. In particular, Petrarchanism, with its continuous postponement of consummation, and the idealisations of Neoplatonism and pastoral, are eroticised and urbanised in Nashe's story of the young lover who sought his 'bonnie Bell' (3.406) in 'the merie moneth of Februarie' (3.403), only to find her in a brothel.[9] *The Choise of Valentines* is a dirty story that also questions the literary status quo and Nashe invokes Ovid and the specifically Ovidian form of the 'wanton Elegie' (3.403) to challenge genres such as pastoral, complaint, and sonnet. The poem shamelessly vaunts the fact that it breaks taboo by 'painting forth the things that hidden are' (3.403), using its transgressive subject matter to promote the author's originality. However, it asserts a paradoxical supremacy by maintaining that the narrator achieves success by courting failure. As the narrator points out in the dedication: 'But of loves pleasure's none did ever write/ That hath succeeded in theis latter times.' Thus he asserts his originality through the fact that none have written about love in this way, while simultaneously acknowledging that this will not bring him success. Evidently the author of the text that was known as 'Nashe's Dildo' in early manuscripts could expect scant reward from society, although its elusive dedicatee, Lord S, may well have been pleased with what he read. My reading of *Hero and Leander* places the poem in the context of such ribald poetry which elaborates a link between sexual explicitness, modernity and literariness. Nashe's brief poem describes a sexual encounter between the narrator and his beloved mistress, Frances, but unfortunately the narrator finds he is impotent and, in exasperation, Frances satisfies herself with a dildo. Nashe's text eroticises scribal activity and defines the dildo as 'this womans secretarie' (3.413), eliding sexual and scribal functions. Nashe produces a poem whose pornographic excess points to the naïveté of contemporary forms and what he sees as their hypocritical idealisations of chastity. Ovid sanctions Nashe's anti-establishment gesture, just as he does in the epyllion, where eroticism is elaborated for similar purposes to interrogate the precise nature of literary activity and its moral status.[10] This particular interface between classical tradition and contemporary poetics was used to challenge contemporary definitions of author, text, and canon, and to assert not only the existence but also the peculiar value of an independent aesthetic space.

Like Ovid's *Metamorphoses*, *Hero and Leander* stands in oblique relationship to epic and triviality is endemic to Marlowe's text, whether it is expressed in the frivolous tone or in the brevity of the poem. The term epyllion means little epic and so, by definition, the epyllion is a reduction, truncation and trivialisation of epic. Indeed, some of the formal and thematic content of epic finds its way into *Hero and Leander*'s heroic couplets. For example, epic periphrasis is imitated by Marlowe's elaborate description of night (187–91), and of the dawn (813–18). The moral gravity of the heroic world is imitated by Marlowe's sententiae, and the heroic descent to the underworld is replayed in Cupid's flight to 'the pallace of the destinies' with the request that Hero and Leander might be allowed to be happy in love (377–84). Nevertheless, the poem presents these conventions through a mock-heroic perspective which registers a sense of anachronism, and a self-conscious distance between Marlowe's perspective and that of epic. Indeed, while Marlowe's sententiae recreate epic, they also point to the ways in which Marlowe deviates from epic and they impart amorous wisdom, rather than martial or political wisdom. Thus we learn that love is inescapable, '*Such force and vertue hath an amorous looke*' (166), and that women are won by rhetoric, not force, 'Maids are not woon by brutish force and might,/ But speeches full of pleasure and delight' (419–20). Yet, in a poetic world ruled by fickle fate it is hard to see how anything of universal value can be derived from such flux. While the epic appeals to the shared values of a community it both reflects and creates, Marlowe's poem expresses a process of subjectification in its philosophical perspective and, as I will later argue, in its aesthetic perspective. In Marlowe's poetic world there can only be coincidences, not commonplaces, and *Hero and Leander*'s inconclusive and contradictory sententiae undermine the existence of a shared perspective. Moreover, as our choices are not determined by the exercise of morality or reason, we may legitimately wonder whether there is any point to didacticism.

The marginality of *Hero and Leander* is reinforced by its status as an unfinished poem and it also resists closure in a variety of other ways. It is far more interested in processes and beginnings than in endings. Objects lose their single nature – they assume other forms, or they are misinterpreted and taken to be other things. The gods in Venus' pavement are preserved 'in sundrie shapes' (143), while the victims of their love suffer change. On the material level, even Hero's buskins are not simply buskins but sparrows too. The rapturous description of Hero's appearance at the start of the poem (5–50) is an attempt to recreate the fecundity and variety of nature in art, but the grotesque image collapses into comedy with the description of the buskins that end in sparrows at the knee. This marvellous, but hollow, sculpture is made from pearl and gold. Thus it confuses associations of chastity, luxury, and eroticism, through the purity of white pearl, combined with the costliness of gold, and the sparrow, which is the symbol of Venus. The buskins are filled with water which spills out of the sparrows' beaks as Hero walks around thereby imitating the chirruping noise of the birds which, one hopes, can still be heard above the squelch of her feet:

> Buskins of shels all silvered, used she,
> And brancht with blushing corall to the knee;
> Where sparrowes pearcht, of hollow pearle and gold,
> Such as the world would woonder to behold:
> Those with sweet water oft her handmaid fils,
> Which as shee went would cherupe through the bils.          (31–6)

The multifarious nature of the material world reflects the unpredictability of fate which can turn humans to love or hate. Desire itself is equally indiscriminate in its effects. In a narrative where everyone is the victim of arbitrary forces, even the most wilful individual is subject to the capricious authority of fate, just as the reasons for our preferences, including our aesthetic preferences, are unpredictable:

> It lies not in our power to love, or hate,
> For will in us is over-rul'd by fate;
> When two are stript long ere the course begin,
> We wish that one should loose, the other win.
> And one especiallie doe we affect,
> Of two gold Ingots like in each respect,
> The reason no man knowes, let it suffise,
> What we behold is censur'd by our eies.          (167–74)

In such a cosmos where things are rarely single or predictable, closure would be a falsehood – it would impose an end-point, a fixed point from which a pattern could be imposed on the realities of process. Thus the unpredictability of existence is echoed on the structural level by the unpredictability of Marlowe's narrative with its fits, starts, interpolations, and final incompletion. In the Stationer Edward Blount's phrase, the poem is an '*unfinished Tragedy*', and while there is a sexual close in the sense that Hero and Leander embrace, there is no narrative close.

It may be objected that the end is inscribed in the beginning of the poem as the very first line, 'In Hellespont guiltie of True-loves blood', as Professor Summers points out, invokes the fate of Leander who drowns in Musaeus' version, provoking Hero's suicide. Yet I would suggest that *Hero and Leander*'s status as a 'twice-told tale' directs attention from the tale to the telling of the tale, from content to form, and raises issues of originality and authority. In fact, the poem's constant references to the traditional ending make the text's failure to supply that ending all the more surprising. They highlight

Marlowe's originality, simultaneously casting it as errant, as he takes a commonplace story and defamiliarises it. *Hero and Leander* is thus an extravagant text, it is both flashy and vagrant, as it stuffs its body with digressions and periphrases that disrupt our narrative expectations, just as the abruptly unorthodox ending does. Thus both the digressiveness and the incompleteness of the text result in a process of subjectification where attention is directed to the idiosyncratic author as the origin of the text, and to the process of reading with its assumptions, dissatisfactions and peculiar fulfilments. The text forces us to become self-conscious about reading, through a narrator who is insistently there, responding to the lovers, betraying his attraction to Leander and his inability to stick to the point. Thus we are not only cast as participants in the events, but as readers of someone's interpretation of events. Self-consciousness is also promoted by conflicting responses to the story, which are imposed by the emphasis on unpredictability and the mixing of forms. Thus Marlowe prompts us to think about what we do and why we do it. Given the poem's view that 'What we behold is censur'd by our eies', we are forced to conclude that our response to the text is dangerously subjective, perhaps even narcissistic, as we read what we want to read and oscillate between critical self-awareness and self-absorption.

The fragmentary nature of *Hero and Leander* is the product of its digressions and multiple allusions. However, Marlowe's individual style is determined by the way these components are put together, and his originality is determined by the difference between his text and its models. In fact, Marlowe's poem draws attention to its components and discovers the cracks and disjunctions in its structure because it is precisely this fragmentariness that leaves space for the expression of the author's individuality. Fragmentariness asserts authorial control as it presents the reader with a product that carries its maker's mark, rather than with a seamless product that conceals its constructedness and the labour that went into it.

From one point of view the polysemous and polymorphous narrative of *Hero and Leander* may be imperfect, but these imperfections are also assertions of authorial work and control. This curious way of promoting the self through deficiency is, of course, central to the paradoxical encomium and *Hero and Leander* is a paradoxical encomium, or a defence of the indefensible, in that it asserts the dignity of an unconventional and even scandalous kind of authorship. It draws attention to its guilty, errant, and marginal status and to its wantonness, and bases its defence on precisely these things because, in so doing, Marlowe finds a way to speak in specifically literary terms. It is striking that when Marlowe undertakes a defence of the literary community in the attack on the perversion of reward that favours sycophantic and greedy people over the Muses' sons who should really be the recipients of honour (469–82), he does so in a digression within a digression within a digression – it is a sideline to the story of Mercury and the country-maid, which is itself a digression from the story of why the destinies dislike Cupid, which is itself a digression from the main narrative. This is a paradoxical kind of self-assertiveness but its complexities are yet more involved and unsettling because the voice Marlowe discovers in *Hero and Leander* is also a feminised voice. This is authorship in drag – one which acknowledges an analogy between the aesthetic and the feminine.[11] Paradoxically, Marlowe's authorial self-assertiveness also invokes a concomitant feminisation, a simultaneous assertion and loss of power, although in the free-wheeling world of *Hero and Leander* this loss is not condemned and only causes momentary anxiety. The authorial subjectivity defined through the epyllion is Ovidian, but it is not 'the subject in crisis', rather it is an authorial subject asserted and celebrated through disjunction.[12] The author of *Hero and Leander* is both subject and object, both in control of the text and the object fashioned by the text. Thus the author as artefact is both the perpetrator of the voyeuristic gaze as he surveys Hero and Leander, and the object of that gaze, who desires to be the centre of vision. Following the model established by Freud in his essay, 'Instincts and Their Vicissitudes', voyeurism is usually interpreted as a one-way transaction from powerful male voyeur to passive female object. However, this transaction is undone by an object that looks back and exercises its own influence, as Hero does in Marlowe's poem. While the narrator joins the crowds gazing on Hero, these voyeurs are undone by her beauty: 'But far above, the loveliest *Hero* shin'd,/ And stole away th'inchaunted gazers mind' (103–4). Thus the narrator occupies both the feminised object position, and the powerful subject position, with the result that the categories of subject and object, male and female, are elided through visual transactions that transfer pleasure, as well as power.[13]

As I have suggested, Marlowe's little epic presents itself as a supplement to the masculine world of epic. In *The Aeneid*, for example, public duty always takes priority over love and activities associated with the feminine sphere, and Aeneas abandons Dido to pursue his epic destiny as founder of a new empire.[14] Ironically, not only does love matter come into focus through the story of Hero and Leander, but love matter is revealed to be the motivating force behind all epics. Even Homer's *Iliad*, which is the origin of the genre, has its own origins in love, and '*Venus* glasse' (142), which is a visual anthology of negative experiences of love, contains some unexpectedly heroic examples, including that of Troy:

> Blood-quaffing *Mars*, heaving the yron net,
> Which limping *Vulcan* and his *Cyclops* set:
> Love kindling fire, to burne such townes as *Troy*,
> *Sylvanus* weeping for the lovely boy.                    (151–4)

Thus private emotional experience supplants public duty, fickle fate supplants providence, and the origins of epic are revealed to lie in love. Moreover, not only is Marlowe's poem unheroic, but its very hero/Hero is a woman! Rather than hide the fact that his poem promotes what had been marginalised in epic, Marlowe shamelessly draws attention to the deviancy of his poem. Indeed, Leander is compared to a hero, to 'Theban *Hercules*', when he succeeds in Marlowe's alternative field of action – the amatory field when, as the text coyly puts it, he enters 'the orchard of *Th'esperides*' and makes love with Hero (769–70). In this way, the poem is quite shameless about its deficiencies and it provides a model for the self-promotion of a literary community whose products had long been dismissed as trivial. The narrator bases his authority on the extravagance of his style and behaviour, and exalts decorative and recreative activities. Thus his self-promotion is based on the unashamed promotion of the trivial, negative, and peripheral aspects of authorial occupation. In so doing, the author deliberately pursues a process of emasculation and *Hero and Leander* supplies what was excluded from epic – love matter, female heroes and female concerns.[15]

Thus *Hero and Leander* celebrates the rites of Venus as opposed to the rites of epic. As a consequence the text, and all textual activity, whether it be reading or writing, is eroticised as the characters speak about sex, the author writes about sex, and we read about sex. A direct correlation between desire and eloquence is suggested, as we are told that the greater the desire, the greater the rhetorical power of the subject:

> Therefore unto his bodie, hirs he clung,
> She, fearing on the rushes to be flung,
> Striv'd with redoubled strength, the more she strived,
> The more a gentle pleasing heat revived,
> Which taught him all that elder lovers know,
> And now the same gan so to scorch and glow,
> As in plaine termes (yet cunningly) he crav'd it,
> Love alwaies makes those eloquent that have it.          (549–56)

The members of the textual community that are assembled by *Hero and Leander* are like the 'wandring guest[s]' (94) who congregate at Sestos during the festival of Adonis. They come to encounter love, and indeed no one leaves empty-handed, as 'such as had none at all,/ Came lovers home, from this great festivall' (95–6). Even the narrator finds love there and he betrays his indecent attraction to Hero the nun and, perhaps even more scandalously, to Leander whose delights he seems to have sampled. While one can gaze from afar, the gustatory and tactile analogies in the description of Leander suggest a far greater degree of intimacy: 'Even as delicious meat is to the tast,/ So was his necke in touching' (63–4). Hero is not the only 'dish' in the poem. In fact there is nothing innately masculine or feminine about Hero or Leander: they are the products of various discourses of desire, even the same discourses of desire. Both are, for example, constructed through the conventions of Petrarchanism, a discourse that usually defines feminine beauty with the result that, in Leander's case, 'Some swore he was a maid in mans attire,/ For in his lookes were all that men desire' (83–4). All that men desire consists of 'A pleasant smiling cheeke, a speaking eye,/ A brow for love to banquet roiallye' (85–6) and Leander's beauty is established by the blazon and his worth, like Hero's, is established by emphasising his desirability to others. In this way Hero and Leander become the object of other people's desires, the focus of other people's stories and colonise all forms of desire, even incest:

> But this is true, so like was one the other,
> As he [Cupid] imagyn'd *Hero* was his mother.
> And oftentimes into her bosome flew,
> About her naked necke his bare armes threw.
> And laid his childish head upon her brest,
> And with still panting rockt, there tooke his rest.          (39–44)

Thus Hero and Leander are both the motivation for discourse and the product of that discourse. They embody the desire aroused by language, and the desired object fashioned by that language. As such they are synecdoches for the text as a whole, for the object fashioned through language, and for the desire that is aroused by language and is shared by writer and reader.

The author as artefact has much in common with the woman as artefact and Marlowe explores the correlation between the aesthetic, the feminine, and the processes of the imagination in his particular narrator. When Marlowe praises Hero he concentrates on her clothes, her jewels, and her habit. The description of her kirtle, for example, is a *tour de force* of the imagination, a poetic artefact that associates its own artifices with those of Hero:

> Upon her head she ware a myrtle wreath,
> From whence her vaile reacht to the ground beneath.
> Her vaile was artificiall flowers and leaves,
> Whose workmanship both man and beast deceaves.
> Many would praise the sweet smell as she past,
> When t'was the odour which her breath foorth cast,
> And there for honie, bees have sought in vaine,
> And beat from thence, have lighted there againe.          (17–24)

The artificiality and the deceptiveness attributed to Hero turn her into a kind of hyper-woman. She is the most desirable of women and a compound of mother, maid, and lover, but her description provokes a self-remarking poeticism from the narrator, which associates literariness with femininity and with wantonness.[16] As I have argued, metamorphosis is associated with wit, but it is also true that women are supposed to be the quintessentially changeable beings. In fact, the changeability of process that is endemic to *Hero and Leander* effeminises author, reader, and reality, as our sublunary status not only makes us changeable, it also makes us prey to emotion. Moreover, the narrator suggests that the very structure of *Hero and Leander* is effeminised. The exquisite artificiality of the text, its deceptions, its abandonment to love and to the pleasures of affection and emotion undermine the author's status as a proper man but, so too, does his narrative. The digressions in the story sharpen the readers' narrative desires by frustrating them, just as Hero denies Leander to excite him further: 'Thereat she smild, and did denie him so,/ As put thereby, yet might he hope for mo' (311–12). The narrative coyness also settles the narrator's worth. Just as Hero uses coyness to make herself more desirable, so the narrator asserts his control of text and reader, and promotes his own ambitions by putting us off in order to bring us on.

Whether we like it or not, as readers we not only share the desire for Hero and Leander, we are also teased and excited by the narrative. Unsurprisingly, the concept of guilt is introduced in the very first line of the poem, 'In *Hellespont* guiltie of True-loves blood'. Our sense of guiltiness is kept in mind through the allusions to the 'guilt starres' (10) on the purple lining of Hero's garments, the very colour of the lining serving as an uncomfortable reminder of defloration. Thus our fear of impropriety is itself aestheticised, transformed into pleasing 'guilt starres' and even ridiculed by the trifling pun on guilt/gilt. Of course, *Hero and Leander* is predicated on the breaking of taboos, whether they are broken by falling in love with a nun, or by writing or reading, and thus entering into the scandalous matter of indiscriminate desire and the suppressed intentions behind the most innocent of gesture and language:

> As she spake this, her toong tript,
> For unawares (*Come thither*) from her slipt,
> And sodainly her former colour chang'd,
> And here and there her eies through anger rang'd.     (357–60)

From Donne's *Elegies* to Nashe's *Choise of Valentines*, literary innovation is associated with the frank treatment of desire, an association reinforced by Elizabethan readings of wanton Ovid, the most modern of the ancients. Yet *Hero and Leander* goes even further than this by turning reading and writing themselves into erotic activities. Thus, it is not simply that the epyllion deals with sexual subject matter and breaks taboo, but the relation between reader, writer, and text, a relation mediated by rhetoric, is eroticised. Such a definition of literature is indeed threatening and is acknowledged to be threatening by the poem when Leander points out that the rites of Venus, which are violent, degraded, and painful, also include artistic and literary rites. He associates literature with appetite, eros, recreation, deception, and with everything that is evil. Rather than presenting the text as seemly, moral or useful, Marlowe redefines it as shameless and prodigal:

> The rites
> In which Loves beauteous Empresse most delites,
> Are banquets, Dorick musicke, midnight revell,
> Plaies, maskes, and all that stern age counteth evill.     (299–302)

*Hero and Leander* is a masterpiece of wit and a technical *tour de force*. However, through celebrating its artistic accomplishments and by making matter out of its guiltiness, it finds a way of speaking in specifically literary terms and defines a space for literature within the conceptual framework of late Elizabethan culture. The poem's shameless eroticism finds its correlative in its literariness. It is a pageant of styles, a locus of sensual and poetic pleasures for both writer and reader. In this way the author proves his own excellence in a variety of styles and demonstrates the versatility of his creative talent, but the celebration of artifice is dependent on the erotic nature of the poem. Marlowe can be self-consciously literary because he is also being self-consciously wanton. To return to Leander's list of the rites of Venus, literature is one of the things accounted evil by society: it is immoral, wanton, and prodigal. Thus by emphasising the immoral, wanton and prodigal nature of his text, Marlowe finds a way to speak in specifically literary ways. The artificiality of Marlowe's verse is exaggerated, even to the point of preciousness, and the contrivance which is fundamental to all literature, becomes even more contrived and comes to the fore as couplets are turned with facility and images run wild, as they do in the description of Hero's buskins. Thus what we could term the sporadic crudities of *Hero and Leander* proclaim it to be a work of art and hail its status as a *manufactured* object, celebrating and promoting the singular and prodigal author within the text.

As a fragment, Marlowe's poem invites completion and endings were supplied by George Chapman and Henry Petowe in 1598. In fact, Marlowe's poem survives in more oblique ways as well, since its most striking features find their way into other texts where they become the focus for intra-community competition, as authors try to outwit Marlowe. At the beginning of the *Metamorphoses*, Ovid refers to his poem as a '*perpetuum carmen*', a perpetual or unending song, and as Marlowe's story is taken up by other voices it too becomes a '*perpetuum carmen*'. Allusions to *Hero and Leander* in these texts serve two purposes, they prove the author's literary skill, provoking a self-conscious inflation of wit, and they generate a sense of community, both between writers, and between writers and readers, by promoting the in-joke. Thus the poem's iconic status provoked Thomas Nashe to parody in *Lenten Stuffe* (1599). *Hero and Leander* is both an inspiration and a challenge to Nashe's ambitions and in particular his praise of Yarmouth as the 'delicate paramour of *Neptune*' (3.172) is challenged by Marlowe's epyllion which describes a rival paramour in a striking passage that presents the hapless Leander as the focus of Neptune's desires. Nashe acknowledges Marlowe's poem to be the work of 'a diviner Muse' (3.195) than Musaeus but, as a result, it also threatens his own claims to supremacy, and the struggle for professional priority in the 1590s is translated into the comic rivalry of the red herring, in Nashe's corner, versus Leander, now transformed by Nashe into a blue-lipped sturgeon. Nashe's witty adaptation of *Hero and Leander* runs for several pages (3.195–201) and, while it proclaims his allegiance to the ideals of Marlowe and to those of the epyllion vogue of the 1590s, it also outdoes the epyllion at its own game by exaggerating such characteristic elements as the confusion of the sexes (3.196), mock sententiae (3.196, 197), and aetiological fictions (3.200–1). Unlike other contemporaries, Nashe sees their story as a source of witty creativity and Marlowe's marine narrative is used to explain why fish goes with mustard, why the ling lives near Iceland, and why the herring lives near England. Yet Nashe also makes space for his own voice, and for all its strengths, *Hero and Leander* is an old tale that can only be briefly revived by Nashe as he turns it into nourishment for his own imagination. In fact, *Hero and Leander* is only a short-cut for Nashe, one which he invokes to avoid tedium, and while it epitomises the values of metamorphic wit, Nashe outdoes Marlowe by turning to a 'new lesson' and he eventually transforms the humble red herring into nothing less than the glorious golden fleece! This is certainly all a little too fishy, a little too clever, and Nashe flaunts the fact that his text is an extravagant hoax. His celebration of *Hero and Leander*, is a celebration of the metamorphic power of the imagination. *Lenten Stuffe* describes fish as '*Protaeus* heards' (202) and Proteus, the god of change, is also carved into the walls of the Temple of Venus in Marlowe's poem. Nashe, Marlowe and the classical god Proteus all derive their power from their ability to take many shapes and Nashe's praise of *Hero and Leander* is a shameless exercise in authorial self-defence and self-promotion, a localised instance of the paradoxical encomium, where Marlowe, Leander and the epyllion stand for a particular kind of literariness, one that is skilful, cunning, and trivial, although, as I attempt to show, important because it is trivial.

In fact, the rhetorical and sexual are linked through Elizabethan interpretations of the elegy which could be an erotic lyric in the tradition of Ovid's *Elegies*, as well as a poem of commemoration. In his dedication of *Hero and Leander* to Sir Thomas Walsingham, Edward Blount presents the publication of the epyllion as a memorial to Marlowe, as an elegiac gesture which will gather his friends in shared activities of commemoration and celebration. Thus the publication of *Hero and Leander* both constructs and reflects a literary community, establishing its identity and its goals in relation to Marlowe's poem:

Sir, wee thinke not our selves discharged of the dutie wee owe to our friend, when wee have brought the breathlesse bodie to the earth: for albeit the eye there taketh his ever farwell of that beloved obiect, yet the impression of the man, that hath beene deare unto us, living an after life in our memory, there putteth us in mind of farther obsequies due unto the deceased. And namely of the performance of whatsoever we may iudge shal make to his living credit, and to the effecting of his determinations prevented by the stroke of death.

Paradoxically, the concerns of Marlowe's epyllion are acutely social. While it asserts the subjective authority of author and reader, it also extols the virtues of a community defined by the quality of its emotional and aesthetic responses: 'And who have hard hearts, and obdurat minds,/ But vicious, harebraind, and illit'rat hinds?' (701–2). Such responses indicate one's level of cultivation, but by assembling his cultivated readers through *Hero and Leander,* Marlowe pursues the cultivation of English letters. Just as Marlowe defines his modernity through and against Ovid, contemporaries like Thomas Nashe define their own modernity through and against Marlowe. The redefinition of text and author as self-consciously marginal and effeminised in *Hero and Leander* becomes the catalyst for the formation of a literary canon and a literary community in late Elizabethan England.

CHAPTER 11

# *Marlowe's politic women*

### *Joanna Gibbs*

Given the widespread interest in representations of women that has characterised Shakespeare studies since the 1980s, it is, perhaps, surprising that so little critical attention has been paid to Marlowe's female characters. In part, of course, such neglect might be justified by the simple reminder that five of the six major plays focus on the fortunes of their eponymous male protagonists. Nevertheless, the discovery in Marlowe of a war of the sexes in which women function as apolitical, moral arbiters and men as monstrous Machiavells often derives from the belief that all Marlowe's women (not to mention his men) share similar, gender specific, characteristics.[1] Accordingly, it is common to assume that the plays present a world of relatively uncomplicated gender roles in which emotions are the preoccupation of women and power the preserve of men. But, while it is true that Marlowe was writing at a time when women were beginning to be characterised as private and emotional, men as public and politically directed, it is important to remember that it was not until the late seventeenth century that sex roles and gender related characteristics began regularly to be conceived of in this way.[2]

Adequately to appraise Marlowe's women we thus need to jettison anachronistic conceptions of gender roles and attend more carefully to the particularities of the plays' handling of sexual politics. In Marlowe's plays women often *are* allowed to make inroads into male space and actively to engage in statesmanship. What is more, those of Marlowe's women who do make authoritative interventions adopt attitudes at odds with the critical conception of them as inclining towards privacy and harbouring feelings relating to matters of the heart to the exclusion of issues of policy.

If we turn first to *Edward II*, we can see that reading Isabella in terms of a paradigm predicated solely upon a rigid notion of separate spheres and sex-related characteristics has led many critics to miss the ways in which Marlowe eschews any straightforward conformity to the constraints of that model. The Queen's sudden metamorphosis from loving wife to duplicitous adulteress is, according to various critics, symptomatic of Marlowe's broader lack of sympathy with women.[3] More often, however, the apparent inconsistencies of Isabella's character are read as an index of her emotional orientation, with her need for the love of a man driving her to behave in what appears to be a contradictory fashion. When understood as motivated by a yearning for love, Isabella's initial support for Edward, her attempt to have Gaveston reinstated, and her subsequent complicity in schemes to topple both men, no longer appear as inconsistencies at all. Rather, these ostensible confusions translate into symptoms of an emotional neediness which renders the Queen 'a mere puppet'[4] in the hands of Edward and Mortimer, both of whom take advantage of her vulnerability to further their own ends.

Viewed as an irrational victim of her own feelings, Isabella is understood as necessarily lacking the tactical insight required, for instance, to recognise that she is 'taken up by Mortimer only when he needs her to consolidate his position'.[5] Those commentators who perceive Isabella in this way tend also, as Kathleen Anderson contends, to characterise the Queen as an essentially 'private individual'[6] – the corollary of which is to ignore the ways in which Isabella's affections are informed by the operations of politics. However, when Isabella's public dimension is brought into view, the relationship between her attempt to find love and her pursuit of authority becomes apparent.

In the society of *Edward II* the discourse of 'love' is, as Simon Shepherd argues, 'structured within reward and patronage' (Shepherd, p. 204). Hence, for low-ranking individuals, the search for love invariably involves a quest for power. Given that Edward is, initially, the play's locus of authority, his favour is sought – indirectly by the 'upstart' Spenser and directly by the 'base' born Gaveston – as a means to advancement. Spenser seeks Gaveston's love because he 'hath the favour of [the] king' and may thus 'with one word advance us' (2.1.7–8). Gaveston in turn attempts to secure his place in the King's 'bosom' in order that he might forgo having to 'stoop' and 'bow' (1.1.14, 18–19) to those more mighty than himself. Yet Edward's love not only confers authority on these subordinate males, but also imparts power to the Queen. That Isabella's political strength derives from her proximity to Edward means, as Anderson suggests, that 'Edward's action of disavowing Isabella robs her of her influence'.[7] While it has been claimed that the 'Queen's rejection mirrors that of other factions within the state' (Bartels, p. 163), there is a crucial difference between Isabella and, for instance, the barons. Although, like these men, the Queen is of high social standing, unlike them she is a woman in a patriarchal structure. Accordingly, while her social position gives her a degree of ascendancy, her gender marks her out as a second-class citizen. Thus, losing Edward's love – and thereby involuntarily relinquishing his endorsement of her sovereignty – Isabella's sway is significantly diminished. Consequently, she clings to her position as mother of the prince, a role which partly reaffirms her social status. Nevertheless, without Edward's favour, she is primarily a woman adrift in a world geared towards protecting the interests of men.

To see that Isabella's desires are directly connected to the operations of the play's social and political structures enables us to recognise that her pursuit of love, first from Edward and, failing that, from Mortimer, is not a mere symptom of a needy disposition. Rather, it is an index of the pragmatic grasp of statecraft which allows Isabella to recognise the far-reaching consequences of losing the protection afforded her by the love of a high-ranking male. When we first meet Isabella, moving 'fast' across the stage and claiming '[t]o live in grief and . . . discontent;/ . . . now . . . the King regards me not' (1.2.48–9), her personal 'grief' is best understood in the context of political 'discontent'. It is, after all, the fear of being banished which haunts her, surfacing to punctuate her subsequent speeches like a refrain, reminding us that her emotional instability is the result of political flux. Without Edward's 'regard' she is, she knows, less likely to be perceived as the wife of the King than as a forlorn woman who stands to be 'banished' to the peripheries of power.

Just as Edward's love affords Isabella protection, so Edward's affection allows Gaveston – albeit temporarily – to surmount the obstacle posed by his position as a male of low social standing in a society highly conscious of rank. As the barons are constantly reminding Gaveston, he is 'hardly. . . a gentleman by birth' (1.4.29). In the hierarchical world of *Edward II*, Gaveston, like Isabella, bears the stigma of a foreignness which goes beyond that of being a French subject in an English court. Within this society, in which Isabella is of the right rank to command deference but of the wrong gender, Gaveston has the advantage of being male, but is simultaneously disadvantaged by his subordinate social position. Similarly compromised – for either to assume authority in their own right would be to transgress the laws governing the social hierarchy – Gaveston and Isabella thus share an equally pressing need for Edward's love. His favour can absolve them of their 'otherness', devolving power onto two otherwise powerless subjects by allowing them to 'command' (1.1.169) in the King's name. Thus when – by dint of circumstances in Gaveston's case and by his own volition in Isabella's – Edward withdraws his favour, Gaveston and Isabella stand alike to be subjected to the commands of the barons. Comprising a male group whose ancestry derives 'from . . . heraldry' (2.2.244), the barons constitute this society's privileged, and therefore dominant, elite. Consequently, to avoid being subjugated by the barons, Gaveston and Isabella must both strive ceaselessly to secure Edward's love.

In the fourth scene of Act One, we witness Isabella drawing Mortimer aside from the barons to plead in dumb-show for the revoking of Gaveston's banishment, a task which has been set her by Edward on the condition that, should she succeed, she will regain his love. Initially, Mortimer appears intractable. Nevertheless, after whispering in dumb-show with Isabella, he returns to the barons and suggests, as Isabella has requested, that Gaveston be brought back from France – albeit with the aim of having him killed. The Queen's physical separation at this point from the barons might be seen simply as a succinct dramatic metaphor for the actual relations between the sexes in later sixteenth-century society. Thus, for Shepherd, Isabella seems to be presented here as a peripheral figure, her silence when the men enter and her insistence on speaking in dumb-show with Mortimer indicative of her inability to figure herself in the public terms that patriarchy reserves for men. Stepping automatically into a private sphere in which her words carry neither to the barons in the centre of the stage nor to the audience in the auditorium, Isabella's language in this scene might indeed be read as 'private and non-functional' (Shepherd, p. 191). Yet, if Gaveston seeks to win Edward's affections by actually staging shows, Isabella here too assumes a role in so far as she puts on an act as a strategy through which to secure the love and related protection of a male patron.

Mortimer, stepping back out of the space in which Isabella has placed herself and into the arena where the barons are located, remarks that, prior to his interchange with Isabella, the idea of murdering Gaveston was one which the men had 'not thought upon' (1.4.275). Mortimer's comment here implies, as Claude Summers notes, that the plot to murder Gaveston stems from Isabella. Yet Summers' assumption that the Queen is a 'subtle schemer'[8] who, having been rejected by a man, is caught up in a passionate turmoil that prompts her to behave maliciously is surely questionable. Isabella's subtlety here is as characteristic of what Jonathan Dollimore calls the 'theatricality [and] dissimulation . . . essential for the practice of *realpolitik*'[9] as it is of the cliché of the 'woman scorned'. Isabella figures in this interchange not as a character operating according to the lineaments of the latter stereotype, but rather as a woman acting out a part designed to consolidate her political position. While the dramaturgy might indeed suggest a world of naturally separate and gendered spheres, Marlowe complicates the model by having Isabella resist it from within.

Stage-managing the space, Isabella constructs a peripheral arena within the collective domain. In this way she figures herself as marginal. Stepping aside from the male group and affecting a posture at once self-abnegating and deferential, she assumes the position which a male-dominated society deems appropriate to women. By so doing, the Queen is able to do what the men least expect – subversively to reinscribe herself within the dominant group. Dextrously manipulating the perception of women as naturally self-effacing, Isabella causes Mortimer to embrace her own plan of action without appearing to intervene in the male realm where policies are promoted and decisions are made. Making a bid for centrality while appearing to affirm her own marginality, she is thus able to participate in the barons' power play – prompting them to believe that their chosen course of action has not in effect been chosen for them. As Jean Howard suggests in a discussion of *As You Like It*, this type of 'self-conscious staging' presents women 'act[ing] out the parts scripted for [them] by [their] culture . . . and shows a woman manipulating those [parts] in her own interest'.[10]

Certainly, Isabella acts in this sequence to further her own interests rather than advance those of either Edward or the barons. Ostensibly, she acts on behalf of Edward and Mortimer. Effecting the annulment of Gaveston's banishment, Isabella gratifies Edward's desires. Equally, by mooting the murder of Gaveston, she gratifies

Mortimer's. Yet at the same time, the strategy of ingratiating herself with both Edward and Mortimer enables Isabella to act on her own behalf. At once successfully revoking the decree which has caused the banishment of Gaveston and setting up Gaveston's murder, for which Mortimer, and not she, will take any blame, Isabella strikes out the obstacle blocking her path to Edward's favour. But, should Edward fail in his promise to reinstate her in his affections, her proposal that Gaveston be murdered ingratiates her with Mortimer, and thereby paves the way for his future favour. Showing Isabella maximising her chances of securing Mortimer's favour by engendering a moment of intimacy between them, Marlowe once again uses the stage space to full effect.

The dumb-show dialogue between Isabella and Mortimer not only establishes a bond which will open the way for her adulterous liaison with him, but also echoes the moment of suit in the male client–patron relationship. Like Bosola – the marginalised malcontent of Webster's *The Duchess of Malfi* who sues for patronage to the Aragonese brothers in the midst of a communal space – Isabella appeals to Mortimer in a space sectioned off from, but located within, the public domain. It might, therefore, be argued that during this sequence Isabella manipulates the codes governing not only the relations between the sexes, but also between the client and patron in a patronage structure.[11] Isabella's manoeuvring signifies to Mortimer that as a woman she is malleable but, equally, that as a courtier she is willing to do his bidding. Mortimer duly reciprocates by favouring Isabella at once sexually and politically, protecting her as a lover and promoting her as a patron would a client whose usefulness renders them worthy of advancement.

Isabella's recognition that 'love' is inseparable from politics is in marked contrast to Edward's niece whose naïveté reduces her to a pawn in her uncle's policy for advancing Gaveston. Conversely, Isabella, adopting the guise of a loving wife suing for the annulment of the decree that has banished her husband's minion, renders Edward and Gaveston alike pawns in her own project for self advancement. The dumb-show scene demonstrates Isabella's tactic of acquiring control by affecting the posture, uncritically accepted by Edward's niece, of acquiescing to men in return for their 'entire love' (2.1.62). That said, in the fourth scene of Act Four, Isabella presumes to relinquish that posture. Instead of waiting for Mortimer to speak on her behalf, Isabella appropriates the male prerogative of

public speaking by addressing a crowd in her own right. Consequently, she no longer appears deferential and dependent, but seems
rather to be aggressively set on usurping male space. Mortimer
immediately responds to Isabella's assertive speech – retorting 'Nay,
madam, if you be a warrior,/ You must not grow so passionate in
speeches' (4.4.15–16) – by pressing her back into the role of the
'passionate' woman. Constructing Isabella as incapable of assuming
control because too brimming with feelings to do so, Mortimer
figures Isabella as intemperate, unreasonable, and, consequently, ill
equipped to command in the manner of a man. Mortimer's sexist
figuration of 'woman' has often been read as a reflection of
Marlowe's own attitude. Yet if Mortimer's retort marks the beginning of his brutal suppression of Isabella, it does not in fact signal
the end of her political progress. Tellingly, of the three central
characters who 'overreach' the positions allotted them in this society
– Gaveston, Mortimer, and Isabella – it is Isabella who is the last to
survive.

Isabella continues into the play's concluding moments to play the
parts that in this society men deem appropriate to women. So
convincing is she in her final role as a blameless mother appealing to
her son for protection that, even as the young Edward commands
that Isabella be taken to the tower, his command collapses into a
plea that she be removed before pity cause him to revoke his edict:
'Away with her! Her words enforce these tears,/ And I shall pity her,
if she speak again' (5.6.85–6). Although the child King's utterance
should confirm the absolute authority of male control, it admits to a
sympathy which in turn undermines it. Qualified in the very
moment of delivery, the royal command loses its status as an absolute
decree. Having said that he will show his mother no pity, Isabella's
son promptly admits to pitying her. In light of these contradictions,
Marlowe leaves open the possibility that Isabella may yet escape
death. Although banished to the tower, she is not, like Mortimer and
Gaveston, necessarily beheaded. For a character who has been
described as 'figuratively speaking . . . lack[ing] a head of her
own',[12] Isabella thus proves impressively capable of consolidating
her position in a society hostile to female power.

Like Isabella, Dido tends to be read as a woman for whom 'the
emotional life is everything' (Steane, p. 38). All too often, Dido
appears to critics to be the 'ticing dame' (4.3.31) that Achates
perceives her to be, a woman whose sole purpose is to draw Aeneas

into an emotional world at odds with the serious business of founding a new Trojan empire. The Dido of this approach is a woman who dies for love because unable to comprehend, and therefore accommodate herself to, the male preoccupation with issues of government and of policy. Unsurprisingly, perhaps, Dido's perceived lack of statecraft tends, like Isabella's, to be traced to her gender. Yet if Dido strives to be loved, there is nonetheless in this play, as in *Edward II*, a clear political logic to her desires.

Emily Bartels has pointed out that, having acquired dominion by persuading the men of Africa, figured in the person of Iarbas, to 'divide' their 'laws and land' (4.2.14) with her, Dido's powerful position is precarious. Hence, if Dido 'speaks in terms of desire and marriage . . . her need for Aeneas is [nevertheless] as political as is his for her. To embrace him as husband is a way of signalling and confirming her royal rights, autonomy and control' (Bartels, p. 46). Thus Dido's preoccupation with love can be partly understood as a quest to validate her sovereignty. The royal suitors whose portraits line Dido's gallery walls are displayed as 'signs and subjects of [Dido's] dominance' (Bartels, p. 47). Furthermore, in the fourth scene of Act Four, Aeneas is figured as a spectacle by means of which Dido displays her might. Led forth to be 'gazed' on while Dido plans to observe from a turret above, Aeneas is here scripted into a tableau stage managed by Dido to afford her a superior vantage point from which to 'command' him and her subjects alike. That Dido appears to those ranked beneath her as 'goddess of all' (4.4.77) she surveys suits her strategic purpose – her project being to use the stranger Aeneas 'to obscure the fact that she is herself a stranger [and] the ground is not naturally hers' (Bartels, p. 50).

By focusing attention on Dido's tactics for securing her supremacy, Bartels' reading reminds us of what the Queen shares with Tamburlaine. Where Dido reduces men to 'sights of power',[13] Tamburlaine appropriates women at once as signs of his magnanimity and of his projected invincibility. In *Tamburlaine Part II*, for example, Tamburlaine forces the Turkish concubines to submit to his soldiers' lust. The Turkish women's misery is thus made into a mark of Tamburlaine's benevolence, figuring his willingness to share with his male subjects the spoils of war. Similarly, in *Tamburlaine Part I*, the Virgins of Damascus are reduced by Tamburlaine to signs in a system designed to represent his conquest of Damascus as justly enacted according to a providential schema. The colour code which Tamburlaine deploys in his siege of Damascus corresponds, as Malcolm Kelsall notes, with the tripartite colour scheme which, in the sixth chapter of Revelation, prefigures the 'day of God's wrath when no king can stand'.[14] By such symbolism, Tamburlaine presents himself as a deity and the Virgins as mortal man opposing his divine decree. The death of the Virgins – 'hoisted' (5.2.68) up on his horsemen's lances and 'symbolically violated'[15] – thus serves, like the rape of the Turkish concubines, to magnify Tamburlaine's might and to make him appear immortal.

It is, of course, Zenocrate who is most systematically produced as a 'mirror . . . in which [Tamburlaine's] self-image is reflected'.[16] Tamburlaine's panegyric to Zenocrate – in which he figures her as 'Fairer than whitest snow' (1.2.89) – aestheticises his bride-to-be. Controlling her by 'situating her in an environment of frosty inaccessibility', his speech, as Mark Thornton Burnett suggests, is an 'act of appropriation or colonization' in which, by fashioning Zenocrate as the object of his own and of his subjects' gaze, 'Tamburlaine mark[s] out the extent of his empire'.[17] Just as Dido seeks to consolidate her hold over Carthage by producing a controlled representation of Aeneas, so Tamburlaine marks out his empire by aestheticising Zenocrate. Indeed, where, as we have seen, the portraits of Dido's suitors function as signs of her dominance, the 'picture' (*Part II*: 3.2.25) that Tamburlaine erects of Zenocrate after her death likewise signifies his might. Resurrecting his beloved by recreating her image and embalming her body, Tamburlaine proposes to cheat death by constructing Zenocrate as immortal and thereby further enhancing his own godlike image.

The regularity with which women are reduced to signs in Tamburlaine's rhetoric of mastery has meant that the *Tamburlaine* plays have often been categorised as misogynist. Dido's comparable strategies should, however, at least alert us to the dangers of ascribing Tamburlaine's uncomplicated sexism to Marlowe. To be sure, there are temptations to read the plays as simply endorsing patriarchal perceptions of women. If Dido uses Aeneas to validate her empire, Aeneas too uses Dido to further his imperial project, rejuvenating himself in Carthage prior to embarking on his mission to found a new Troy. Moreover, Zenocrate, unlike Dido, makes no move to resist her beloved's attempts to reduce her to a sign signifying his supremacy. As the *Tamburlaine* plays progress, Zenocrate becomes increasingly silent, her muteness being indicative,

according to Harry Levin, of her growing 'weakness'[18] in the face
of Tamburlaine's authority. Whilst the wife's silence was occasionally posited as a sign of recalcitrance – as, for example, in William
Gouge's *Of Domesticall Duties* (1622) – to claim Zenocrate's muteness
as resistance to, rather than acceptance of, Tamburlaine's rule
would be to read against the grain of these dramas. Ultimately, as
*Tamburlaine Part II*'s concluding juxtaposition of Zenocrate's hearse
with Tamburlaine's chariot suggests, Zenocrate is rendered passive,
encased, and encoded within meanings made for her, and fashioned
out of her, by Tamburlaine, the active and assertive male. Furthermore, just as Zenocrate is subjugated by Tamburlaine, Aeneas uses
Dido to consolidate his position as surely as Mortimer uses Isabella
to secure his. Both Mortimer and Aeneas are indebted to women
for enabling them to further their ambitions, Mortimer to Isabella
for the leverage afforded him by the protectorship of her son, and
Aeneas to Dido for succouring him in his hour of need. Yet both
deny they owe anything to, and thus are potentially in the power
of, women. As Bartels points out, by 'reducing Dido's gestures to
"female drudgery"', Aeneas 'depoliticiz[es] her desires [and
thereby] places himself beyond obligation' (Bartels, p. 43). Likewise
Mortimer's reading of Isabella as 'passionate' censors out the
possibility that she might have aided him by advancing his own
schemes.

For all the apparent compulsion of such evidence for the prosecution, Marlowe seems nevertheless concerned at crucial points in the
plays to complicate any simple reduction of women to positions of
servility. Dido's death by fire may appear to suggest a destructive
desire which subsumes reason, and the addition of the suicides of
Anna and Iarbas, who follow Dido into the fire, to hint at the
grotesque comedy of the closing scenes of the *Jew*. However, Bartels'
suggestion that the proximity of Anna's and Iarbas' suicides to
Dido's serves to contrast the 'comic senselessness' of their deaths
with Dido's 'gesture of power' (Bartels, p. 51) provides a persuasive
counter to such contentions.

However we read Dido's death, Zenocrate's finds her, as we have
seen, unambiguously subsumed in her husband's grand scheme. Yet
in *Tamburlaine Part II*, the Tamberlaine–Zenocrate relationship is
significantly paralleled and finally qualified by Marlowe's dramatisation of Theridamas' interaction with Olympia. Unlike Zenocrate in
her relations with Tamburlaine, Olympia denies Theridamas the

privilege of monopolising language. Thus she prevents him from securing access to a medium central to defining woman as the subject who submits before male authority. Refusing to be reduced to the type of the silent woman, and colonised by Theridamas in the manner that Tamburlaine marks out the extent of his empire by means of his aestheticisation of Zenocrate, Olympia appropriates the male prerogative of deploying 'working words' (*Part I*: 2.3.25). Hastily capitalising on the opportunity to turn the tables on a male tormentor who has failed to take into account that women too might have the capacity to mobilise language and thereby take charge of a situation, Olympia sets about convincing Theridamas that she possesses a magical ointment which makes hers a 'charmed skin' (1.2.179). Having persuaded her captor that because of this ointment her skin is capable of resisting any assault made upon it, Olympia tricks Theridamas into stabbing her – a desperate strategy which does, however, liberate her from captivity and imminent rape. Departing from his source for this episode, Ariosto's *Orlando Furioso*, Marlowe tellingly has his beleaguered woman anoint her throat rather than her 'neck and brests, and shoulders'.[19] Thus Marlowe directs his audience's attention towards Olympia's organs of speech. In so doing, he adds a fresh dimension to an inherited plot in which events resolve themselves in the manner desired by the woman rather than that anticipated by the man. What is stressed here is female language and particularly its efficacy. Like Isabella, to whom Edward proffers the gift of a 'golden tongue' (1.4.330) and who claims, in the fourth scene of Act One, neither to speak for men nor to have them speak for her, Olympia too reclaims the right to speak and hence to represent herself. If the capacity to intervene verbally and represent oneself is denied Zenocrate in the main plot, it is, therefore, grasped by Olympia in the subplot. The subplot consequently allows for an alternative figuration of woman to that projected by Tamburlaine.

Of course, Olympia seeks a release from male power only in order that she may remain a chaste and faithful wife – taking charge of her life solely that she might relinquish her hold on it. Moreover, the extremity of her method of finding a way out of the predicament in which Theridamas has placed her raises questions about whether she is in fact released from, or is rather effaced by, male power. Even so, Olympia demonstrates an ability to comprehend the operations of power and to intervene accordingly. The capacity for intervention differentiates Olympia, as it does Isabella and Dido, from Zenocrate, Edward's niece and, indeed, from Abigail – the naïve and trusting daughter of the Jew of Malta. Unlike Isabella, who claims that it is 'for myself I speak, and not for him' (1.4.221), Abigail's first words are '[n]ot for myself, but . . . / Father, for thee' (1.2.233–4). Professing to understand the 'difference of things', Abigail sees power operating only where there is lack of 'piety' (3.3.68, 54). Consequently, she fails to account for the gendering of power, accepting it to be the order of things. That this order is both produced and sustained by specific cultural discourses escapes her and, although she 'tries to write her own story',[20] her intervention takes the form of a confession occasioned by guilt at relinquishing the daughterly duties which she associates with filial love. Failing to comprehend that 'love' is informed by a power relation, Abigail is duped, as is Edward's niece, by a male authority figure. Murdered by Barabas who believes she has put his fatherly authority in jeopardy, Abigail dies in a scene often read, like Dido's death scene, as comic and thus complicit in the cynicism expressed about women by the male characters in the play. But both the deceit practised upon Edward's niece and the scene of Abigail's death work to reveal the oppressiveness of a system in which, if women misunderstand the operations of power, they are either marginalised or eliminated. As such, Abigail's death serves to illuminate, as much as to perpetuate, the workings of patriarchy.

If Marlowe's women are all immersed in cultural and political mechanisms which function to sustain male power, then the playwright also seems determined to elaborate on the particularities of women's encounters with sexist social structures. Differentiating between women – some of whom seek subversively to reinscribe themselves within patriarchy while others acquiesce to it, or simply misunderstand it and suffer accordingly – Marlowe does more than reduce women to apolitical vessels of feeling who are nothing but adjuncts of his male characters. If we dispense with the notion that the plays are necessarily informed by binary divisions between male and female spheres and gender roles, we can recognise the extent to which Marlowe's women share with his men a motivation that is as much political as emotional. While important differences nevertheless remain between Marlowe's male and female characters, such differences are finally related to questions of motivation. Where Marlowe's men tend to seek power for the purpose of determining the destinies of others, those of Marlowe's women who pursue power more often do so in order that they may determine their own destinies. Amongst Marlowe's women, the quest for power is more a quest for self-determination than for the self-aggrandisement that so often characterises the political aspirations of his male characters. Hence not all women are presented as either morally repelled by, or unable to comprehend the operations of, politics. On the contrary, Marlowe allows many of his female characters to intervene in, and offer resistance to, the male-orientated social structures which govern the worlds of his plays.

# CHAPTER 12

# 'Edward II', Derek Jarman, and the state of England[1]

## Lawrence Normand

The title of Derek Jarman's book *Queer Edward II* indicates his intention in his film *Edward II*: to represent being queer, that is to have a certain sexuality and consequent political stance in Britain in the 1980s and 1990s. On the other hand, Jarman seemed to ignore politics when he declared that he 'chose this play solely for its subject' 'a gay love affair' (Jarman, p. 26, Preface), a characterisation of Marlowe's play that foregrounds a twentieth-century notion of a same-sex relationship. It looks as though Marlowe's play was just a pretext for Jarman to make a film that is really about being queer in 1991. The name 'Marlowe' carried enough cultural authority to help him find money to make the film: 'can you imagine an original script on "Edward II" finding funds?', Jarman asked; and went on, '[h]ow to make a film of a gay love affair and get it commissioned. Find a dusty old play and violate it' (Jarman, p. 110, Preface). In some ways that is what he does: he cuts and changes the text of Marlowe's *Edward II*, and gives it a modern setting. But Jarman's remarks are misleading if they suggest that he was indifferent to the qualities of this Renaissance play. He turned to the English Renaissance in *The Tempest* (1979) and *The Angelic Conversation* (1985) for material that advanced his project of producing images of England's history that speak to the present. Jarman's response to *Edward II* was to produce a film that is as scrupulous in its sexual politics as Marlowe's play, though their relations to historical circumstances are necessarily different. Jarman's statement, 'Marlowe outs the past – why don't we out the present?' (Jarman, Preface), is accurate if it means that Marlowe's dramatisation of homoerotic love is honest and critical: and it is the starting point of this essay which shows that configurations of same-sex desire are historically relative, and implicated in a field of complex social and political forces.

I

When Lear's Fool wants the King to attend to reality he tells him,
'He's mad that trusts in the tameness of a wolf, a horse's health, a
boy's love, or a whore's oath'.[2] Here 'a boy's love' is unremarkable,
merely another commonplace. In *Twelfth Night* similarly it is a cause
of no specific comment that Antonio should be in love with
Sebastian, and express that love in direct and passionate terms.
There are enough other examples of male homoerotic relationships
represented on the Elizabethan and Jacobean stage – for example
Jove and Ganymede, Orlando and 'Ganymede', Achilles and Patroclus, Coriolanus and Aufidius – to suggest that audiences could
watch at least some homoerotic relationships with comparative ease
and comprehension.[3] Stephen Orgel suggests that one reason for
lack of anxiety about homoeroticism was that in the Renaissance 'it
was precisely the world of public discourse that was the space of
homoerotic relationships', and so the 'love between men was open
and public', though with the effect that it was not possible to tell
from this language of love the sexual content of any relationship for
'it is a language that implies everything and nothing'.[4] One difference between the late sixteenth and early seventeenth centuries and
the twentieth century is that in the earlier period male homoeroticism was given expression in different social forms and discourses:
homoeroticism in each period was subjected to a different range of
tolerances and oppressions. The habit of twentieth-century readers,
acquired from the general cultural repression of homoeroticism, to
search out coded signs of hidden passion, is consequently inappropriate as an interpretative tactic with Renaissance texts that
make no secret of homoeroticism. But that merely shifts the
challenge of reading from deciphering hidden signs to making sense
of what is on the surface. The differences between the early modern
and the modern in their representation of homoeroticism are
ultimately social and political.

But if male same-sex passion was represented on the stage, what
then of that other early modern concept of sodomy that not only
signified one of the worst imaginable forms of evil but was also the
subject of legal prohibition? This crime is aligned, in the writings of
moralists, satirists and legal writers, with everything that is negative
and destructive. In *Basilicon Doron* in 1598, James VI put it alongside
'Witch-craft, wilfull murther, Incest . . . poisoning, and false coine'

as a crime that a monarch should not tolerate.[5] Alan Bray suggests that the apparent incompatibility between homoeroticism and sodomy in sixteenth-century English culture is explained by the fact that the concept of sodomy was not attached to most sexual or emotional relationships between men.[6] A gulf existed in people's minds between sodomy and actual homoerotic relationships they might be involved in or aware of. Legal records show that prosecutions for sodomy were rare. Homoerotic attachments among men and boys were generally taken to be part of the normal social scene, and so hardly worth commenting on, as the Fool's comment on boys' love suggests. Far from intense male–male attachments incurring disapproval or reprobation, they were an integral part of patriarchal social structures; but only when they were formally recognisable as friendship: an arrangement in which emotional closeness guaranteed financial and social support.

However, unproblematical representations of male–male attachments in the Renaissance must be balanced against Bray's identification of social relations which prompted anxiety. Bray argues that the signs of sixteenth-century friendship could easily be read by contemporaries (and by us) as either friendship or sodomy: kissing and embracing, bestowing patronage, sharing a bed, speaking the language of love, entering into bonds of mutual support. Such ambiguity could be a source of cultural anxiety, for between friendship and sodomy, though absolutely different conceptually, there was in practice no clearly signifiable difference. Bray urges us to recognise in Marlowe's play the discourse of male friendship: 'friend', along with 'minion', are terms that sound in the play to name the central relationship. Edward's patronage of Gaveston, and his embraces, are signs of strong feeling, but do not in themselves prove that the relationship is sexual. Sixteenth-century 'friendship', in which physical intimacy and emotional expressiveness were acceptable and not regarded as sexual, may describe much of Edward's and Gaveston's behaviour, but not all. The conventional signs of friendship in the play seem to be exceeded and to point to something else: 'Marlowe describes in this play what could be a sodomitical relationship, but he places it wholly within the incompatible conventions of Elizabethan friendship, in a tension which he never allows to be resolved' (Bray, 'Homosexuality and the signs', 10). The play's power, Bray argues, comes from its tapping growing anxieties in the 1590s as the signs of friendship came to be readable as sodomy,

which was not just forbidden sex but sex that signified the breaking
of class barriers as lower-class men found favour with their superiors
through the conventions of increasingly suspect 'friendship'. This
anxiety about defining intense male relationships is ultimately
political, as lower-class men were increasingly able to become the
intimate dependants of their betters (Bray, 'Homosexuality and the
signs', 10–13). The language of sodomy could be used to denigrate a
relationship that prompted social disapproval by crossing class
boundaries, and such language thus acquired its own political force.
Marlowe is aware of these political effects, and dramatises material
conflicts partly through conflicting definitions of the King's relationship with Gaveston.

Male homoeroticism in early modern England is not represented
as one thing: it is a constellation of behaviour, feeling, social relationships, and language that is figured differently across a range of
discourses that shape its meaning and value. The notion of 'homosexual' certainly does not help in understanding Marlowe's play, for
neither the word nor the concept existed in 1592. There is no early
modern category of homosexuality: same-sex desire may appear in a
range of relationships such as friendship, patronage, master–pupil
relations, and sodomy. So we may be looking for something which
we believe in (homosexuality) but which did not exist then as that
concept. A historical understanding of same-sex desire requires us to
dissolve the category of homosexuality, and describe same-sex
feelings in the terms in which they were then understood. We have
to perform not a suspension of disbelief concerning what they
believed, but a suspension of belief concerning what we believe.

II

Jarman's film, on the other hand, is fully sexualised. It demonstrates
the Foucauldian dictum that in the modern world the truth of the
subject's sexuality is an effect of power. Gaveston reads Edward's
letter while two sailors are having sex, and when he first meets
Edward on his return from exile their kiss on the lips is sexual.
Power and sex are more obviously entwined than in Marlowe: the
Bishop of Winchester is humiliated by being stripped and forced by
Gaveston into mock fellatio. Edward's neglect of Isabella appears as
his not responding to her kiss. Mortimer, the epitome of a violent
masculinity, is seen having masochistic sex with two Wild Girls.

Gaveston wins momentary power over Isabella by teasingly trying to kiss, then mocking her. Edward's ferocious stabbing of the policeman who killed Gaveston comes after he tenderly combs his hair. Isabella's cruelty is signalled by her vampirish killing of Kent. [In these incidents and imagery sex is entwined with power, and power is realised through sex.] And there is no ground which defines the natural or the authentic: power is realised as the satisfaction of sexual desire, sexual desire as the effect of the play of power, and sex as the means to power. Isabella and Mortimer come to desire each other as the advantage of their political co-operation becomes clear; and the fulfilment of their political desires appears as their both sitting on the throne bubbling with sexual intimacy – repeating the image of Gaveston and Edward sharing the throne at the start.

Marlowe's play also dramatises the power–sex interplay, and reading it through the film highlights that. But Jarman is specifically modern in producing a film that centres on sexual politics. Kate Chedgzoy identifies the complexity of Jarman's ideology in which a 'post-modern aesthetic combines with a passionate commitment to radical sexual politics and an equally deeply-felt love of the English cultural past'.[7] I would like to pursue some of the implications of this. The film's postmodernity is evident in the eighty or so short scenes using minimal Marlovian dialogue; the formal, painterly composition in the film frame; and the mixing of contemporary and historical references.[8] The film's historical framings slip easily from modern to Renaissance to medieval, and this fluidity provokes the viewer into seeing aspects of these historical moments in each other. Unlike researchers of sexuality who generally insist on its historical relativity, Jarman's 'commitment to radical gay politics', which is founded on a sense of 'a shared sexual identity',[9] combines with his ambition of 'reclaiming . . . the Queer Past'[10] to produce a film that insists on the historical continuity of gay oppression and the trans-historicity of gay sexuality. The screenplay reshapes the play, but improvised fragments of dialogue, and the highlighting of other lines, make the contemporary and fictional historical scenes inter-penetrate. Transforming the Poor Men into sailors having sex on a bed in the same room as Gaveston and Spenser makes explicit the gay subculture shared by these young men. Gaveston's line, 'there are hospitals for such as you' (1.1.35), which in the play sneers at the men's poverty, is translated into a sexual sneer associating homo-sexuality with AIDS. Jarman, like Marlowe, characterises Gaveston as contemptuous of others, and Jarman is unconstrained in showing Gaveston's, as well as Isabella's behaviour, as cruel or repellent in ways that might seem anti-gay or mysogynist. Jarman's 1990s' sexual context transforms non-sexual or ambiguous lines from the play into sexual ones in the film, such as Lancaster's, 'arm in arm, the king and he doth march' (1.2.20). The purpose of this radical transforming of the play into the contemporary is, as Chedgzoy suggests, political. The homophobia of the Conservative government found legal expression in 1988 in the passing of Section 28 of the Local Government Act which threatened local authorities with prosecution for actions that 'promoted' homosexuality. For many younger lesbians and gay men it was the first time they had faced a threat from the state against their ways of life, and for many older men like Jarman it was the return of the state oppression that prevailed before the 1967 Sexual Offences Act partially decriminalised male homosexuality. The Conservative government's intention to restrict and stigmatise homosexuality by legal action was Jarman's evidence that English state power had depended since at least the time of Edward II on the repression of homosexuality. This political thesis underpins the film's aesthetic that combines a Renaissance play with the contemporary sexual political scene. As Colin MacCabe writes, '[f]rom the moment that Mortimer appears with the dress and bearing of an SAS officer in Northern Ireland, the equations between past and present, between state and sexuality, are clearly visible on the screen'.[11]

Jarman's sexual politics can be clearly differentiated from Marlowe's. First, Jarman produces a history based on gay identity. The film shows contemporary history in rollups and Walkmans, OutRage! and protests against state-sponsored homophobia; but it also connects with Marlowe and the 1590s; and beyond that to the 1310s and 20s when Edward was King. So a gay history is produced, or rather a gay myth, of English ruling-class power being founded on the repression of homosexuality. From the point of view of the dominant class, to allow homosexuality to become fused with power is to risk undoing the ideological structure that is used to capture and hold power. As Gregory Bredbeck has shown, that discursive structure, defined in the early modern period as sodomy, represents same-sex desire as the very epitome of disorder, subversion, and rebellion, and therefore the very thing that has to be repressed for order to emerge. If homosexuality did not exist it would be necessary for the ruling class to invent it in order to have something sufficiently threatening to justify its political repression. By giving the play a modern context Jarman turns Marlowe's aristocracy into the bourgeoisie as the dominant class. Marlowe's barons disappear and only Mortimer remains as the military leader of a bourgeois nexus; he is an SAS officer, and following him are churchmen, police, and civilians who look like a Conservative constituency association. The banishment which Edward is forced to sign is written on House of Commons notepaper dated 1991. The sexual relationship between Edward and Gaveston appears contemporary too: they are about the same age, and have a relationship of equality. The word 'minion' almost disappears from Jarman's script and along with it the quite different ways of seeing a homoerotic relationship between men that Marlowe offers us, including Marlowe's construction of a powerful king and his dependent sexual partner. For Jarman sexuality is the basis for personal identity and a radical politics that contests established power structures. The riot scene is between straights and queers, with Edward shouting, 'March with me my friends', to a crowd of lesbians and gay men from OutRage! in a scene which, Jarman wrote, should resemble 'the Poll Tax riot'. Spenser joins Edward on Gaveston's recommendation as 'one of us' (a Thatcher phrase ironically reversed), and Lightborn spares the King when he falls in love with him. The power struggle is between groups defined by their sexuality. Figures not defined by this binary are either torn between both sides like Kent, or, like the young Prince Edward, forced to construct an identity within it.

### III

If Marlowe did not have the notion of sexual identity to work with, in what sense can one talk about sexual desire in Marlowe's play? Is sex, as Bray suggests, only ambiguously there? Marlowe does give us signs of sex between men, but they are always used for ulterior, selfish, political motives. Isabella's designating Gaveston as 'Ganymede' encodes sexual meanings, but in a self-justifying scenario with herself as wronged Juno: 'For never doted Jove on Ganymede/ So much as he on cursed Gaveston' (1.4.181–2). Sexual pleasures are projected in Gaveston's imagined masques; and the boy acting Diana hides 'those parts which men delight to see', genitals ambiguously sexed. When Gaveston imagines embracing Edward, 'upon whose bosom let me die', the embrace will last till he dies, or has an orgasm. Gaveston imagines deploying his sexual attractiveness to the king as a political and financial resource. Mortimer speaks sex metaphorically when he tells Edward that his gifts to Gaveston 'have drawn thy treasure dry/ And made thee weak' (2.2.158),[12] conflating inappropriate financial generosity and sexual depletion.[13] But these specific, if indirect, sexual references do not exhaust the ways in which desire can be written in the play.

In Marlowe's play sex is always political, and it engages with contemporary social and political concerns of the 1590s in ways that are similar to Jarman's engagement with the 1990s.[14] Claude Summers has argued that the 'radicalism of *Edward II* resides in the play's intersection of sex and politics and in Marlowe's refusal to moralize either'.[15] Jarman, by contrast, moralises both. Bredbeck argues, more radically, that the 'rhetoric of homoerotic passion, which in other tales marks the place where politic concerns end and temporal ones begin, is, in this play, a *part* of the politic' (Bredbeck, p. 59). Marlowe repeatedly dramatises the instability and violability of the social order to demonstrate that social and political values are expedient. Warwick ambushes Gaveston as he is being taken by Pembroke and Arundel for a last meeting with Edward and murders him. One of Pembroke's men protests at Warwick's breaking his word, 'Your lordship doth dishonour to yourself,/ And wrong our lord, your honourable friend' (3.1.9–10); and Edward later protests that Gaveston's killing is ''gainst law of arms' (3.3.54). However, it is when Warwick claims that his actions are done in 'my country's cause' (3.1.11) that the radical political implications become clear, for Marlowe is demonstrating that values are routinely and casually subordinate to political advantage. With the possible exception of Edward's final scenes, Marlowe demonstrates this throughout the play, and it is this radical politicisation that suited the play to the thoroughgoing politicisation in contemporary terms that Jarman effected. But while for Jarman the politics of sexual identity were central, for Marlowe sexual desire was an element in another identity, that of the King.

For Marlowe's barons the offence that Gaveston represents is not self-evidently sexual. This is unlike the twentieth century when someone's homosexuality is often seen as the predominant aspect of their identity that overwhelms, and virtually excludes, all others. But for the barons Gaveston is objectionable because his access to favour

means their exclusion, and their anger is expressed in political
terms. Lancaster protests, ' "My lord of Cornwall" now at every
word!/ And happy is the man whom he vouchsafes,/ For vailing of
his bonnet' (1.2.17–19). They detest Gaveston's lower-class origins
(changed from the aristocratic ones of Marlowe's sources): Mortimer
is touchiest on this, calling Gaveston 'villain . . . / That hardly art a
gentleman by birth' (1.4.28–9). Not only did Marlowe choose to
lower Gaveston's social status from the historical Gaveston's, he also
seems to have raised Mortimer from 'Sir Roger Mortimer, a
Marcher Lord and the master of Wigmore'[16] to a noble equal to
Warwick and Lancaster. The old noble class hates lower-class men
who win advancement. Baldock's self-advancement, like Marlowe's
and indeed Jarman's, comes through education. Leicester's hatred is
evident when, arresting the King along with Spenser and Baldock,
he refuses to recognise the latters' noble names: 'Spenser and
Baldock, by no other names,/ I arrest you of high treason here'
(4.6.56–7). Class rather than sexual hatred seems to impel the peers
to persistent, irreconcilable opposition to Edward. In fact, at one
remarkable moment Mortimer Senior actually suggests that the
nobles might tolerate Edward's relationship with Gaveston since it is
of no great political import: 'The mightiest kings have had their
minions;/ Great Alexander lov'd Hephaestion,/ The conquering
Hercules for Hylas wept,/ And for Patroclus stern Achilles droop'd'
(1.4.393–6). Homoeroticism is placed in a classical frame in which it
becomes a familiar kind of passion that expresses royal or heroic
greatness. Mortimer Senior's advice is to let Edward have his lover
since 'riper years will wean him from such toys' (1.4.403), a version of
the familiar 'it's a stage you're going through' argument that
tolerates present homoerotic attachments in the expectation that
there will be a turn to orthodox sexual, and therefore orthodox
social and political, ones in the future. Surprisingly perhaps, Mortimer's first response is to agree with his uncle that the King's
attachment to Gaveston is insignificant, a matter merely of 'his
wanton humour' (1.4.404). But in a brilliant, odious piece of political
rhetoric, he restates his opposition to Gaveston in class terms, that
'one so basely born/ Should by his sovereign's favour grow so pert,/
And riot it with the treasure of the realm' (1.4.405–7); and then goes
on to represent Gaveston in the discourse of the Elizabethan satirist
expressing indignation at the sodomite and his supposed subversion
of social and political norms. Mortimer singles out the signs of

Gaveston's foreign clothes, proud manners, and familiarity with the King: 'Midas-like, he jets it in the court,/ With base outlandish cullions at his heels'; and 'wears a short Italian hooded cloak,/ Larded with pearl, and in his Tuscan cap/ A jewel of more value than the crown'; and 'the king and he/ From out a window laugh at such as we' (1.4.410–11, 415–17, 418–19). The suggestion of pride and wealth exceeding even the crown's goes along with contempt in the phrase 'base outlandish cullions' that combines class, foreignness, and sex ('cullions' can mean testicles). Mortimer's response to his uncle's version of the King's relation with Gaveston as temporary and politically innocuous is to refashion that relation in recognisably sodomitical terms, for this figuration authorises his opposition to Edward. He recognises the necessity for some such authority earlier: 'For, howsoever we have borne it out,/ 'Tis treason to be up against the king' (1.4.282–3).

The barons see Edward's relation with Gaveston as primarily political rather than sexual, and their sexual discourses are deployed only in so far as they serve their political interests. The displacement of patronage from the nobility to the upstart newcomers enrages the barons, whether Edward's motive for that redirection is partly homoerotic in Gaveston's case, or not in Spenser's and Baldock's. Edward's redirected patronage does not first of all signify to the nobles same-sex desire, but rather political disadvantage. Jarman gives the 'mightiest kings' speech to Kent as a direct apologia for his brother, thus deleting the complex political functioning it has in Marlowe as the nobles' testing the best ways to exploit Edward's passion for Gaveston to their advantage.

The complex relation between Edward and Gaveston in Marlowe's play is the subject of a discursive struggle among several competing versions of it that are designed to achieve particular political effects. The play has no one dominant discourse that would account for this complex relation; unlike the twentieth-century discourse of 'homosexuality' that claims precisely that, and with which Jarman engages. Homoerotic desire appears in the play as one strand in discourses that are not simply sexual: namely, sodomy, friendship, and patronage. Marlowe's characters test out different ways of representing the Edward–Gaveston relationship, and the best version for each is the one that is most persuasive in achieving their political ends. Edward, for example, uses the language of friendship in an attempt to legitimate in the eyes of the court a blend of personal love and political favour: 'Thy worth, sweet friend, is far above my gifts:/ Therefore, to equal it, receive my heart.' (1.1.161–2.)

It is a significant instance of the historical relativity of ideas of same-sex desire that for Marlowe the King's passionate attachment to his favourite does not denote a 'homosexuality' that excludes marriage. Edward arranges Gaveston's marriage to Gloucester's niece so that Gaveston can become his kin. For Marlowe there is no gender blurring involved in Gaveston's marrying; same-sex desire is not incompatible with marriage, and does not threaten masculinity. Jarman cut Gaveston's marriage, presumably because it would have confused the 1990s difference of straight/gay that the film maintains. In the play it is assumed that male sexual desire can be directed at either sex, and that Gaveston's marriage has political, not sexual, significance. The marriage denotes friendship, and attempts to combine that with the kinship ties of the royal and noble families. Marlowe shows kinship and friendship to be potentially reconcilable relations, with passionate male friendship inscribed in the midst of these bonds. Jarman accurately depicts the contemporary situation in which homosexuality is commonly seen as a feature of a type of person who is, or should be, excluded from heterosexual relations, and in which homosexuality threatens the masculine–feminine divide: when Jarman's Mortimer kills Spenser he hisses the word 'girlboy' at him.

Homoerotic desire in Marlowe, then, appears – and disappears – in several competing discourses. When Edward is seen lamenting his banished lover in Act One, Lancaster cries '*Diablo*, what passions call you these?' (1.4.321). He has no name for what he sees though his Italian oath hints at devilish sodomy. Edward's account of his friendship with Gaveston takes a Neoplatonic turn when he asks, 'know'st thou not who I am?/ Thy friend, thyself, another Gaveston!' (1.1.142–3). Implicit here is the notion of equality with two men being so mutually involved that they share a common soul and body. But these fragments of Neoplatonic idealism do not persuade the King's enemies, and such idealism is unsustainable as a way of articulating same-sex desire. Patriarchy demands that a king should embody the principle of sovereign power, but by redefining his position in relation to a friendship discourse entailing equality, Edward allows patriarchal political hierarchy to seem disturbed. While Marlowe pursues the implications of this, Jarman is uninterested in Edward's function in patriarchy. In the play Edward's representing himself as friend gives his enemies the chance to justify their rebellion by casting Edward as enemy of the state; for example in Mortimer's typical assertion, 'Your king hath wrong'd your country and himself' (4.5.78). This rejects the interpretation of Edward's choice of favourites as a legitimate reshaping of political relationships within the king's prerogative, and reasserts the nobles' claims on political favour by erecting past practice as a timeless political principle on which the safety of the state depends.

Once Edward yields up his crown Mortimer and Isabella attempt systematically to destroy him. But what connection is there in Marlowe's play between this final sequence of events and Edward's relation with Gaveston? What are his enemies seeking to destroy? Obviously they aim at Edward's body, by holding him in a stinking dungeon, feeding him on bread and water, tormenting him with continual noise, and finally murdering him. More importantly, Edward's status as a king comes under attack; and as it does so the play asks the question that *King Lear* was to ask fifteen or so years later, 'Is it possible to destroy a king?' Edward voices his sense of royal identity repeatedly in the final scenes: he asks 'sweet God of heaven' to let him despise the crown's 'transitory pomp' (5.1.107–8); his final words call on a tender God to help his soul enter heaven when he dies (5.5.111); and he tells Lightborn, 'Know that I am a king' (5.5.91). It is possible to read Edward's final assertion of himself as a king either as an Aristotelian *anagnorisis* in which he discovers royal power and selfhood, or as the last of the series of flimsy self-fashionings that he attempts throughout the play. In the former, Edward represents himself positively as the anointed king suffering martyrdom. In the latter, Edward's Christian heaven is similar to Gaveston's Elysium of pleasure in being one of a sequence of representations of 'a politically impossible, utopian space'[17] that are attempted, prove inadequate and are replaced. This reading can be challenged, however, by seeing Edward's behaviour in the last scenes as qualitatively different from his earlier behaviour, as being self-aware and aware of others. Even though it is belated and limited, Edward's transformation is most evident in his recognising the truth of himself as king. His words carry weight as he refuses obfuscating discourse and asserts this new sense of self and events. When Spenser offers the comforting platitude that when he and the King are separated, 'so will the angry heavens', Edward replies, 'The gentle heavens have not to do in this' (4.6.74, 76). And Edward refutes the nobles' oft-repeated self-serving ideology voiced by Winchester: 'it is for England's good/ And princely Edward's right we crave the crown': Edward replies, 'No, 'tis for Mortimer' (5.1.38–40). Like Faustus, Edward realises the truth of himself and his situation just as he is about to lose his life.

These opposed interpretations of Edward have come to centre on the meaning of Edward's death, and in both Marlowe and Jarman the endings are subject to authorial reshaping of their sources (which for Jarman is Marlowe's play, of course). Ever since William Empson suggested that Marlowe's dramatisation of Edward's death, by thrusting a red-hot poker into the anus, invoked the anal sex that Edward and Gaveston were supposed to have practised, editors, critics, and directors have responded to this idea. Homophobic critics have been happy to see this death as a punishment for presumed sexual acts of which they disapproved. Such a punitive, moralising reading of the protagonist dispels the ironies that are characteristic of Marlowe's other tragedies, and aligns itself with, say, Ferneze's view of Barabas, or the Chorus' of Faustus. In these plays (including the B-text of *Doctor Faustus*) the protagonists' deaths are brought about by acute physical suffering, and that suffering itself offers a problem of interpretation. But other critics sympathetic to King Edward's homoeroticism have also emphasised the sexual meanings of the killing of the King.[18] In these cases it has been interpreted as being so terrible in its extreme, homophobic cruelty that the audience sympathises with the victim, as it does with Barabas. This attempt by Edward's enemies to destroy his body and his royalty, according to this reading, reveals Mortimer and Isabella to be the true destroyers of the social order, and therefore the true sodomites in trying to dissolve the created order of monarch and state. The sodomy that most critics have identified in Marlowe, and that Jarman isn't interested in because he has no concept of sodomy, is faced by Edward alone, and concerns the dissolution of his identity as king. Jarman cuts and disperses the speeches that Marlowe assigns to Edward in the last scenes throughout the film. This avoids what a modern audience is unlikely to find of much concern – the dissolution of the sacred category of king, and the revelation that kingship is not intrinsic to the person, nor affirmed by God, but dependent on power. In Marlowe's play Edward suffers this attempted dissolution not as a homosexual, as in Jarman's film, but as a king. Jarman

includes and displaces what editors and critics have assumed to be
Edward's staged death with a spit (the authority for which comes
from Holinshed), representing it as a nightmare from which Edward
awakes to find Lightborn transformed from murderer to lover.
Jarman places scenes between Edward and Lightborn throughout
the film, making the audience expect Marlowe's violently rendered
death, but then overturns that by confirming instead the film's focus
on the truth and power of sex. It is Lightborn's emergent love for
Edward that makes him switch loyalties from Isabella and Mortimer;
he abandons his promise to Isabella to kill Edward and becomes the
king's lover and political supporter, signalled by a tender kiss.
Jarman's reversing the action of the play invites an active response
from viewers, which might include identifying with a sexual desire
that is so powerful as to subvert state power and establish its own
loyalties: '[w]ith this kiss a whole history of homophobia and
violence is annulled, a whole new history becomes possible'.[19] This
is one of many moments which engage viewers' wishes, anxieties or
desires, and open up various possibilities of interpretation and
response.

Jarman's rewriting of Marlowe's ending is anticipated in
Marlowe's rewriting of Holinshed's account of Edward's death; and
in both cases the changes work to diminish homophobia. But the
critical assumption that Marlowe stages Edward's death in the
manner detailed in Holinshed is probably wrong. Orgel notes (see
also p. 114) that the insistence on the red-hot spit shows a wish to
make the murder 'precisely what Marlowe refuses to make it, a
condign punishment, the mirror of Edward's unspeakable vice'; and
he argues that Marlowe may have designed the play so that its
scrutiny of power can be screened by Edward's sexuality, 'a way of
protecting the play, a way of keeping what it says about power
intact'.[20] Readings of the play that insistently focus on sexuality, in
Orgel's view, obscure its dramatisation of power. This insistence on
sexuality is evident in the added stage directions in Act Five, Scene
Five of the 1995 'World's Classics' edition of David Bevington and
Eric Rasmussen. The editors state that they only add stage directions
'where they seem clearly intended to be performed' (p. xxv), but the
added stage direction '[*Matrevis and Gurney bring in a table and a red-hot
spit*]' (p. 398) is unwarranted in indicating what was intended for
stage performance.[21] Although Lightborn tells Matrevis and Gurney
to 'get me a spit, and let it be red-hot' (5.5.32), no further mention is

made of the spit. Then Lightborn asks Gurney and Matrevis for 'A table and a feather-bed', and the dialogue continues:

GURNEY: That's all?
LIGHTBORN: Ay, ay: so, when I call you, bring it in.                    (5.5.35–7)

When the murder starts Lightborn calls only for the table (5.5.112) – which, as Orgel notes, is something that requires two people to carry – and then orders Matrevis and Gurney to 'lay the table down, and stamp on it,/ But not too hard, lest that you bruise his body' (5.5.114–15). The red-hot spit is redundant to Lightborn's Machiavellian intention of murdering the King without marking his body, which is done by crushing with a table without bruising (perhaps also with the mattress of 'this bed' [5. 5. 74] that Lightborn invites Edward to lie on). Stamping on a table along with Edward's 'cry' (5.5.116) would be enough to suggest the grotesque violence of the death. If this reading of Marlowe's staging of Edward's death is correct then Marlowe anticipated Jarman in redirecting attention away from the chronicles' homophobic accounts to a dramatisation that emphasises political meanings: Edward's responses as king in the face of a designedly low and treacherous death.

IV

Jarman's *Edward II*, like other of his films, uses the history and literature of the English Renaissance to explore what he saw as the grim English present under a Conservative government. 'English' is the right word, for Jarman was a cultural conservative who loved that country's landscapes and literature, while also detesting what he saw as its hypocritical, repressive political values.[22] His homosexuality was the source of his political radicalism, which increased in the late 1980s as the government supported homophobic legislation, including Section 28, at the same time as gay men were suffering most from HIV disease. Jarman's HIV positive status had been diagnosed in 1986, and by the time he made *Edward II* he was involved in the gay activist group OutRage!, and had become the most prominent public figure to talk openly about being HIV positive. The making of *Edward II* was an integral part of the personal and political strands of his life. The presence of members of OutRage! in *Edward II* indicates the precise logic of Jarman's sexual politics. Queer love in the film is not confined to the private realm but is political; OutRage!'s demonstrations, often theatrical or parodic and always high profile, are designed to make the same point. Both represent a kind of protest through performance that is 'self-consciously imitative of actual events, providing a polemical antithesis to spectatorship and passivity'.[23]

I have been discussing the film and play as if the film worked with fixed sexual identities and the play worked without sexual identities, but rather with sex dispersed through other discourses. I want to end by complicating that impression. In the film we see not the fixity of sexual identities but their terrifying contingency. In the scene after Isabella has been accused by Edward of fawning on Mortimer and causing Gaveston's exile we see her changing. Tilda Swinton plays the speech beginning 'Would, when I left sweet France, and was embarked,/ That charming Circe, walking on the waves,/ Had chang'd my shape' slumped on her knees in the bottom of the frame, facing the camera, her body symmetrically composed and motionless. As she speaks, we witness the birth of a new consciousness as the power exerted on her by Edward produces the knowledge that she must act differently to create power for herself: 'I must entreat him, I must speak him fair' (1.4.172–3, 184). Circe, then, is the apt reference, for Isabella's new-found power leads to sexual pleasure with Mortimer. Edward too changes to become, for example, a butcher-like killer of Gaveston's killer, though he is constant in his love for Gaveston. But the pre-eminent figure in whom identity is unfixed and in the process of being formed as the film goes on is Prince Edward. As he wanders around the set directing a torch's beam at sights that amaze him – a naked rugby scrum, his father's violence directed at his mother, a huge opened carcass – the audience shares his point of view and his bewilderment at this fearful semiotic excess. Neither play nor film ends with Edward's death, but rather with the return of Prince Edward as the new king. Marlowe and Jarman diverge markedly in their treatment of young Edward, with Marlowe's Prince voicing patriarchal continuity, and Jarman's constructing an improvised subjectivity from various signs of power he has previously encountered. In Marlowe's astonishingly swift final scene the Prince is transformed from being 'yet a child' to a sovereign uttering words of judgement and condemnation, the power of which comes from his occupying authoritatively the patriarchal place vacated by his father: 'in me my loving father speaks,/ And plainly saith, 'twas thou that murder'dst him' (5.6.17,

41–2). The new king's subjectivity, as Marlowe dramatises it, is split in a way that intensifies rather than undermines his power, between the voicing of royal authority and the weeping of a loving son. The final tableau, ordered by Edward, of Edward II's hearse with Mortimer's head on it effects a reordering of events that re-establishes royal legitimacy and sovereignty. Jarman's prince improvises a new subjectivity through partial identifications that we have seen him make through the film: from Mortimer's world he wears a soldier's uniform and fires a toy machine gun; from Edward, whose letters he delivered and read, he picks up family loyalties; from Isabella he acquires ruthlessness and a cold heart, and some remarkable earrings. The little boy dancing to 'The Sugar Plum Fairy' on top of the cage containing Isabella and Mortimer is uncanny, scary – you might say, queer. He has no certain place in ideology; he is a self-assembled figure constructed of signs of power from others (who all fail), a bricolage of partial identifications that do not construct anything like a simple sexual identity, but will enable him to capture and exercise enough power to survive in what lies ahead (which includes being queer as well as being king). This is a long way from Marlowe's new king's orthodoxy but perhaps no less radical in its analysis of sex and power.

# *Notes*

INTRODUCTION

1 Michel Foucault, 'What is an Author?', in Josué V. Harari (ed.), *Textual Strategies: Perspectives in Post-Structuralist Criticism* (London: Methuen, 1979), pp. 141–60 (especially p. 159).
2 Robert Greene, from *Perimedes The Blacke-Smith*, quoted in Millar MacLure (ed.), *Marlowe: The Critical Heritage* (London, Boston and Henley: Routledge and Kegan Paul, 1979), p. 30.
3 Roland Barthes, 'The Death of the Author', in *Image Music Text*, trans. Stephen Heath (Glasgow: Fontana/Collins, 1977), p. 147.
4 David Bevington and Eric Rasmussen (eds.), *Doctor Faustus and Other Plays* (Oxford and New York: Oxford University Press, 1995), p. vii.


1. MARLOWE: FACTS AND FICTIONS

1 Anthony Burgess, *A Dead Man in Deptford* (London: Hutchinson, 1993); Robin Chapman, *Christoferus, or, Tom Kyd's Revenge* (London: Sinclair-Stevenson, 1993); Judith Cook, *The Slicing Edge of Death* (London: Simon and Schuster, 1993); Liam Maguire, *Icarus Flying: The Tragical Story of Christopher Marlowe* (Morden Park: Ormond, 1993); Charles Nicholl, *The Reckoning: The Murder of Christopher Marlowe* (London: Jonathan Cape, 1992).
2 For the earlier history of this phenomenon, see Dabbs, *passim.*
3 Register of Baptisms of St George the Martyr, Canterbury, now in the Archives of the Cathedral Chapter Library, cited in A. D. Wraight and Virginia F. Stern, *In Search of Christopher Marlowe: A Pictorial Biography* (Chichester: Adam Hart (Publishers) Ltd, 1993), p. 2 (a valuable source for reproductions of the scanty primary materials for Marlowe's life).

There is no authority for the statement repeated in numerous works about Marlowe that he was born on 6 February 1564. We do not know the date of his birth.
4 Wraight and Stern, *Christopher Marlowe*, p. 38. He received his first quarterly payment on 25 March 1579 (Canterbury Cathedral Archives and Library, CAC Misc. Accounts 40).

5 University Matriculation Registry, cited in Frederick S. Boas, *Christopher Marlowe: A Biographical and Critical Study* (Oxford: Clarendon Press, 1940), p. 10. He is listed as 'Marlin' in the College Admission Book. See Wraight and Stern, *Christopher Marlowe*, p. 54. However, the buttery books of Corpus Christi reveal that, although he did not replace Christopher Pashley as a Parker scholar until 7 May 1581, Marlowe was in residence by the second week of December 1580. See Boas, *Christopher Marlowe*, p. 10.

6 Ibid., p. 6. I am not persuaded that the 12-year-old 'Christopher Mowle' who was a witness to a case of sexual assault in 1573 was Christopher Marlowe the playwright. See Andrew Butcher, ' "onelye a boye called Christopher Mowle" ', in Darryll Grantley and Peter Roberts (eds.), *Christopher Marlowe and English Renaissance Culture* (Aldershot: Scolar Press, 1996), pp. 1–16.

7 Boas, *Christopher Marlowe*, p. 15; Wraight and Stern, *Christopher Marlowe*, p. 84.

8 See Boas, *Christopher Marlowe*, pp. 12–15. Marlowe was in Canterbury in the autumn of 1585, when he attested to the will of Katherine Benchkyn. The will is reproduced in William Urry, *Christopher Marlowe and Canterbury* (London: Faber & Faber, 1988), pp. 123–7. Marlowe was called upon to read the will aloud, which he did 'plainely and distinktly'. See the evidence of John Moore, the husband of Marlowe's sister, Jane, also reproduced ibid., pp. 127–9.

We have no information about Marlowe's other apparent absences from Cambridge in these years.

9 Wraight and Stern, *Christopher Marlowe*, p. 88.

10 Peter Roberts, 'The "Studious Artizan": Christopher Marlowe, Canterbury and Cambridge', in Grantley and Roberts (eds.), *Christopher Marlowe*, p. 25.

11 In the buttery books for 1583, for instance, the name of 'Marlyn' is prefixed by a 'D', indicating that he was 'Dominus Marlyn', and therefore a graduate. Marlowe actually graduated in 1584.

12 Robert Greene, *Perimedes The Blacke-Smith* (London, 1588), 'To the Gentlemen readers', sig. A3.

13 'It is therefore unnecessary to labour the internal evidence. The arresting music of the blank verse, unique in its combination of sonorous ring and liquid flow, the cosmic imagery, the pervading impress of an endlessly aspiring mind stamp both Parts of *Tamburlaine* with the unmistakably authentic Marlovian signature' (Boas, *Christopher Marlowe*, p. 70). Cf. Nicholl, *The Reckoning*, p. 203: 'There are one or two obscurities about the passage, but the gist is clear. This is an attack on Marlowe, identified by the allusion to *Tamburlaine*, and by the pun on "Merlin" and Marlowe.'

14 Gabriel Harvey, *A New Letter of Notable Contents* (London, 1593), sig. D3: 'Weepe Powles, thy *Tamberlaine* voutsafes to dye.' Does this refer to

*Tamburlaine* the play, or Tamburlaine the character? If the latter, then all it may be doing is drawing parallels between the 'high astounding terms' voiced by Tamburlaine, and the 'monstruous opinions' attributed to Marlowe by Thomas Kyd and others (see above, pp. 28–9).

For other problems with Harvey's account, see Nicholl, *The Reckoning*, pp. 60–4.

15 'Pd. to Thomas Dekker, the 20th of Desember, 1597, for adycyons to Fosstus twentye shellinges, and fyve shellinges more for a prolog to Marloes Tamburlan: so in all I saye payde twentye fyve shellinges.' (Cited in Dabbs, p. 62.)

16 We do not even know when he left Cambridge, although he took his MA in July 1587.

17 Middlesex Sessions Roll 284, cited in Boas, *Christopher Marlowe*, p. 103.

18 What a curious word to use in the circumstances.

19 Public Record Office, S.P. 84/44, fol. 60, cited in R. B. Wernham, 'Christopher Marlowe at Flushing in 1592', *English Historical Review* 91 (1976), 344–5.

20 There are two versions of the Baines note: BL Harleian MS 6848, fols. 185–6; and BL Harleian MS, 6853 fols. 307–8. The former is reproduced in Wraight and Stern, *Christopher Marlowe*, pp. 308–9.

21 BL Harleian MS 6848, fols. 187–9, reproduced in Wraight and Stern, *Christopher Marlowe*, pp. 314–15.

22 Nicholl's sole new fact about Marlowe is that Burghley signed a warrant for the payment of £13 6s 8d to Sidney's ensign 'for bringing of letters from ye said Sir Robert Sidney, knight, importing Her Majesty's special service, together with three prisoners committed to his charge' (Nicholl, *The Reckoning*, p. 239).

23 See Charles Nicholl, ' "At Middleborough": Some Reflections on Marlowe's Visit to the Low Countries in 1592', in Grantley and Roberts (eds.), *Christopher Marlowe*, p. 39.

24 BL Harleian MS 6848, fols. 187–9, reproduced in Wraight and Stern, *Christopher Marlowe*, pp. 314–15.

25 All details of the fight between Marlowe and Corkyn are taken from Urry, who also prints the relevant documents (Urry, *Christopher Marlowe*, pp. 130–1).

26 Reproduced in Wraight and Stern, *Christopher Marlowe*, p. 284. We do not know why the Privy Council was interested in Marlowe. On this point, see Nicholas Davidson, 'Christopher Marlowe and Atheism', in Grantley and Roberts (eds.), *Christopher Marlowe*, pp. 140–1.

27 Details are taken from the Coroner's report, reproduced in Wraight and Stern, *Christopher Marlowe*, pp. 292–3.

28 Reproduced ibid., p. 305.

29 Arthur Freeman, 'The Deptford Killer', *TLS*, 28 May 1993, p. 30.

30 Frederick S. Boas, *Marlowe and His Circle* (Oxford: Oxford University Press, 1931), p. 108.

31 Stephen Orgel (ed.), Christopher Marlowe, *The Complete Poems and Translations* (Harmondsworth: Penguin Books Ltd, 1971), p. 9.
32 Recently, Nicholl has suggested that the imprint might be a genuine one. See Nicholl, ' "At Middleborough" ', in Grantley and Roberts (eds.), *Christopher Marlowe*, pp. 40–2.
33 On this point, see Davidson, 'Christopher Marlowe and Atheism', Grantley and Roberts (eds.), *Christopher Marlowe*, pp. 137–42.

## 2. MARLOWE AND THE ROSE

1 Henslowe's diary and papers have been edited by a number of scholars: W. W. Greg, *Henslowe's Diary* (London: A. H. Bullen, 1904–1908); W. W. Greg, *Henslowe Papers, being documents supplementary to Henslowe's Diary* (London: A. H. Bullen, 1907); R. A. Foakes and R. T. Rickert (eds.), *Henslowe's Diary* (Cambridge: Cambridge University Press, 1961); C. C. Rutter, *Documents of the Rose Playhouse* (Manchester: Manchester University Press, 1984).
2 The most comprehensive account of the excavations to date is Julian Bowsher, *The Rose Theatre; an Archaeological Discovery* (London: Museum of London, 1998), which contains full references to all comparative material.
3 See Mark Eccles, *Christopher Marlowe in London* (Cambridge, Mass.: Harvard University Press, 1934), pp. 122–4.
4 References to Marlowe in the Henslowe papers have proved to be forgeries. See Greg, *Henslowe's Diary*, I, xxxix. So have references to Marlowe being at the Curtain. See E. K. Chambers, *The Elizabethan Stage* (Oxford: Clarendon Press, 1923), III, 418.
5 Letter of Philip Gawdy, cited ibid., II, 135; cf. Rutter, *Documents of the Rose Playhouse*, p. 42.
6 Cited in Chambers, *The Elizabethan Stage*, II, 423. The Theater was pulled down in 1598 but *Faustus* had been in the Admiral's Company's repertoire at the Rose since at least 1594.
7 William Prynne, *Histriomatrix* (London, 1633), cited in Chambers, *The Elizabethan Stage*, II, 423.
8 C. F. Tucker Brooke, *The Life of Marlowe and the Tragedy of Dido, Queen of Carthage* (London: Methuen, 1930), p. 48.
9 A reference to 'Dido & Eneus' in Henslowe's diary is not thought to refer to Marlowe's play. See Chambers, *The Elizabethan Stage*, III, 426.
10 Alleyn's purchase is reproduced in Greg, *Henslowe's Papers*, p. 31; cf. Rutter, *Documents of the Rose Playhouse*, pp. 42–3.
11 Ibid., p. 73.
12 It was sold to Henslowe on 18 January 1602. See Chambers, *The Elizabethan Stage*, III, 425–6. Rutter suggests that Alleyn bought the play on the disbandment of Strange's Company in 1593, and took it with him to Sussex's Company (see Rutter, *Documents of the Rose Playhouse*,

p. 78). See also Scott McMillin, 'The Ownership of *The Jew of Malta*, *Friar Bacon*, and *The Rangers Comedy*', *English Language Notes* 9 (1972) 249–52.

13 Peter Whelan, *The School of Night* (London: Warner Chappell Plays, 1992). See Act 2, Scenes 3 and 4.

14 Foakes and Rickert (eds.), *Henslowe's Diary*, pp. 304–6. It should be noted that the agreement stated that the building was to be used exclusively for playing and enterludes.

15 Described as 'ye new plaie house' in the Surrey & Kent Commission of Sewers, fol. 148$^v$, noted in Chambers, *The Elizabethan Stage*, II, 407; complaints about playing on the Sabbath are noted in a Privy Council Minute dated 29 October 1587, reproduced ibid., IV, 304–5.

16 See S. Loengard, 'An Elizabethan Lawsuit', *Shakespeare Quarterly* 34 (1983), 309.

17 Reproduced in Foakes and Rickert (eds.), *Henslowe's Diary*, pp. 9–13.

18 See C. W. Wallace, *The First London Theatre* (Lincoln, Nebr.: Nebraska University Press, 1913), pp. 69–70, 76; Herbert Berry, 'Aspects of the Design and Use of the First Public Playhouse' in Herbert Berry (ed.), *The First Public Playhouse: The Theatre in Shoreditch, 1576–1598* (Montreal: McGill-Queen's University Press, 1979), p. 32.

19 On this point, it is convenient to consult R.A. Foakes, *Illustrations of the English Stage 1580–1642* (London: Scolar Press, 1985), pp. 52–5.

20 Foakes and Rickert (eds.), *Henslowe's Diary*, p. 13.

21 Ibid., p. 319.

22 There is a discussion of stage sizes in Bowsher, *The Rose Theatre*, p. 65, *n.* 9.

23 See Foakes, *Illustrations of the English Stage*, pp. 48–51.

24 Glynne Wickham, *Shakespeare's Dramatic Heritage* (London: Routledge & Kegan Paul, 1969), pp. 121–31; J. L. Simmons, 'Elizabethan Stage Practice and Marlowe's *Jew of Malta*', *Renaissance Drama* 4 (1972) 93–104; Ernest K. Rhodes, *Henslowe's Rose, the Stage and Staging* (Lexington: Kentucky University Press, 1977); Scott McMillin, 'Staging at the Rose', in *The Elizabethan Theatre and the Book of Sir Thomas More* (Ithaca: Cornell University Press, 1987), pp. 113–34; Andrew Gurr, 'What the Plays Might Tell Us About the Stage', in F. J. Hildy (ed.), *New Issues in the Reconstruction of Shakespeare's Theatre* (New York: Peter Lang, 1990), pp. 119–34.

25 Large properties are suggested in McMillin, 'Staging at the Rose', p. 132, but see the 1598 list in Foakes and Rickert (eds.), *Henslowe's Diary*, pp. 316–25.

26 See Wickham, *Shakespeare's Dramatic Heritage*, pp. 125–6; and Glynne Wickham, '"Heavens", Machinery and Pillars', in Berry (ed.), *The Theatre in Shoreditch*, p. 4.

27 Simmons, 'Elizabethan Stage Practice', 94, 96–97, 99, 101. Traffic on and off the stage is also discussed in J. W. Sanders, 'Vaulting the Rails', *Shakespeare Survey* 7 (1954), 69.

28 Foakes and Rickert (eds.), *Henslowe's Diary*, pp. 316–25.
29 It is almost certainly the Rose to which Thomas Dekker refers in this way in 1599 in the prologue to *Fortunatus*.

### 3 MARLOWE AND THE EDITORS

1 Quoted in Leslie Hotson, *The Commonwealth and Restoration Stage* (Cambridge, Mass.: Cambridge, 1928; repr. New York, 1962), p. 305.
2 These altered and added scenes are reprinted in C. F. Tucker Brooke (ed.), *Works of Christopher Marlowe* (Oxford: Clarendon Press, 1929), pp. 195–229.
3 Robert D. Hume, *The Development of English Drama in the Late Seventeenth Century* (Oxford: Clarendon Press, 1976), p. 375.
4 William Mountfort, *The Li[f]e and Death of Doctor Faustus, Made into a Farce* (London, 1688), sig. E1$^v$.
5 Verna An Foster, '*Dr Faustus* on the Stage', *Theatre Research* 14 (1974), 18–44, cited in William Tydeman, *Dr Faustus: Text and Performance* (London and Basingstoke: Macmillan, 1984), p. 66.
6 Ibid., p. 50.
7 *Mr. William Shakespeares Comedies, Histories, & Tragedies* (London, 1623), sig. A3.
8 *Tamburlaine the Great* (London, 1590), sig. A2.
9 Roma Gill (ed.), *The Complete Works of Christopher Marlowe* (Oxford: Clarendon Press, 1987), I, 122.
10 Fredson Bowers (ed.), *The Complete Works of Christopher Marlowe* (Cambridge: Cambridge University Press, 1973; 2nd edn., 1981), I, ix.
11 Ibid., I, x.
12 J. P. Postgate, 'Textual Criticism', *Encyclopedia Britannica*, cited in W. W. Greg, *The Tragical History of the Life and Death of Doctor Faustus by Christopher Marlowe. A Conjectural Reconstruction* (Oxford: Oxford University Press, 1950), p. [iv].
13 David Bevington and Eric Rasmussen (eds.), *Doctor Faustus, A- and B-texts (1604, 1616), Christopher Marlowe and his collaborators and revisers* (Manchester: Manchester University Press, 1993).
14 Gill (ed.), *Complete Works*, II, xxviii–xxi.

### 4. MARLOWE AND THE METAPHYSICS OF MAGICIANS

1 David Bevington and Eric Rasmussen (eds.), Christopher Marlowe, *Doctor Faustus and Other Plays*, World's Classics (Oxford and New York: Oxford University Press, 1995), p. 141. Unless indicated otherwise, further references to *Doctor Faustus* are from the A-text in this edition, and are cited parenthetically in the body of the text.
2 (1) *The Tragicall History of D. Faustus* (1604, the A-text), followed in A. W. Ward (ed.), Christopher Marlowe, *The Tragicall History of Dr Faustus*,

(Oxford: Clarendon Press, 1868) and C. F. Tucker Brooke (ed.), *Works of Christopher Marlowe* (Oxford: Clarendon Press, 1929); (2) *The Tragicall History of the Life and Death of Doctor Faustus* (1616, the B-text); (3) John D. Jump (ed.), Christopher Marlowe, *Doctor Faustus* (London: Methuen, 1962); (4) Fredson Bowers (ed.), *The Complete Works of Christopher Marlowe* (Cambridge: Cambridge University Press, 1973; 2nd edn., 1981), who here follows the suggestion of Greg, who conjectured 'Signes'. See W. W. Greg (ed.), *Marlowe's Doctor Faustus 1604–1616* (Oxford: Clarendon Press, 1950), p. 301; (5) Roma Gill (ed.), *The Complete Works of Christopher Marlowe* (Oxford: Clarendon Press, 1987); (6) David Ormerod and Christopher Wortham (eds.), Christopher Marlowe, *Dr Faustus: The A-Text* (Nedlands, Western Australia: University of Western Australia Press, 1989); (7) Michael Keefer (ed.), *Christopher Marlowe's Doctor Faustus: A 1604–Version Edition* (Peterborough, Ontario: Broadview Press, 1991).

3 '[E]ironeia, quae diversum ei quod dicit intellectum petit' (Quintilian, *Institutio Oratoria*, VI, 15).

4 For this debate see R. H. West, 'The Impatient Magic of Dr. Faustus', *English Studies in Canada* 4 (1974), 218–19; Keefer (ed.), *Marlowe's Doctor Faustus*, pp. xiii–xvi; Max Bluestone, '*Libido speculandi*: Doctrine and Dramaturgy in Contemporary Interpretations of Marlowe's *Doctor Faustus*', in Norman Rabkin (ed.), *Reinterpretations of Elizabethan Drama* (New York and London: Columbia University Press, 1969), pp. 33–88; Bevington and Rasmussen (eds.), *Doctor Faustus*, pp. 15–31.

5 Leo Kirschbaum, 'Marlowe's Faustus: A Reconsideration', *Review of English Studies* 19 (1943), 229.

6 Wilbur Sanders, *The Dramatist and the Received Idea: Studies in the Plays of Marlowe and Shakespeare* (Cambridge: Cambridge University Press, 1968), p.194; West, 'Impatient Magic', 224, esp. *n.* 10.

7 See Michael Hunter, 'The Problem of Atheism in Early Modern England', *Transactions of the Royal Historical Society* 35 (1985), 135–57; Nicholas Davidson, 'Marlowe and Atheism', in Darryll Grantley and Peter Roberts (eds.), *Christopher Marlowe and English Renaissance Culture* (Aldershot: Scolar Press, 1996), pp. 129–47. Cf. Downie, 'Marlowe: facts and fictions', above pp. 28–9.

8 Helen Gardner (ed.), John Donne, *The Elegies and the Songs and Sonnets* (Oxford: Clarendon Press, 1965), pp. 3, 117.

9 On the desire for an 'original' *Doctor Faustus*, see Michael J. Warren, '*Dr. Faustus*: The Old Man and the Text', *English Literary Renaissance* 11 (1981), 111–17.

10 Ibid.; Constance Brown Kuriyama, 'Dr. Greg and Dr. *Faustus*: The Supposed Originality of the 1616 Text', ibid., 5 (1975), 171–97; Michael Keefer, 'Verbal Magic and the Problem of the A and B texts of Dr. *Faustus*', *Journal of English and Germanic Philology* 82 (1983), 324–46.

11 George Doidge Willcock and Alice Walker (eds.), George Puttenham,

*The Arte of English Poesie* (Cambridge: Cambridge University Press, 1936), p.154; Henry Peacham, *Garden of Eloquence* (London, 1577), sig. D3$^v$.

12 'Nulla est scientia, quae nos magis certificet de divinitate Christi, quam Magia & Cabala', quoted in Frances Yates, *Giordano Bruno and the Hermetic Tradition* (London: Routledge & Kegan Paul, 1964), p. 105.

13 BL Royal MS XVII.A.XLII, fol. 9$^v$. This is a fifteenth-century MS in English of the *Liber Juratus*. The Latin text runs 'nam magus per se Philosophus graece, hebraice scriba, latine sapiens dicitur' (BL Sloane MS 3885, fol. 61).

14 King James, *Dæmonologie* (Bodley Head Quartos, 1924), I, 8.

15 'There is in the prayer a holiness [*sanctimonia*] not only in itself, but by the recalling of sacred things, such as holy scripture, history, works, miracles, effects, graces, promises, sacraments, sacramentals and the like' ([Pseudo-]Agrippa, *Liber Quartus*, in Agrippa, *De Occulta*, p. 539).

16 Compare, for example, Girolammo Menghi, *Flagellum Daemonum, seu Exorcismi terribiles, Potentissimi, et Efficaces* (Bologna, 1582), p. 119 with BL Add. MS 36,674, fol. 71.

17 See Keith Thomas, *Religion and the Decline of Magic: Studies in Popular Belief in Sixteenth- and Seventeenth-Century England* (London: Weidenfeld and Nicolson, 1971), pp. 477–92; D. P. Walker, *Unclean Spirits: Possession and Exorcism in France and England in the Late Sixteenth and Early Seventeenth Centuries* (London: Scolar Press, 1981).

18 A similar point is made by Michael H. Keefer, 'Right Hand and Left Heel: Ideological Origins of the Faustus Legend', *Mosaic* 22 (1989), 82.

19 Clearly, there are some differences in these works caused by time, religious confession and geography, but on large issues they are remarkably unanimous. See Stuart Clark, 'Protestant Demonology: Sin, Superstition and Society (c.1520–c.1630)' in Bengt Ankarloo and Gustav Henningsen (eds.), *Early Modern Witchcraft: Centres and Peripheries* (Oxford: Clarendon Press, 1993), pp. 45–81.

20 Paul H. Kocher, *Christopher Marlowe: A Study of his Thought, Learning and Character* (New York: Russell and Russell, 1962), pp. 139 *n.* 1, 170–1, 172.

21 Warren, '*Dr. Faustus*', 117. See also Keefer's comment on 'how intimately related textual decisions are to critical and ideological orientations' (Keefer [ed.], *Marlowe's Doctor Faustus*, p. viii).

22 R. H. West, *The Invisible World: A Study of Pneumatology in Elizabethan Drama* (Athens, Georgia: University of Georgia Press, 1939), pp. 118, 110–35.

23 Moelwyn Merchant, 'Marlowe the Orthodox' in Brian Morris (ed.), *Christopher Marlowe* (London: Ernest Benn, 1968), pp. 179–92.

24 George Giffard, *A Dialogue concerning Witches and Witchcraftes*, Percy Society, vol. 8, 1842, pp. v, 8, 12.

25 Henry Holland, *A Treatise against Witchcraft* (Cambridge, 1590), sig. B.

26 Thomas, *Religion and the Decline of Magic*, pp. 179–206.

27 'For such of them as are in great miserie and pouertie, he allures to follow him, by promising vnto them greate riches, and worldlie commoditie' (*Dæmonologie*, II, 32). See also Dekker, Ford and Rowley, *The Witch of Edmonton* in Peter Corbin and Douglas Sedge (eds.), *Three Jacobean Witchcraft Plays* (Manchester: Manchester University Press), II.i.

28 'The dewill apperit to him [Dr. Fian] with quhyte rayment quhair he spak to him In thir termes or ever he spak to him will 3e be my serwand and adore me and my serwandis and 3e sall never want' (Scottish Record Office, J. C. 2/2, fol. 195).

29 'When I go but into my closes, I am afraid for I see now and then a hare, which my conscience giveth me is a witch' (Giffard, *Dialogue concerning Witches*, p. 8); and in the second Lancashire trial of 1634, little Edmund Robinson testified to witches taking the shape of greyhounds (BL Harley MS 6854, fols. 22–22$^v$).

30 See J. P. Brockbank, *Marlowe: Dr. Faustus* (London: Edward Arnold, 1962), p. 57.

31 E. K. Chambers, *The Elizabethan Stage* (Oxford: Oxford University Press, 1923), III, 424. The Exeter performance was presumably that of the B-text, since its record of 'a certain number of Devels' accords better with the stage direction at the beginning of B, 1.3: '*Thunder. Enter LUCIFER and four Devils*', than with A.

32 Samuel is the name of one of Giffard's interlocutors in his *Dialogue*; Orthodoxus is the orthodox Protestant spokesman in Deacon and Walker's *Dialogicall Discourses*; 'Owin Lordinge' apparently wrote the conjuring book which is BL Harley MS 2267 (see fol. 1).

33 A reads 'Orientis princeps Belsibub, inferni ardentis monarcha' and B 'Orientis Princeps Belzebub, inferni ardentis monarcha'. Editors conjecture 'Orientis princeps Lucifer, Beelzebub, inferni ardentis monarcha' for the sort of reasons adduced by Greg (ed.), *Marlowe's Doctor Faustus*, p. 312 and A. E. Taylor, 'Marlowe's *Dr. Faustus*', *TLS*, 6 Dec. 1917, p. 597.

34 'Gehenna' as a word for hell appears, as far as I can see, only in the Vulgate, where it occurs, for example, in the Gospels (Matthew 5.22 and 29, 10.28; Mark 9.42 and 46; Luke 12.5) and not in the Bishops' or Geneva bibles.

35 Samuel Rowland, *The Knave of Clubs* (?1615), sig. D2$^v$.

36 The debate over the efficacy of words was important in discussions of magic; see Stuart Clark, 'The Rational Witchfinder: Conscience, Demonological Naturalism and Popular Superstitions' in Stephen Pumfrey, Paolo L. Rossi, and Maurice Slawinski (eds.), *Science, Culture and Popular Belief in Renaissance Europe* (Manchester and New York: Manchester University Press, 1991), pp. 222–48. For the rejection of the innate efficacy of words by English demonologists, see George Giffard, *A Discourse of the Subtill Practises of Devilles* (1587), sigs. E3$^v$–E4; William Perkins, *A Discourse of the Damned Art of Witchcraft* (Cambridge, 1608),

pp.136–9, 143–7; James Mason, *The Anatomie of Sorcerie* (1612), p. 48; Alexander Roberts, *A Treatise of Witchcraft* (1616), pp. 66–70; Thomas Cooper, *The Mystery of Witchcraft* (1617), pp. 158–66.

37 Giffard, *Dialogue concerning Witches*, pp. 20–30.

38 Compare 'And vile blasphemous Conjurers to call/ On Jesus name' (John Donne, 'If faithfull soules', Helen Gardner (ed.), *The Divine Poems* (Oxford: Clarendon Press, 1952), p. 14). Greene's Friar Bacon repents that his magic renewed 'those wounds those bloody Jews did pierce,/ Which by thy magic oft did bleed afresh' (Daniel Seltzer (ed.), Robert Greene, *Friar Bacon and Friar Bungay* (London: Edward Arnold, 1963), xiii. 101–2).

39 King James says that one of the two necessities for conjuration is 'holy water (whereby the Deuill mockes the *Papistes*)' (*Dæmonologie*, I, 17).

40 'Tremor umbris tenebrosi phlegetontis. Amor incredibilis caelicolarum. Pavor invincibilis tartareorum', cited by Charles Zika, 'Reuchlin's *De verbo Mirifico* and the Magical Debate of the Late Fifteenth Century', *Journal of the Warburg and Courtauld Institute* 39 (1976), 104–38, 117 n. 41.

41 West, *The Invisible World*, pp. 131–2; cf. Taylor, 'Marlowe's *Dr. Faustus*', 597.

42 A is also more precise than B about the particular issue of the inefficacy of magic words: 'Did not my conjuring speeches raise thee? Speak' (A, 1.3.45); 'Did not my conjuring raise thee? Speak' (B, 1.3.42).

43 Keefer has to claim that this moment, which contradicts his reading of a coherent undermining of verbal magic in A, is a revision (Keefer, 'Verbal Magic', 342–3, n. 45).

44 'That he might be a spirit in shape and quality' (John Henry Jones (ed.), *The English Faust Book* (Cambridge: Cambridge University Press, 1994), p. 96).

45 See Kocher, *Christopher Marlowe*, p. 138; L. C. Knights, 'The Strange Case of Christopher Marlowe' in *Further Explorations* (London: Chatto & Windus, 1965), p. 96; Warren, '*Dr. Faustus*', 113–15.

46 Ibid., pp. 115–16.

47 Giffard, *Dialogue concerning Witches*, p. 119.

## 5. MARLOWE'S 'THEATRE OF CRUELTY'

1 See *The Observer Magazine*, 19 December 1976, pp. 12–15.

2 Antonin Artaud, *The Theater and its Double*, trans. Mary Caroline Richards (New York: Grove Press, 1958). Correspondences between Marlowe and Artaud have also been formulated by N. S. Sahu in his brief introduction to *Christopher Marlowe and Theatre of Cruelty and Violence: A Shaping Thought* (New Delhi: Associated Press, 1990). In comparison, my emphasis is more on performative violence than the metaphysics of Artaud's writings.

3 For a transcript of Baines's 'note' see Christopher Marlowe, *Complete*

*Plays and Poems*, E. D. Pendry and J. C. Maxwell (eds.) (London, 1976), pp. 511–14.

4 Jonathan Goldberg, 'Sodomy and Society: The Case of Christopher Marlowe', in David Scott Kastan and Peter Stallybrass (eds.), *Staging the Renaissance: Reinterpretations of Elizabethan and Jacobean Drama* (New York and London: Routledge, 1991), pp. 80–1.

5 The exception is Constance Brown Kuriyama, *Hammer or Anvil: Psychological Patterns in Christopher Marlowe's Plays* (New Brunswick, NJ: Rutgers University Press, 1980).

6 The now classic theory is associated with Harry Levin, *Christopher Marlowe: The Overreacher* (London: Faber & Faber, 1961). See also Michael Goldman, 'Marlowe and the Histrionics of Ravishment' in Alvin Kernan (ed.), *Two Renaissance Mythmakers: Christopher Marlowe and Ben Jonson* (Baltimore: Johns Hopkins University Press, 1977), pp. 22–40 and Lawrence Danson, 'Christopher Marlowe: the Questioner', *English Literary Renaissance* 12 (1982), 3–29.

7 C. L. Barber, *Creating Elizabethan Tragedy; the Theatre of Marlowe and Kyd*, Richard P. Wheeler (ed.), (Chicago and London: University of Chicago Press, 1988), p. 46.

8 I. H. Jeayes (ed.), *Letters of Philip Gawdy of West Harling, Norfolk and of London to various members of his family, 1579–1616* (London, 1906), p. 23.

9 The so-called 'Sieve portrait' of Elizabeth I (*c.*1583) has behind the figure of the Queen a richly jewelled and engraved column sculptured with imperial imagery including the story of Dido and Aeneas. Elizabeth was compared to Aeneas who, resisting the temptation of Dido, achieved his true destiny of founding the Roman Empire. See *Dynasties: Painting in Tudor and Jacobean England 1530–1630* (London: Tate Publishing, 1995), p. 85. In his vacillating image of Aeneas, Marlowe ignores such imperial associations.

10 Thomas Lodge, *A Defence of Poetry, Music and Stage-Plays* (London: Shakespeare Society, 1853), p. 4.

11 For an analysis of Marlowe's strategy of producing minimal resistance to audience enjoyment of fantasy fulfilment see Cartelli, pp. 162–80.

12 See Catherine Minshull, 'Marlowe's "Sound Machiavell"', *Renaissance Drama* 13 (1982), 35–53.

13 Katherine Duncan-Jones and Jan Van Dorsten (eds.), *Miscellaneous Prose of Sir Philip Sidney* (Oxford: Clarendon Press, 1973), p. 96.

14 Artaud, 'Metaphysics and the Mise en Scène', in *The Theater and its Double*, p. 37.

15 See Artaud, 'Oriental and Occidental Theater', in *The Theater and its Double*, pp. 70–3.

16 George Puttenham, *The Arte of English Poesie* (1589), p. 5.

17 Such visual symmetry was strongly pronounced in the 1976 National Theatre production of *Tamburlaine*.

18 For a detailed response to Marlowe's integration of verbal and visual

images, see Clifford Leech, *Christopher Marlowe: Poet for the Stage*, Anne Lancashire (ed.) (New York: AMS Press, 1986).

19 Artaud, *The Theater and its Double*, p. 76.
20 Robert Greene and Thomas Lodge, *A Looking Glass for London and England* (1587–91).
21 Artaud, 'Oriental and Occidental Theater', in *The Theater and its Double*, p. 72.
22 Artaud, 'The Theater and the Plague', in *The Theater and its Double*, pp. 28–30.
23 Jonathan Crewe, 'The Theater of the Idols: Theatrical and Anti-theatrical Discourse', in *Staging the Renaissance*, pp. 49–57.
24 Thomas Lodge, *A Reply to Stephen Gosson's Schoole of Abuse* in *A Defence of Poetry*, pp. 14–15. See Arthur Kinney, *Markets of Bawdrie: The Dramatic Criticism of Stephen Gosson*, Salzburg Studies in English Literature 4 (Salzburg, 1974), p.14, *n.* 33. Kinney interprets the reference as being to one of Gosson's own (lost) plays.

### 6. MARLOWE ONSTAGE: THE DEATHS OF THE AUTHOR

1 On the importance of the Mermaid editions, see Dabbs, pp. 129–34.
2 Humphrey Carpenter, *OUDS, a Centenary History of the Oxford University Dramatic Society 1885–1985* (Oxford and New York: Oxford University Press, 1985), p. 47.
3 See Lois Mai Chan, *Marlowe Criticism: A Bibliography* (Boston: G. K. Hall & Co. 1978), pp. 181–3, for a list of plays inspired by the life of Marlowe. Dabbs, pp. 156–7, *n.*, 53, discusses the Horne play.
4 *Kit Marlowe's Death* is printed in W. L. Courtney, *Dramas and Diversions* (London: Chapman and Hall, 1908), p. 103. An opera inspired by Courtney's play, by Herbert Bedford, was published in 1898.
5 Horne's play, oddly enough, also followed Marlowe's death with this quotation from *Doctor Faustus*.
6 See George L. Geckle, *Tamburlaine and Edward II* (Basingstoke and London: Macmillan, 1988), p. 51.
7 J. S. Cunningham (ed.) *Tamburlaine the Great* (Manchester and Baltimore: Manchester University Press and Johns Hopkins University Press, 1981), p. 83.
8 See Simon Callow, *Orson Welles: the Road to Xanadu* (London: Jonathan Cape, 1995), pp. 264–7.
9 Both parts, directed by Alison Brown for the First Bite Theatre Company, were, however, performed by a cast of ten in a London pub theatre on alternate nights from 10 October to 3 November 1991.
10 See Nancy T. Leslie, '*Tamburlaine* in the Theatre: Tartar, Grand Guignol, or Janus?', *Renaissance Drama* 4 (1971), 110, 112.
11 Geckle, *Tamburlaine and Edward II*, pp. 55, 65. This version was later performed both at Harvard and the Everyman Theatre in Cheltenham.

12  Ibid., p. 74.
13  This doubling had already been used effectively in the *Tamburlaine* at the Tower Theatre, Canonbury, in 1964; another significant double in this production was that of Agydas, Arabia, and Calyphas, who, as the director noted, represented three kinds of opposition to Tamburlaine's power. See Leslie, '*Tamburlaine* in the Theatre', 117.
14  See Peter Hall, *Peter Hall's Diaries, the Story of a Dramatic Battle*, John Goodwin (ed.) (London: Hamish Hamilton, 1983), p. 256.
15  J. S. Cunningham and Roger Warren, '*Tamburlaine the Great* Rediscovered', *Shakespeare Survey* 31 (1978), 155–62, 158. Cf. Geckle, *Tamburlaine and Edward II*, p. 71.
16  Cutting and (in *Part II*) rearrangement of the scenes also affected the tone (ibid., p. 73).
17  F. W. Hawkins, *The Life of Edmund Kean* (London: Tinsley Bros., 1869), I, 39–43, quoted in Millar MacLure (ed.), *Marlowe: The Critical Heritage* (London, Boston and Henley: Routledge & Kegan Paul, 1979), p. 108.
18  Reviews are quoted in James L. Smith, 'The Jew of Malta in the Theatre', in Brian Morris (ed.), *Christopher Marlowe* (London: Benn, 1968), pp. 4–5, 6–10, and in MacLure (ed.), *Marlowe: The Critical Heritage*, pp. 70–7.
19  Since it was Revill's performance that I saw, any unattributed comments will apply to it. For some comparative remarks, see Smith, 'Jew of Malta', in Morris (ed.), *Christopher Marlowe*, p. 20. Note that, where no review is footnoted, I am relying on my own recollections of a production. These may sometimes be inaccurate, or may be true of some performances and not others – but they are better than nothing, especially for the period before in-house videos became commonplace.
20  Ibid., p. 18.
21  See William Tydeman, *Dr Faustus: Text and Performance* (London and Basingstoke: Macmillan, 1984), pp. 58–9.
22  It is the most frequently quoted line in reviews and often seems genuinely to have taken the reviewer by surprise.
23  Michael L. Greenwald, *Directions by Indirections, John Barton of the Royal Shakespeare Theatre Company* (Newark, London, and Toronto: Delaware University Press, 1985), p. 202.
24  John D. Jump's note on this passage credits W. W. Greg with a suggestion which apparently inspired this bit of business. See John D. Jump (ed.), Christopher Marlowe, *Doctor Faustus* (London: Methuen, 1962)
25  Lyric, Hammersmith, reviewed by Sybil Truchet, *Cahiers Elisabéthains* 18 (Oct. 1980), 96.
26  See W. Bridges-Adams, *The Irresistible Theatre* (Cleveland, Ohio, and New York: World Publishing Co., 1957), p. 129; see also Robert Speaight, *William Poel and the Elizabethan Revival* (Cambridge, Mass.: Harvard University Press, 1954), pp. 114–15.

27 See Carpenter, *OUDS, a Centenary History*, p. 134.
28 Jeffrey Wainwright, review in *Independent on Sunday*, 30 Oct. 1992; Jenny Naish, review in *Research Opportunities in Renaissance Drama* 10 (1977), 70; Tydeman, *Dr Faustus*, p. 77; Nottingham Playhouse Production directed by Philip McDermott, 6–12 Nov. 1992), reviewed by Alistair Macaulay, *Financial Times*, 10 Nov. 1992; stage history in Jump (ed.), *Doctor Faustus*.
29 See Peter Holland in *Research Opportunities in Renaissance Drama* 10 (1977), 62. For the Baines note, see above pp. 21–2.
30 See Peter Holland and Jenny Naish in *Research Opportunities in Renaissance Drama* 10 (1977), 69; Andy Lavender, *City Limits*, 2 Mar. 1981. For some interesting suggestions about the playing of *Faustus*, see also Ernst Honigmann, 'Ten Problems in *Dr. Faustus*', in Murray Biggs, Philip Edwards, Inga-Stina Ewbank, and Eugene M. Waith (eds.), *The Arts of Performance in Elizabethan and Early Stuart Drama* (Edinburgh: Edinburgh University Press, 1991), pp. 171–91.
31 See Geckle, *Tamburlaine and Edward II*, p. 95.
32 Joy Leslie Gibson, *Ian McKellen, a Biography* (London: George Weidenfeld and Nicolson, 1986), p. 59.
33 Speaight, *William Poel*, p. 180.
34 Clifford Leech, *Christopher Marlowe: Poet for the Stage*, Anne Lancashire (ed.) (New York: AMS Press, 1986), p. 200. Professor Leech died in 1977 and, according to Professor Lancashire, had been working on the book 'for the last ten or fifteen years of his life' (p. vii).
35 Kate Bassett, *Times*, 26 May 1993.
36 See McKellen's article in the *Sunday Express*, 23 May 1993.
37 Peter J. Smith, review of *Doctor Faustus* on 10 May 1989, in *Cahiers Elisabéthains* 36 (Oct. 1989), 104.
38 Martin Wiggins, review of *Tamburlaine*, ibid., 44 (Oct. 1993), p. 82.
39 See *The Guardian*, 25 Mar. 1988.
40 J. M. Maguin, review in *Cahiers Elisabéthains* 32 (Oct. 1987), 111.
41 Michael Coveney, *Financial Times*, 24 Mar. 1988; Christopher Edwards, *Spectator*, 2 Apr. 1988. (Similarly, the Tamburlaine of Anthony Sher in 1992–3 reminded many of Saddam Hussein. Racism or a parody of racism?)
42 Margaret Shrewring and J. R. Mulryne (eds.), *This Golden Round* (Stratford-upon-Avon: Shewring/Mulryne, 1989), p. 75.
43 Unsigned review in *Blackwood's Magazine* (May 1818), III, 209–10, in MacLure (ed.), *Marlowe: The Critical Heritage*, p. 72; cf. David Nathan: 'it is clearly played as a test of Ithamore's capacity for future villainy' (*Jewish Chronicle*, 1 Apr. 1988).
44 Shrewring and Mulryne (eds.), *This Golden Round*, p. 129.
45 *Jewish Chronicle*, 1 Apr. 1988. Other Jewish reviewers agreed with Nathan; however, Melanie Phillips, in the *Guardian*, claimed that the caricature devices had accentuated the play's anti-semitism.

46 See Della Coulin, *The Tablet*, 2 Apr. 1988; see also Victoria Radin, in *The New Statesman*, 1 Apr. 1988.
47 Review (10 May 1989), *Cahiers Elisabéthains* 36 (Oct. 1989), 104.
48 Ibid., 44 (Oct. 1993), p. 81.
49 John Peter, *Sunday Times*, 6 Sep. 1992.
50 *Guardian*, 3 Sep. 1992.
51 *New Republic*, 13 Feb. 1956, p. 20, quoted in Leslie, '*Tamburlaine* in the Theatre', p. 115.
52 See Geckle, *Tamburlaine and Edward II*, p. 57.
53 *Independent on Sunday*, 6 Sep. 1992.
54 This theory is also used in another (otherwise very different) play called *The School of Night*, by Stephen Place, which was given at Edinburgh and on tour in 1992. Martin Hoyle's review in *The Times* (10 Sep. 1992) gives a full account of it.
55 Jane Gilbey, interview with Peter Whelan, *Plays International*, Nov. 1992.
56 Peter Whelan, *The School of Night* (London: Warner Chappell Plays, 1992), p. 113.
57 Joseph A. Porter, *Shakespeare's Mercutio, His History and Drama* (Chapel Hill and London: University of North Carolina Press, 1988), suggests that Romeo's responsibility for the death of Mercutio shows 'Shakespeare's unconscious assumption of responsibility for Marlowe's death' (p. 141). For other references to the possibility that Mercutio is Marlowe, see esp. p. 233, *n.* 12.

### 7. A BIT OF RUFF: CRITICISM, FANTASY, MARLOWE

1 N. W. Bawcutt (ed.), *The Jew of Malta* (Manchester: Manchester University Press, 1978), p. 55.
2 Ibid., p. 37.
3 Stanley Wells, 'Theatricalizing Shakespeare's text', *New Theatre Quarterly* 26 (1991), 184–6.
4 Jonathan Goldberg, 'Sodomy and society: The case of Christopher Marlowe', in David Scott Kastan and Peter Stallybrass (eds.), *Staging The Renaissance: Reinterpretations of Elizabethan and Jacobean Drama* (New York and London: Routledge, 1991), p. 80.
5 Stephen Orgel, 'What is a text?' in ibid., p. 84.
6 Alan Sinfield, *Faultlines: Cultural Materialism and the Politics of Dissident Reading* (Berkeley: University of California Press, 1992), p. 23.
7 James Shapiro, ' "Tragedies naturally performed": Kyd's representation of violence', in Kastan and Stallybrass, p. 103.
8 Ibid., pp. 460–1.
9 J. A. Symonds, introduction to Havelock Ellis (ed.), *Christopher Marlowe* (1887) (London: Ernest Benn, 1948), p. xxxiv.
10 Publicity flyer for A. D. Wraight and Virginia F. Stern, *In Search of*

*Christopher Marlowe: A Pictorial Biography* (Chichester: Adam Hart (Publishers) Ltd, 1993).

11 Alan Bray, 'Homosexuality and the signs of male friendship in Elizabethan England', in Jonathan Goldberg (ed.), *Queering the Renaissance* (Durham and London: Duke University Press, 1994), pp. 42, 49.

12 Stephen Orgel, *Impersonations: The Performance of Gender in Shakespeare's England* (Cambridge: Cambridge University Press, 1996), pp. 47, 48.

## 8. 'WRIT IN BLOOD': MARLOWE AND THE NEW HISTORICISTS

1 Terry Eagleton, *William Shakespeare* (Oxford: Blackwell, 1986), pp. ix–x.

2 Michel Foucault, *Discipline and Punish: The Birth of the Prison*, trans. Alan Sheridan (Harmondsworth: Penguin Books, 1979), p. 25.

3 Michel Foucault, *The History of Sexuality: Volume I: An Introduction*, trans. Robert Hurley (Harmondsworth: Penguin Books, 1981), p. 93.

4 Stephen Greenblatt, 'Invisible Bullets: Renaissance Authority and its Subversion, *Henry IV* and *Henry V*', in Richard Wilson and Richard Dutton (eds.), *New Historicism and Renaissance Drama* (London: Longman, 1992), p. 108.

5 Michel Foucault, *Language, Counter-Memory, Practice* (Ithaca: Cornell University Press, 1977), p. 34, quoted in Dollimore, pp. 114–15. Dollimore applies Foucault's dictum to Faustus.

6 Michel Foucault, *Madness and Civilization: A History of Insanity in the Age of Reason*, trans. Richard Howard (London: Tavistock, 1967), p. 39. The conference proceedings were published as *Two Renaissance Mythmakers: Christopher Marlowe and Ben Jonson: Selected Papers of the English Institute, 1975–76*, Alvin Kernan (ed.) (Baltimore: Johns Hopkins University Press, 1977). See especially Margaret Higonnet, 'In Memoriam: William K. Wimsatt', ibid., pp. 199–200.

7 For Foucault's fascination with the labyrinth, shared with Jacques Lacan and Gilles Deleuze, see James Miller, *The Passion of Michel Foucault* (London: HarperCollins, 1993), pp. 144–7.

8 Margery Garber, ' "Infinite Riches in a Little Room": Closure and Enclosure in Marlowe', in Kernan (ed.), *Two Renaissance Mythmakers*, pp. 3–21, esp. pp. 11–13.

9 Roland Barthes, 'Inaugural Lecture, College de France', in Susan Sontag (ed.), *Barthes: Selected Writings* (London, Fontana, 1983), pp. 475–8, esp. 461.

10 Ibid., pp. 460–1.

11 Ibid., p. 459.

12 Michel Foucault, *Death and the Labyrinth: The World of Raymond Roussel*, trans. Charles Ruas (London: Athlone Press, 1987), p. 80.

13 Michel Foucault, 'Discourse and Repression' and 'Infantile Sexuality', trans. John Leavitt, unpublished typescripts in the Bibliothèque du Saulchoir and the 'History of the Present' Collection, University of

Berkeley. See David Macey, *The Lives of Michel Foucault* (London: Hutchinson, 1993), pp. 338–9.

14  Harry Levin, *Christopher Marlowe: The Overreacher* (London: Faber & Faber, 1961), pp. 41–2, 183–4.

15  Foucault, *History of Sexuality*, p. 12.

16  Stephen Greenblatt, 'Marlowe and Renaissance Self-Fashioning' in Kernan (ed.), *Two Renaissance Mythmakers*, pp. 41–69 (p. 62).

17  For Greenblatt's defection from Wimsatt's 'mystery cult' see his *Learning to Curse: Essays in Early Modern Culture* (London: Routledge, 1990), pp. 1–2.

18  For the French antecedents of Greenblatt's categories, see for example, Elisabeth Roudinesco, *Jacques Lacan*, trans. Barbara Bray (Cambridge: Polity Press, 1997), pp. 95–8, 229.

19  Greenblatt, *Learning to Curse*, p. 2.

20  Stephen Greenblatt, 'Marlowe, Marx and Anti-Semitism', *Critical Inquiry* 5 (1978), reprinted in *Learning to Curse*, pp. 40–56 (pp. 54–5).

21  See, for example, Edward Pechter, 'The New Historicism and its Discontents', *PMLA* 102 (1987), 292–303 (p. 292).

22  Greenblatt, *Learning to Curse*, p. 55; Bernard-Henri Levy, 'What is Left-Wing Anti-Semitism?', in *Adventures on the Freedom Road: The French Intellectuals in the 20th Century*, trans. Richard Veasey (London: Harvill, 1995), pp. 81–4, esp. p. 83.

23  Greenblatt, *Learning to Curse*, p. 56.

24  Ibid., p. 53; Jean-François Lyotard, *Economie libidinale* (Paris: Editions Minuit, 1974), p. 136.

25  Greenblatt, *Learning to Curse*, pp. 45–7, 52–3.

26  Michel Foucault, 'The Discourse of Power', in *Remarks on Marx: Conversations with Duccio Trombadori*, trans. Anon. (New York: Semiotext(e), 1991), pp. 173–4.

27  Michel Foucault, 'Power and Strategies', in Colin Gordon (ed.), *Michel Foucault, Power/Knowledge: Selected Interviews and Other Writings, 1972–1977* (Brighton: Harvester, 1980), p. 138.

28  André Glucksmann, *La Cuisinère et la mangeur d'hommes* (Paris: Seuil, 1977), p. 11. For a discussion of Foucault's influence on the New Philosophy, see Macey, *Lives of Michel Foucault*, pp. 381–8.

29  Michel Foucault, *The Use of Pleasure: The History of Sexuality II*, trans. Robert Hurley (Harmondsworth: Penguin, 1987), p. 11.

30  Frank Lentricchia, *Criticism and Social Change* (Chicago: Chicago University Press, 1983), p. 15; Gilles Deleuze, 'Gilles Deleuze contre les "nouveaux philosophes"', *Le Monde*, 19 June 1977, p. 16, quoted in Macey, *Lives of Michel Foucault*, p. 385.

31  Jacques Rancière, 'Objectif '78', *Le Nouvel Observateur*, 25 July 1977, p. 40, quoted in Macey, *Lives of Michel Foucault*, p. 385.

32  Greenblatt, *Learning to Curse*, p. 3.

33  Barthes, 'Inaugural Lecture', in Sontag (ed.), *Barthes: Selected Writings*, pp. 461–2.

34 Frank Lentricchia, 'Foucault's Legacy: A New Historicism?', in Aram Veeser (ed.), *The New Historicism* (London: Routledge, 1989), pp. 231–42 (p. 241).
35 Ibid., p. 241.
36 Quoted in Miller, *Passion of Michel Foucault*, p. 264.
37 Jean-François Lyotard, *Just Gaming*, trans. Walter Godzich (Manchester: Manchester University Press, 1985), p. 5: 'The difference between what I write and literature is that, in principle, what I write is not fiction. But I do wonder more and more: Is there a real difference between theory and fiction?'
38 Raphael Samuel, 'Reading the Signs', *History Workshop Journal* 32 (1991), 88–109 (pp. 90–1, 103).
39 Margery Garber, ' "Here's Nothing Writ": Scribe, Script, and Circumscription in Marlowe's Plays', *Theatre Journal* 36 (1984), 301–20 (p. 301).
40 Umberto Eco, 'Language, Power, Force', *Faith in Fakes: Essays*, trans. William Weaver (London: Secker & Warburg, 1986), pp. 239–55, esp. p. 245.
41 Jacques Lacan, 'Sur Les Rapports entre la mythologie et ritual', *Bulletin de la Société française de philosophie* 3 (1956), 114, commenting on the influence of Claude Lévi-Strauss and quoted in Roudescino, *Jacques Lacan*, p. 212.
42 Garber, ' "Here's Nothing Writ" ', 312–13, 316.
43 Michel Foucault, *The Order of Things: An Archaeology of the Human Sciences*, trans. Anon. (London: Routledge & Kegan Paul, 1970), p. 387.
44 Michel Foucault, 'On the Genealogy of Ethics: An Overview of Work in Progress' in Paul Rabinow (ed.), *The Foucault Reader* (Harmondsworth: Penguin, 1986), pp. 340–72, esp. 341.
45 Jonathan Goldberg, 'Sodomy and Society: The Case of Christopher Marlowe', *Southwest Review* 69 (1984), 371–8? (380).
46 Jonathan Goldberg, 'Play the sodomites, or worse', *Sodometries: Renaissance Texts, Modern Sexualities* (Stanford: Stanford University Press, 1992), pp. 125–43.
47 Ibid., pp. 129,141.
48 Foucault, *History of Sexuality*, p. 94.
49 Dollimore, p. 115.
50 W. H. Auden, 'Musée des Beaux Arts', *Selected Poems* (Harmondsworth: Penguin, 1958), p. 61.

## 9. *HERO AND LEANDER*: THE ARBITRARINESS OF DESIRE

1 Rather than classify previous writers on the poem as moralisers or celebrants, I will observe that at least the moralisers have the virtue of taking the work seriously even if they tend to distort it. My own position is similar to that of J. B. Steane who observes that 'we are insensitive if our amusement is not held in check by something almost fiercely

serious within the verse' (*Marlowe: A Critical Study* (Cambridge: Cambridge University Press, 1965), p. 321). Steane's chapter and that of William Keach in *Elizabethan Erotic Narratives: Irony and Pathos in the Ovidian Poetry of Shakespeare, Marlowe, and Their Contemporaries* (New Brunswick, NJ: Rutgers University Press, 1977) remain the fullest and most persuasive discussions of the poem.

2 My assumption is that Marlowe's *Hero and Leander* is a completed poem in its own right, independent of Chapman's continuation. For arguments in support of this position see, e.g. Louis Martz, 'Introduction', *Hero and Leander: A Facsimile of the First Edition* (New York: Johnson Reprint Corporation, 1972), pp. 1–22; Marion Campbell, ' "Desunt Nonnulla": The Construction of Marlowe's *Hero and Leander* as an Unfinished Poem', *ELH* 51 (1984), 241–68; and Theresia de Vroom, 'Mediating Myth: The Art of Marlowe's *Hero and Leander*', *CLAJ* 37 (1994), 425–42. The fact that Marlowe chose to depict a tragic story comically says a great deal about his delight in thwarting expectations and in dealing with familiar material in original ways. Allusions within the poem, however, indicate that he was well aware that the famous couple were indeed destined to a tragic end.

3 Marlowe's representation of homosexuality has been the focus of intense scrutiny. See, for example, Gregory W. Bredbeck, *Sodomy and Interpretation: Marlowe to Milton* (Ithaca, NY: Cornell University Press, 1991), *passim*; Jonathan Goldberg, *Sodometries: Renaissance Texts, Modern Sexualities* (Stanford, CA: Stanford University Press, 1992), pp. 105–43; Goldberg, 'Sodomy and Society: The Case of Christopher Marlowe', *Southwest Review* 69 (1984), 371–8; M. Morgan Holmes, 'Identity and the Dissidence It Makes: Homoerotic Nonsense in Kit Marlowe's *Hero and Leander*', *English Studies in Canada* 21 (1995), 151–69; Bruce R. Smith, *Homosexual Desire in Shakespeare's England: A Cultural Poetics* (Chicago: University of Chicago Press, 1991), pp. 92–3, 131–6, 204–23; Claude J. Summers, 'Marlowe and Constructions of Renaissance Homosexuality', *Canadian Review of Comparative Literature/Revue Canadienne de Littérature Comparée* 21 (1994), 27–44; Summers, 'Sex, Politics, and Self-Realization in *Edward II*', in Kenneth Friedenreich, Roma Gill, and Constance B. Kuriyama (eds.), *'A Poet & a Filthy Play-maker': New Essays on Christopher Marlowe* (New York: AMS, 1988), pp. 221–40; and Gregory Woods, 'Body, Costume, and Desire in Christopher Marlowe', in Claude J. Summers (ed.), *Homosexuality in Renaissance and Enlightenment England: Literary Representations in Historical Context* (New York: Haworth, 1992), pp. 69–84. Most of the earlier discussions of homoeroticism in *Hero and Leander*, including those of Steane and Keach, are vitiated by homophobia.

4 On the tensions between sodomitical and non-sodomitical constructions of homosexuality in Marlowe, see Summers, 'Marlowe and Renaissance Constructions of Homosexuality', 34–42.

5 All quotations from *Hero and Leander* follow the text of Millar MacLure (ed.), *The Poems: Christopher Marlowe*, (London: Methuen, 1968) and are cited by sestiad and line numbers within parentheses.

6 See Bredbeck, *Sodomy and Interpretation*, pp. 113–14.

7 See Judith Butler, 'Imitation and Gender Insubordination', in Diana Fuss (ed.), *Inside/Out: Lesbian Theories, Gay Theories* (New York: Routledge, 1991), pp. 13–31.

8 Holmes, 'Identity and the Dissidence It Makes', 157.

9 Marlowe's immediate source, Musaeus' *Hero and Leander*, may indeed have been intended as a Christian Neoplatonist allegory. See the introduction to Musaeus' poem by Thomas Gelzer in the Loeb Library edition (London: Heinemann, 1975), pp. 316–22.

10 Clifford Leech, ' "Venus and the Nun": Portraits of Women in Love in Shakespeare and Marlowe', *Studies in English Literature* 5 (1965), 252, 254. I find unconvincing the argument of W. L. Godshalk, '*Hero and Leander*: The Sense of an Ending', in Freidenreich, Gill and Kuriyama (eds.), '*A Poet & a Filthy Play-maker*', pp. 293–314, that Marlowe intends a distinction between the amorality of the gods and the moral sense of the humans.

11 Joanne Altieri, '*Hero and Leander*: Sensible Myth and Lyric Subjectivity', *John Donne Journal* 8 (1989), 164. In contrast, William P. Walsh, 'Sexual Discovery and Renaissance Morality in Marlowe's "Hero and Leander"', *Studies in English Literature* 12 (1972), 33–54, simply (and, in my view, quite inappropriately) imposes Neoplatonic attitudes on the poem.

12 On the poem's progression from an emphasis on sight to an emphasis on touch, see Godshalk, '*Hero and Leander*', in Freidenreich, Gill and Kuriyama (eds.), '*A Poet & a Filthy Play-maker*', pp. 298–300.

13 It is interesting that the passage quoted above actually echoes some lines in Castiglione's *The Courtier*, that compendium of Neoplatonic attitudes toward love, but in the process transforms them. In Castiglione, the emphasis is simply on the human propensity toward loving and hating; in Marlowe, the emphasis is on the arbitrariness of desire.

14 Brian Morris, 'Comic Method in *Hero and Leander*' in Brian Morris (ed.), *Christopher Marlowe: Mermaid Critical Commentaries* (London: Ernest Benn, 1968), p. 118.

15 David Lee Miller, 'The Death of the Modern: Gender and Desire in Marlowe's *Hero and Leander*', *South Atlantic Quarterly* 88 (1989), 773, 779.

16 On this point, see Godshalk, '*Hero and Leander*', in Freidenreich, Gill and Kuriyama (eds.), '*A Poet & a Filthy Play-maker*', pp. 301–2.

17 Steane, *Marlowe*, p. 316.

18 Werner von Koppenfels, 'Dis-Covering the Female Body: Erotic Exploration in Elizabethan Poetry', *Shakespeare Survey* 47 (1994), 127.

19 On this point, see S. Ann Collins, ' "Sundrie Shapes, Committing Headdie Ryots, Incest, Rapes": Functions of Myth in Determining

Narrative and Tone in Marlowe's *Hero and Leander*', *Mosaic* 4 (1970–71), 120–1.

20 See William Kerrigan and Gordon Braden, 'Milton's Coy Eve: *Paradise Lost* and Renaissance Love Poetry', *ELH* 53 (1986), 27–51. Von Koppenfels, 'Dis-Covering the Female Body', also stresses the influence of *Hero and Leander* on subsequent love poetry. My emphasis on Marlowe's exposure of the inequities and contradictions of the Elizabethan sex-gender is not, of course, tantamount to presenting Marlowe as a proto-feminist. While the poem does, indeed, offer proto-feminist insights, it also contains a misogynistic strain that relishes the comedy at Hero's expense.

## 10. GENDER AND VOICE IN *HERO AND LEANDER*

1 Northrop Frye identifies one of the weaknesses of New Criticism as a desire to remove 'all external goals from literature, thus postulating a self-contained literary universe'. He goes on to note that this practice 'merely restored the aesthetic view on a gigantic scale, substituting Poetry for a mass of poems, aesthetic mysticism for aesthetic empiricism' (*Anatomy of Criticism: Four Essays* (Princeton: Princeton University Press, 1957), p. 350. My essay explores how and why 'aesthetic mysticism' was constructed at a particular point in late Elizabethan culture.

2 The obvious exception to this is Sir Philip Sidney's *Defence of Poetry* which argues that literature is best equipped to reveal truth precisely because of its self-subverting, errant wit which alerts the reader to its own pretensions.

3 Sir Thomas Elyot expresses the standard Humanist view when he asserts that moral and practical wisdom can be extrapolated from literary texts 'Wherfore sens good and wise mater may be picked out of these poetes, it were no reason, for some lite mater that is in their verses, to abandone therefore al their warkes' (Henry Croft [ed.], *The Boke Named the Gouernour* (London: Kegan Paul, 1880), I, 129).

4 All quotations are from Louis L. Martz (ed.), *Hero and Leander By Christopher Marlowe: A Facsimile of the First Edition London 1598* (Washington: The Folger Shakespeare Library, 1972). I normalise the use of *u*, *v* and *s* throughout. Line numbers are included parenthetically in the body of the text.

5 Gordon Braden, *The Classics and English Renaissance Poetry: Three Case Studies*, Yale Studies in English 187 (New Haven and London: Yale University Press, 1978), p. 80.

6 Elizabethan interpretations of Ovid are analysed by Gerald Snare, 'Chapman's Ovid', *Studies in Philology* 75 (1978), 430–50.

7 Clark Hulse, *Metamorphic Verse: The Elizabethan Minor Epic* (Princeton: Princeton University Press, 1981), p. 7.

8 Nashe collaborated with Marlowe on *Dido, Queen of Carthage* and Marlowe remains a fundamental influence on Nashe's self-definition, as I will argue later.

9 All quotations are from R. B. McKerrow (ed.), rev. F. P. Wilson, *The Works of Thomas Nashe* (Oxford: Blackwell, 1966). References are to volume and page number and are included in the body of the text within parentheses. I normalise the use of *u*, *v* and *s*.

10 *The Choise of Valentines* was not published in Nashe's lifetime. One of the surviving manuscripts, Bodleian Library MS Rawl. Poet. 216, is bound with a translation of Ovid's *Ars Amatoria*, underlining the Ovidian heritage of the 'wanton Elegie'. Another manuscript, MS Dyce 44, elaborates the pleasures of revelation in another way as it is written in code, thereby contributing to the fetishisation of script which is one of Nashe's jokes.

11 Naomi Schor argues for an association between detail, femininity, and decadence. (See Naomi Schor, *Reading in Detail: Aesthetics and the Feminine* (New York and London: Methuen, 1987), p. 22). Schor also notes (p. 44) that in the *Institutio Oratoria*, Quintilian equates rhetorical ornament with the artifices of painted women.

12 By contrast Petrarch's transmission of Ovidian models produces 'the subject in crisis'. See Lynn Enterline, 'Embodied Voices: Petrarch Reading (Himself Reading) Ovid', in Valeria Finucci and Regina Schwartz (eds.), *Desire in the Renaissance: Psychoanalysis and Literature* (Princeton: Princeton University Press, 1994), pp. 120–45. Enterline argues that the language of desire both constitutes and impoverishes the self in Petrarch, and while a process of impoverishment also takes place in *Hero and Leander* through the acknowledgement that its strategies are feminised, the subject so defined is confident, shameless, and avoids the self-frustrating complexities of the Petrarchan subject.

13 For a very suggestive reinterpretation of the politics of voyeurism which also takes issue with Freud, see Regina M. Schwartz, 'Through the Optic Glass: Voyeurism and *Paradise Lost*', in Finucci and Schwartz, pp. 146–66. For Freud's essay, see *The Standard Edition of the Complete Psychological Works*, trans. James Strachey (London: Hogarth Press and The Institute of Psycho-analysis, 1953–74), XIV, 109–40.

14 Tamburlaine identifies beauty, love, and lyricism as effeminate in *Tamburlaine Part I*: 5.2.97–127, although the limitations of this attitude are also pointed up by the play. The idea that love and women are inimical to epic is, of course, explored in *Dido*.

15 The epyllion displays a generic interest in female concerns. Thomas Heywood's *Oenone and Paris* (1594), for example, gives space to Oenone's complaint and the opinions of the woman who was abandoned by Paris for Helen. Rather than the great dynastic and political consequences of

the judgement of Paris which are recorded in *The Iliad, Oenone and Paris* focuses on the personal and domestic effects of his famous judgement.

16 David Kuchta, 'The Semiotics of Masculinity in Renaissance England', in James Grantham Turner (ed.), *Sexuality and Gender in Early Modern Europe* (Cambridge: Cambridge University Press, 1993), p. 239, points out that effeminacy is linked to materiality and an immoderate attention to objects, clothes, and ornaments. It is the excessiveness of Marlowe's descriptions, with their over-wrought poeticism, that defines them as effeminate.

## 11. MARLOWE'S POLITIC WOMEN

1 For criticism in which Marlowe's women figure as repositories of positive qualities threatened by negative attributes embodied in his male characters, see: Velma Bourgeoise Richmond, 'Renaissance Sexuality and Marlowe's Women', *Ball State University Forum* 16 (1975), 36–44; Sara Munson Deats, 'The Dialectic of Gender in Four of Marlowe's Plays', *The University of Hartford Studies in Literature* 20 (1988), 13–36; and Barbara Baines, 'Sexual Polarity in the Plays of Christopher Marlowe', *Ball State University Forum* 23 (1982), 3–17. For the view that Marlowe marginalises female characters, see: Steane, p. 83; Jeremy Tambling, 'Abigail's Party: "The Difference of Things" in D. Kehler and S. Baker (eds.), *In Another Country: Feminist Perspectives on Renaissance Drama* (Metuchen: Scarecrow, 1991), pp. 106–9; Roger Sales, *Christopher Marlowe* (Basingstoke: Macmillan, 1991), p. 82; and Bartels, pp. 25–6.

2 See Catherine Belsey, *The Subject of Tragedy: Identity and Difference in Renaissance Drama* (London and New York: Routledge, 1985). Belsey argues that a liberal discourse in which private and public are polarised and '[d]omestic relationships are defined as affective rather than political' arises in the 1660s. She does, however, identify in *The Duchess of Malfi* elements which anticipate that discourse (pp. 193–9 and *passim*).

3 See, for example, Richmond, 'Renaissance Sexuality', 37.

4 Michel Poirier, *Christopher Marlowe* (London: Chatto & Windus, 1951), p. 184, cited in Claude Summers, 'Isabella's Plea for Gaveston in Marlowe's *Edward II*', *Philological Quarterly* 52 (1973), 308.

5 Michael Hattaway, *Elizabethan Popular Theatre* (London and Boston: Routledge, 1982), p. 148.

6 Kathleen Anderson, ' "Stab, as occasion serves": the real Isabella in Marlowe's *Edward II*', *Renaissance Papers* (1992), 31. Anderson's illuminating comparison of Marlowe's *Edward II* with Elizabeth Cary's version incisively critiques, and offers useful examples of, the figuring of Isabella as emotional and apolitical.

7 Ibid., p. 36.

8 Summers, 'Isabella's Plea for Gaveston', 310. Deats, too, subscribes to the view that Isabella acts out the cliché of the 'woman scorned'. See

Deats, 'Edward II: A study in Androgyny', *Ball State University Forum* 22 (1981), 33–4.

9 Jonathan Dollimore, 'Subjectivity, Sexuality, and Transgression: The Jacobean Connection', *Renaissance Drama* 17 (1986), 64.

10 Jean Howard, 'Crossdressing, The Theatre, and Gender Struggle in Early Modern England', *Shakespeare Quarterly* 39 (1988), 435. Anderson, who offers a similar reading of Cary's version of this scene as being one in which 'a woman manipulat[es] the stereotypes of feminine conduct' for political ends, also finds Machiavellian characteristics in Marlowe's Isabella. See Anderson, ' "Stab, as occasion serves" ', 35–6.

11 See *The Duchess of Malfi* (1. 1.29–48), in John Webster, *Three Plays*, ed. D. C. Gunby (Harmondsworth: Penguin, 1972). I am grateful to Gareth Roberts for calling my attention to this comparison.

12 Judith Weil, *Christopher Marlowe Merlin's Prophet* (Cambridge: Cambridge University Press, 1977), p. 158.

13 David Thurn, 'Sights of Power in *Tamburlaine*', *English Literary Renaissance* 19 (1989), 15.

14 Malcolm Kelsall, *Christopher Marlowe* (Leiden: E. J. Brill, 1981), p. 87.

15 Mark Thornton Burnett, '*Tamburlaine* and the Body', *Criticism* 33 (1991), 35.

16 Peter Donaldson, 'Conflict and Coherence: Narcissism and Tragic Structure in Marlowe', in L. Layton and B. A. Schapiro (eds.), *Narcissism in the Text* (New York: New York University Press, 1986), p. 44.

17 Burnett, '*Tamburlaine* and the Body', 34.

18 Harry Levin, *Christopher Marlowe: The Overreacher* (London: Faber & Faber, 1961), p. 63.

19 A. B. Taylor, 'Notes on Marlowe and Golding', *Notes and Queries* 232 (1987), 191.

20 Sales, *Christopher Marlowe*, p. 103.

## 12 *EDWARD II*, DEREK JARMAN, AND THE STATE OF ENGLAND

1 I should like to thank Steve Futter for locating a video of Jarman's *Edward II* for me, and Gareth Roberts and Jonathan Hope for valuable comments on a final version of the essay.

2 William Shakespeare, *The Complete Works*, eds. Stanley Wells and Gary Taylor (Oxford: Clarendon Press, 1988): *The History of King Lear*, 3.13.14–15.

3 I am using 'homoerotic' as a general term to signify same-sex desire without regard to the particular social or subjective formations of sexuality that exist at any particular time or place. 'Sodomy' and 'homosexuality' are examples of such actual, particular formations.

4 Stephen Orgel, *Impersonations: The Performance of Gender in Shakespeare's England* (Cambridge: Cambridge University Press, 1996), p. 42. Orgel's first comment is attributed to Jonathan Goldberg, *Sodometries: Renaissance*

*Texts, Modern Sexualities* (Stanford, CA: Stanford University Press, 1992), pp. 70ff.

5 King James VI and I, *Political Writings*, J. P. Sommerville (ed.), Cambridge Texts in the History of Political Thought (Cambridge: Cambridge University Press, 1994), p. 23.

6 See Alan Bray, 'Homosexuality and the signs of male friendship in Elizabethan England', *History Workshop Journal* 29 (1990), 1–19.

7 Kate Chedgzoy, *Shakespeare's Queer Children: Sexual Politics and Contemporary Culture* (Manchester and New York: Manchester University Press, 1995), p. 195.

8 *Queer Edward II* has 82 sequences but they don't correspond exactly with the film. For example, the first sequence shows the death of Edward I which is absent from the film; and the last sequence has Edward in the throne room speaking: 'But what are Kings, when regiment is gone' – also not in the film. Instead the last shot is of lesbians and gay men from OutRage! standing silent and still as the camera slowly pans across them.

9 Chedgzoy, *Shakespeare's Queer Children*, p. 184.

10 Derek Jarman, *Dancing Ledge*, S. Allen (ed.) (London: Quartet, 1991), p. 7.

11 Colin MacCabe, 'A post-national European cinema: a consideration of Derek Jarman's *The Tempest* and *Edward II*', in Duncan Petrie (ed.), *Screening Europe: Image and Identity in Contemporary European Cinema* (London: BFI Publishing, 1992), p. 14.

12 In this instance, the quotation follows David Bevington's and Eric Rasmussen's text of *Edward II* in the Oxford World's Classics edition of *Doctor Faustus and Other Plays* (Oxford and New York: Oxford University Press, 1995).

13 See Gordon Williams, *A Dictionary of Sexual Language and Imagery in Shakespearean and Stuart Literature*, 3 vols. (London: Athlone Press, 1994), vol. III, *s.v.* 'treasure', p. 1419.

14 See Lawrence Normand, ' "What passions call you these?": *Edward II* and James VI', in Darryll Grantley and Peter Roberts (eds.), *Christopher Marlowe and English Renaissance Culture* (Aldershot: Scolar Press, 1996), pp. 172–97.

15 Claude J. Summers, 'Sex, Politics, and Self-Realization in *Edward II*', in Kenneth Friedenreich, Roma Gill, and Constance B. Kuriyama (eds.), *'A Poet & a Filthy Play-maker': New Essays on Christopher Marlowe* (New York: AMS Press, 1988), p. 222.

16 Christopher Marlowe, *Edward II*, Charles R. Forker (ed.), The Revels Plays (Manchester University Press, 1994), Introduction, p. 45.

17 Normand, ' "What Passions" ', in Grantley and Roberts (eds.), *Christopher Marlowe*, p. 190.

18 See Bredbeck, p. 76; Smith, p. 220; Normand, ' "What passions" ', in Grantley and Roberts (eds.), *Christopher Marlowe*, p. 191.

19 MacCabe, 'Post-national European cinema', in Petrie (ed.), *Screening Europe*, p. 16.

20 Orgel, *Impersonations*, p. 48.
21 The editors are more cautious in their note to 5.5.112–13: 'Whether such a horrible method of murder was simulated by the Elizabethan acting company is not certain' (Bevington and Rasmussen (eds.), *Doctor Faustus and Other Plays*, p. 491).
22 See Michael O'Pray, *Derek Jarman: Dreams of England* (London: BFI Publishing, 1996), pp. 8, 98. 104.
23 Ian Lucas, *Impertinent Decorum: Gay Theatrical Manoeuvres* (London: Cassell, 1994), p. 161. See Chapter 9, 'Queer turf and hetero territory', for a full discussion of OutRage!.

# Select bibliography of works cited

Altieri, Joanne, '*Hero and Leander*: Sensible Myth and Lyric Subjectivity', *John Donne Journal* 8 (1989)

Anderson, Kathleen, ' "Stab, as occasion serves": the real Isabella in Marlowe's *Edward II*', *Renaissance Papers* (1992)

Baines, Barbara, 'Sexual Polarity in the Plays of Christopher Marlowe', *Ball State University Forum* 23 (1982)

Barber, C. L., *Creating Elizabethan Tragedy: the Theatre of Marlowe and Kyd*, Richard P. Wheeler (ed.) (Chicago and London: University of Chicago Press, 1988)

Bartels, Emily, *Spectacles of Strangeness, Imperialism, Alienation and Marlowe* (Philadelphia: University of Pennsylvania Press, 1993)

Belsey, Catherine, *The Subject of Tragedy: Identity and Difference in Renaissance Drama* (London and New York: Routledge, 1985)

Berry, Herbert, 'Aspects of the Design and Use of the First Public Playhouse', in Herbert Berry (ed.), *The First Public Playhouse: The Theatre in Shoreditch 1576–1598* (Montreal: McGill-Queen's University Press, 1979)

Bluestone, Max, '*Libido speculandi*: Doctrine and Dramaturgy in Contemporary Interpretations of Marlowe's *Doctor Faustus*', in Norman Rabkin (ed.), *Reinterpretations of Elizabethan Drama* (New York and London: Columbia University Press, 1969)

Boas, Frederick, S., *Marlowe and His Circle* (Oxford: Oxford University Press, 1931)

    *Christopher Marlowe: A Biographical and Critical Study* (Oxford: Clarendon Press, 1940)

Bowsher, Julian, *The Rose Theatre: an Archaeological Discovery* (London: Museum of London, 1998)

Braden, Gordon, *The Classics and English Renaissance Poetry: Three Case Studies*, Yale Studies in English 187 (New Haven and London: Yale University Press, 1978)

Bray, Alan, 'Homosexuality and the signs of male friendship in Elizabethan England', *History Workshop Journal* 29 (1990)

Bredbeck, Gregory W., *Sodomy and Interpretation: Marlowe to Milton* (Ithaca, NY: Cornell University Press, 1991)

Brockbank, J. B., *Marlowe: Dr. Faustus* (London: Edward Arnold, 1962)

Burnett, Mark Thornton, '*Tamburlaine* and the Body', *Criticism* 33 (1991)

Butcher, Andrew, ' "onelye a boye called Christopher Mowle' ", in Darryll Grantley and Peter Roberts (eds.), *Christopher Marlowe and English Renaissance Culture* (Aldershot: Scolar Press, 1996)

Campbell, Marion, ' "Desunt Nonnulla": The Construction of Marlowe's *Hero and Leander* as an Unfinished Poem', *ELH* 51 (1984)

Cartelli, Thomas, *Marlowe, Shakespeare, and the Economy of Theatrical Experience* (Philadelphia: University of Pennsylvania Press, 1991)

Chambers, E. K., *The Elizabethan Stage* (Oxford: Oxford University Press, 1923)

Chan, Lois Mai, *Marlowe Criticism: A Bibliography* (Boston: G. K. Hall & Co. 1978)

Chedgzoy, Kate, *Shakespeare's Queen Children: Sexual Politics and Contemporary Culture* (Manchester and New York: Manchester University Press, 1995)

Clark, Stuart, 'Protestant Demonology: Sin, Superstition and Society (*c.* 1520–1630)' in Bengt Ankarloo and Gustav Henningsen (eds.), *Early Modern Witchcraft: Centres and Peripheries* (Oxford: Clarendon Press, 1993)

'The Rational Witchfinder: Conscience, Demonological Naturalism and Popular Superstitions', in Stephen Pumfrey, Paolo L. Rossi and Maurice Slawinski (eds.), *Science, Culture and Popular Belief in Renaissance Europe* (Manchester and New York: Manchester University Press, 1991)

Collins, S. Ann, ' "Sundrie Shapes, Committing Headdie Ryots, Incest, Rapes": Functions of Myth in Determining Narrative and Tone in Marlowe's *Hero and Leander*', *Mosaic* 4 (1970–1)

Cooper, Thomas, *The Mystery of Witchcraft* (London, 1617)

Cunningham, J. S., and Roger Warren, '*Tamburlaine the Great* Rediscovered', *Shakespeare Survey* 31 (1978)

Dabbs, Thomas, *Reforming Marlowe: The Nineteenth-Century Canonization of a Renaissance Dramatist* (Lewisburg, London and Toronto: Bucknell University Press and Associated University Presses, 1991)

Danson, Lawrence, 'Christopher Marlowe: the Questioner', *English Literary Renaissance* 12 (1982)

Davidson, Nicholas, 'Christopher Marlowe and Atheism', in Darryll Grantley and Peter Roberts (eds.), *Christopher Marlowe and English Renaissance Culture* (Aldershot: Scolar Press, 1996)

Deats, Sara Munson, 'The Dialectic of Gender in Four of Marlowe's Plays', *The University of Hartford Studies in Literature* 20 (1988)

'*Edward II*: A study in Androgyny', *Ball State University Forum* 22 (1981)

Dollimore, Jonathan, *Radical Tragedy: Religion, Ideology and Power in the Drama of Shakespeare and his Contemporaries* (Brighton: Harvester, 1984)

'Subjectivity, Sexuality, and Transgression: The Jacobean Connection', *Renaissance Drama* 17 (1986)

Donaldson, Peter, 'Conflict and Coherence: Narcissism and Tragic Structure in Marlowe', in L. Layton and B. A. Schapiro (eds.), *Narcissism in the Text* (New York: New York University Press, 1986)

Eagleton, Terry, *William Shakespeare* (Oxford: Blackwell, 1986)

Eccles, Mark, *Christopher Marlowe in London* (Cambridge, Mass.: Harvard University Press, 1934)

Elyot, Sir Thomas, *The Boke Named the Gouernour*, Henry Croft (ed.) (London: Kegan Paul, 1883)

Enterline, Lynn, 'Embodied Voices: Petrarch Reading (Himself Reading) Ovid', in Valeria Finucci and Regina Schwartz (eds.), *Desire in the Renaissance: Psychoanalysis and Literature* (Princeton: Princeton University Press, 1994)

Foakes, R. A., *Illustrations of the English Stage 1580–1642* (London: Scolar Press, 1985)

Foakes, R. A., and R. T. Rickert (eds.), *Henslowe's Diary* (Cambridge: Cambridge University Press, 1961)

Foster, Verna An, '*Dr Faustus* on the Stage', *Theatre Research* 14 (1974)

Freeman, Arthur, 'The Deptford Killer', *TLS*, 28 May 1993

Garber, Margery, ' "Here's Nothing Writ": Scribe, Script, and Circumscription in Marlowe's Plays', *Theatre Journal* 36 (1984)

' "Infinite Riches in a Little Room": Closure and Enclosure in Marlowe', in Alvin Kernan (ed.), *Two Renaissance Mythmakers: Christopher Marlowe and Ben Jonson* (Baltimore: Johns Hopkins University Press, 1977)

Geckle, George L., *Tamburlaine and Edward II* (Basingstoke and London: Macmillan, 1988)

Giffard, George, *A Dialogue concerning Witches and Witchcraftes*, Percy Society, vol. 8, 1842

*A Discourse of the Subtill Practises of Devilles* (London, 1587)

Godshalk, W. L., '*Hero and Leander*: The Sense of an Ending', in Kenneth Friedenreich, Roma Gill, and Constance B. Kuriyama (eds.), '*A Poet & a Filthy Play-maker*': New Essays on Christopher Marlowe* (New York: AMS Press, 1988)

Goldberg, Jonathan, *Sodometries: Renaissance Texts, Modern Sexualities* (Stanford, CA: Stanford University Press, 1992)

'Sodomy and Society: The Case of Christopher Marlowe', in David Scott Kastan and Peter Stallybrass (eds.), *Staging the Renaissance: Reinterpretations of Elizabethan and Jacobean Drama* (New York and London: Routledge, 1991)

Goldman, Michael, 'Marlowe and the Histrionics of Ravishment', in Alvin Kernan (ed.), *Two Renaissance Mythmakers: Christopher Marlowe and Ben Jonson* (Baltimore: Johns Hopkins University Press, 1977)

Greenblatt, Stephen, 'Invisible Bullets: Renaissance Authority and its Subversion, *Henry IV* and *Henry V*', in Richard Wilson and Richard Dutton (eds.), *New Historicism and Renaissance Drama* (London: Longman, 1992)

*Learning to Curse: Essays in Early Modern Culture* (London: Routledge, 1990)
'Marlowe and Renaissance Self-Fashioning', in Alvin Kernan (ed.), *Two Renaissance Mythmakers: Christopher Marlowe and Ben Jonson* (Baltimore: Johns Hopkins University Press, 1977)
*Renaissance Self-Fashioning from More to Shakespeare* (Chicago: Chicago University Press, 1980)
Greene, Robert, *Friar Bacon and Friar Bungay*, Daniel Seltzer (ed.) (London: Edward Arnold, 1963)
*Menaphon* (London, 1589)
*Perimedes The Blacke-Smith* (London, 1588)
Greg, W. W., *Henslowe's Diary* (London: A. H. Bullen, 1904–8)
*Henslowe Papers, being documents supplementary to Henslowe's Diary* (London: A. H. Bullen, 1907)
*The Tragical History of the Life and Death of Doctor Faustus by Christopher Marlowe. A Conjectural Reconstruction* (Oxford: Oxford University Press, 1950)
Gurr, Andrew, 'What the Plays Might Tell Us About the Stage', in F. J. Hildy (ed.), *New Issues in the Reconstruction of Shakespeare's Theatre* (New York: Peter Lang, 1990)
Harvey, Gabriel, *A New Letter of Notable Contents* (London, 1593)
Hattaway, Michael, *Elizabethan Popular Theatre* (London and Boston: Routledge, 1982)
Heywood, Thomas, *Oenone and Paris* (1594)
Holland, Henry, *A Treatise against Witchcraft* (Cambridge, 1590)
Holmes, M. Morgan, 'Identity and the Dissidence It Makes: Homoerotic Nonsense in Kit Marlowe's *Hero and Leander*', *English Studies in Canada* 21 (1995)
Honigmann, Ernst, 'Ten Problems in *Dr. Faustus*', in Murray Biggs, Philip Edwards, Inga-Stina Ewbank and Eugene M. Waith (eds.), *The Arts of Performance in Elizabethan and Early Stuart Drama* (Edinburgh: Edinburgh University Press, 1991)
Hotson, Leslie, *The Commonwealth and Restoration Stage* (Cambridge, Mass.: Cambridge, 1928; repr. New York, 1962)
Howard, Jean, 'Crossdressing, The Theatre, and Gender Struggle in Early Modern England', *Shakespeare Quarterly* 39 (1988)
Hulse, Clark, *Metamorphic Verse: The Elizabethan Minor Epic* (Princeton: Princeton University Press, 1981)
Hume, Robert D., *The Development of English Drama in the Late Seventeenth Century* (Oxford: Clarendon Press, 1976)
Hunter, Michael, 'The Problem of Atheism in Early Modern England', *Transactions of the Royal Historical Society* 35 (1985)
James, King, *Dæmonologie* (Bodley Head Quartos, 1924)
Jones, John Henry (ed.), *The English Faust Book* (Cambridge: Cambridge University Press, 1994)
Keach, William, *Elizabethan Erotic Narratives: Irony and Pathos in the Ovidian*

*Poetry of Shakespeare, Marlowe, and Their Contemporaries* (New Brunswick, NJ: Rutgers University Press, 1977)

Keefer, Michael H., 'Right Hand and Left Heel: Ideological Origins of the Faustus Legend', *Mosaic* 22 (1989)

'Verbal Magic and the Problem of the A and B texts of *Dr. Faustus*', *Journal of English and Germanic Philology* 82 (1983)

Kelsall, Malcolm, *Christopher Marlowe* (Leiden: E. J. Brill, 1981)

Kerrigan, William, and Gordon Braden, 'Milton's Coy Eve: *Paradise Lost* and Renaissance Love Poetry', *ELH* 53 (1986)

Kirschbaum, Leo, 'Marlowe's Faustus: A Reconsideration', *Review of English Studies* 19 (1943)

Kocher, Paul H., *Christopher Marlowe: A Study of his Thought, Learning and Character* (New York: Russell and Russell, 1962)

Koppenfels, Werner von, 'Dis-Covering the Female Body: Erotic Exploration in Elizabethan Poetry', *Shakespeare Survey* 47 (1994)

Kuchta, David, 'The Semiotics of Masculinity in Renaissance England', in James Grantham Turner (ed.), *Sexuality and Gender in Early Modern Europe* (Cambridge: Cambridge University Press, 1993)

Kuriyama, Constance Brown, 'Dr. Greg and *Dr. Faustus*: The Supposed Originality of the 1616 Text', *English Literary Renaissance* 5 (1975)

*Hammer or Anvil: Psychological Patterns in Christopher Marlowe's Plays* (New Brunswick, NJ: Rutgers University Press, 1980)

Leech, Clifford, *Christopher Marlowe: Poet for the Stage*, Anne Lancashire (ed.) (New York: AMS Press, 1986)

' "Venus and the Nun": Portraits of Women in Love in Shakespeare and Marlowe', *Studies in English Literature* 5 (1965)

Leslie, Nancy T., '*Tamburlaine* in the Theatre: Tartar, Grand Guignol, or Janus?', *Renaissance Drama* 4 (1971)

Levin, Harry, *Christopher Marlowe: The Overreacher* (London: Faber & Faber, 1961)

MacCabe, Colin, 'A post-national European cinema: a consideration of Derek Jarman's *The Tempest* and *Edward II*', in Duncan Petrie (ed.), *Screening Europe: Image and Identity in Contemporary European Cinema* (London: BFI Publishing, 1992)

MacLure, Millar (ed.), *Marlowe: The Critical Heritage* (London, Boston and Henley: Routledge & Kegan Paul, 1979)

Marlowe, Christopher, *Christopher Marlowe's Doctor Faustus: A 1604-Version Edition*, Michael Keefer (ed.) (Peterborough, Ontario: Broadview Press, 1991)

*The Complete Plays*, J. B. Steane (ed.) (Harmondsworth: Penguin Books, 1969)

*The Complete Poems and Translations*, Stephen Orgel (ed.) (Harmondsworth: Penguin Books Ltd, 1971)

*The Complete Works of Christopher Marlowe*, Fredson Bowers (ed.), (Cambridge: Cambridge University Press, 1973; 2nd edn., 1981)

*The Complete Works of Christopher Marlowe*, Roma Gill (ed.) (Oxford: Clarendon Press, 1987)

*Doctor Faustus and Other Plays*, David Bevington and Eric Rasmussen (eds.), World's Classics (Oxford and New York: Oxford University Press, 1995)

*Hero and Leander By Christopher Marlowe: A Facsimile of the First Edition London 1598*, Louis L. Martz (ed.) (Washington: The Folger Shakespeare Library, 1972)

*The Poems: Christopher Marlowe*, Millar MacLure (ed.) (London: Methuen, 1968)

*Works of Christopher Marlowe*, C. F. Tucker Brooke (ed.) (Oxford: Clarendon Press, 1929)

Mason, James, *The Anatomie of Sorcerie* (London, 1612)

McMillin, Scott, 'Staging at the Rose', in *The Elizabethan Theatre and the Book of Sir Thomas More* (Ithaca: Cornell University Press, 1987)

Merchant, Moelwyn, 'Marlowe the Orthodox', in Brian Morris (ed.), *Christopher Marlowe* (London: Ernest Benn, 1968)

Miller, David Lee, 'The Death of the Modern: Gender and Desire in Marlowe's *Hero and Leander*', *South Atlantic Quarterly* 88 (1989)

Morris, Brian, 'Comic Method in *Hero and Leander*' in Brian Morris (ed.), *Christopher Marlowe* (London: Ernest Benn, 1968)

Mountfort, William, *The Li[f]e and Death of Doctor Faustus, Made into a Farce* (London, 1688)

Nashe, Thomas, *The Works of Thomas Nashe*, R. B. McKerrow (ed.), rev. F. P. Wilson (Oxford: Blackwell, 1966)

Nicholl, Charles, *The Reckoning: The Murder of Christopher Marlowe* (London: Jonathan Cape, 1992)

' "At Middleborough": Some Reflections on Marlowe's Visit to the Low Countries in 1592', in Darryll Grantley and Peter Roberts (eds.), *Christopher Marlowe and English Renaissance Culture* (Aldershot: Scolar Press, 1996)

Normand, Lawrence, ' "What passions call you these?": *Edward II* and James VI', in Darryll Grantley and Peter Roberts (eds.), *Christopher Marlowe and English Renaissance Culture* (Aldershot: Scolar Press, 1996)

Orgel, Stephen, *Impersonations: The Performance of Gender in Shakespeare's England* (Cambridge: Cambridge University Press, 1996)

Peacham, Henry, *Garden of Eloquence* (London, 1577)

Pechter, Edward, 'The New Historicism and its Discontents', *PMLA* 102 (1987)

Perkins, William, *A Discourse of the Damned Art of Witchcraft* (Cambridge, 1608)

Poirier, Michel, *Christopher Marlowe* (London: Chatto & Windus, 1951)

Porter, Joseph A., *Shakespeare's Mercutio, History and Drama* (Chapel Hill and London: University of North Carolina Press, 1988)

Prynne, William, *Histriomatrix* (London, 1633)

Puttenham, George, *The Arte of English Poesie*, George Doidge Willcock and Alice Walker (eds.) (Cambridge: Cambridge University Press, 1936)

Rhodes, Ernest K., *Henslowe's Rose, the Stage and Staging* (Lexington: Kentucky University Press, 1977)

Richmond, Velma Bourgeoise, 'Renaissance Sexuality and Marlowe's Women', *Ball State University Forum* 16 (1975)

Roberts, Alexander, *A Treatise of Witchcraft* (London, 1616)

Roberts, Peter, 'The "Studious Artizan": Christopher Marlowe, Canterbury and Cambridge', in Darryll Grantley and Peter Roberts (eds.), *Christopher Marlowe and English Renaissance Culture* (Aldershot: Scolar Press, 1996)

Rowland, Samuel, *The Knave of Clubs* (London, ?1615)

Rutter, C. C., *Documents of the Rose Playhouse* (Manchester: Manchester University Press, 1984)

Sales, Roger, *Christopher Marlowe* (Basingstoke: Macmillan, 1991)

Sanders, J. W., 'Vaulting the Rails', *Shakespeare Survey* 7 (1954)

Sanders, Wilbur, *The Dramatist and the Received Idea: Studies in the Plays of Marlowe and Shakespeare* (Cambridge: Cambridge University Press, 1968)

Schwartz, Regina M., 'Through the Optic Glass: Voyeurism and *Paradise Lost*', in Valeria Finucci and Regina Schwartz (eds.), *Desire in the Renaissance: Psychoanalysis and Literature* (Princeton: Princeton University Press, 1994)

Shakespeare, William, *Mr. William Shakespeares Comedies, Histories, & Tragedies* (London, 1623)

Shapiro, James, ' "Tragedies naturally performed": Kyd's representation of violence', in David Scott Kastan and Peter Stallybrass (eds.), *Staging the Renaissance: Reinterpretations of Elizabethan and Jacobean Drama* (New York and London: Routledge, 1991)

Shepherd, Simon, *Marlowe and the Politics of Elizabethan Theatre* (Brighton: Harvester, 1986)

Simmons, J. L., 'Elizabethan Stage Practice and Marlowe's *Jew of Malta*' *Renaissance Drama* 4 (1972)

Smith, Bruce R., *Homosexual Desire in Shakespeare's England: A Cultural Poetics* (Chicago: University of Chicago Press, 1991)

Smith, James L., 'The Jew of Malta in the Theatre', in Brian Morris (ed.), *Christopher Marlowe* (London: Benn, 1968)

Snare, Gerald, 'Chapman's Ovid', *Studies in Philology* 75 (1978)

Speaight, Robert, *William Poel and the Elizabethan Revival* (Cambridge, Mass.: Harvard University Press, 1954)

Steane, J. B., *Marlowe: A Critical Study* (Cambridge: Cambridge University Press, 1965)

Summers, Claude J. (ed.), *Homosexuality in Renaissance and Enlightenment England: Literary Representations in Historical Context* (New York: Haworth, 1992)

'Isabella's Plea for Gaveston in Marlowe's *Edward II*', *Philological Quarterly* 52 (1973)

'Marlowe and Constructions of Renaissance Homosexuality', *Canadian Review of Comparative Literature/Revue Canadienne de Littérature Comparée* 21 (1994)

'Sex, Politics, and Self-Realization in *Edward II*', in Kenneth Friedenreich, Roma Gill, and Constance B. Kuriyama (eds.), *'A Poet & a Filthy Play-maker': New Essays on Christopher Marlowe* (New York: AMS Press, 1988)

Symonds, J. A., introduction to Havelock Ellis (ed.), *Christopher Marlowe* (1887) (London: Ernest Benn, 1948)

Tambling, Jeremy, 'Abigail's Party: "The Difference of Things"' in D. Kehler and S. Baker (eds.), *In Another Country: Feminist Perspectives on Renaissance Drama* (Metuchen: Scarecrow, 1991)

Taylor, A. B., 'Notes on Marlowe and Golding', *Notes and Queries* 232 (1987)

Taylor, A. E., 'Marlowe's *Dr. Faustus*', *TLS*, 6 Dec. 1917

Thomas, Keith, *Religion and the Decline of Magic: Studies in Popular Belief in Sixteenth- and Seventeenth-Century England* (London: Weidenfeld and Nicolson, 1971)

Thurn, David, 'Sights of Power in *Tamburlaine*', *English Literary Renaissance* 19 (1989)

Tyedeman, William, *Dr Faustus: Text and Performance* (London and Basingstoke: Macmillan, 1984)

Urry, William, *Christopher Marlowe and Canterbury* (London: Faber & Faber, 1988)

Vroom, Theresia de, 'Mediating Myth: The Art of Marlowe's *Hero & Leander*', *College Language Association Journal* 37 (1994)

Walker, D. P., *Unclean Spirits: Possession and Exorcism in France and England in the Late Sixteenth and Early Seventeenth Centuries* (London: Scolar Press, 1981)

Wallace, C. W., *The First London Theatre* (Lincoln, Nebr.: Nebraska University Press, 1913)

Walsh, William P., 'Sexual Discovery and Renaissance Morality in Marlowe's "Hero and Leander"', *Studies in English Literature* 12 (1972)

Warren, Michael J., '*Dr. Faustus*: The Old Man and the Text', *English Literary Renaissance* 11 (1981)

Watson, Thomas, *Amintæ Gaudia* (London, 1592)
*Meliboeus* (London, 1590)

Weil, Judith, *Christopher Marlowe Merlin's Prophet* (Cambridge: Cambridge University Press, 1977)

Wells, Stanley, 'Theatricalizing Shakespeare's text', *New Theatre Quarterly* 26 (1991)

Wernham, R. B., 'Christopher Marlowe at Flushing in 1592', *English Historical Review* 91 (1976)

West, R. H., 'The Impatient Magic of Dr. Faustus', *English Studies in Canada* 4 (1974)

*The Invisible World: A Study of Pneumatology in Elizabethan Drama* (Athens, Georgia: University of Georgia Press, 1939)

Wickham, Glynne, '"Heavens", Machinery and Pillars', in Herbert Berry (ed.), *The First Public Playhouse: The Theatre in Shoreditch, 1576–1598* (Montreal: McGill-Queen's University Press, 1979)

*Shakespeare's Dramatic Heritage* (London: Routledge & Kegan Paul, 1969)

Williams, Gordon, *A Dictionary of Sexual Language and Imagery in Shakespearean and Stuart Literature* (London: Athlone Press, 1994)

Woods, Gregory, 'Body, Costume, and Desire in Christopher Marlowe', in Claude J. Summers (ed.), *Homosexuality in Renaissance and Enlightenment England: Literary Representations in Historical Context* (New York: Haworth, 1992)

Yates, Frances, *Giordano Bruno and the Hermetic Tradition* (London: Routledge & Kegan Paul, 1964)

Zika, Charles, 'Reuchlin's *De verbo Mirifico* and the Magical Debate of the Late Fifteenth Century', *Journal of the Warburg and Courtauld Institute* 39 (1976)

# Index

Passing mentions of proper names which give no information about the person have not been indexed. Similarly, only key topics have been indexed. All references to Marlowe's works are indexed under the title of each individual play or poem.